MODERN HUMANITIES RESEARCH ASSOCIATION
TEXTS AND DISSERTATIONS
VOLUME 82

INSTITUTE OF GERMANIC AND ROMANCE STUDIES
(UNIVERSITY OF LONDON)
BITHELL SERIES OF DISSERTATIONS
VOLUME 38

SPACE IN THEODOR FONTANE'S WORKS
THEME AND POETIC FUNCTION

INSTITUTE OF GERMANIC AND ROMANCE STUDIES
BITHELL SERIES OF DISSERTATIONS

Launched in 1978, this series publishes outstanding recent doctoral theses, accepted by universities in the United Kingdom and Ireland, across all fields of Germanic studies. Since 1989 the series has been published in collaboration with the Modern Humanities Research Association.

Recommendations for theses which might be considered for possible inclusion in the series should be made by the supervisor and/or examiner(s), and sent to Professor Ritchie Robertson, Convenor of the Bithell Editorial Board, St John's College, Oxford OX1 3JP. Proposals must be accompanied by a copy of the Examiners' Report and Abstract.

Editorial Board
Dr Judith Beniston, University College London
Professor Sarah Colvin, University of Birmingham
Professor Pól O Dochartaigh, University of Ulster
Professor Ritchie Robertson (*Convenor*), St John's College, Oxford
Professor Bill Marshall,
Institute of Germanic and Romance Studies, University of London
Dr John Walker, Birkbeck College London
Dr Godela Weiss-Sussex,
Institute of Germanic and Romance Studies, University of London
Professor David Wells, Birkbeck College London

MODERN HUMANITIES RESEARCH ASSOCIATION
TEXTS AND DISSERTATIONS

Established in 1970, the series promotes important work by younger scholars by making the most accomplished doctoral research available to a wider readership. Titles are selected and edited by a Board of distinguished experts from across the modern Humanities.

Editorial Board
English: Professor Catherine Maxwell, Queen Mary, University of London
French: Professor William Brooks, University of Bath
Germanic: Professor Ritchie Robertson, University of Oxford
Hispanic: Professor Derek Flitter, University of Exeter
Italian: Professor Brian Richardson, University of Leeds
Portuguese: Professor Thomas Earle, University of Oxford
Slavonic: Professor David Gillespie, University of Bath

Managing Editor: Dr Graham Nelson

Space in Theodor Fontane's Works

Theme and Poetic Function

by
Michael James White

Modern Humanities Research Association
2012

Published by

The Modern Humanities Research Association
1 Carlton House Terrace
London SW1Y 5AF
United Kingdom

© *Modern Humanities Research Association and the*
Institute of Germanic and Romance Studies, University of London, 2012

Michael White has asserted his right under the Copyright, Designs and Patents Act 1988 to be identified as the author of this work. Parts of this work may be reproduced as permitted under legal provisions for fair dealing (or fair use) for the purposes of research, private study, criticism, or review, or when a relevant collective licensing agreement is in place. All other reproduction requires the written permission of the copyright holder who may be contacted at rights@mhra.org.uk.

Copy-Editor: Nigel Hope

First published 2012

ISBN 978-1-907322-29-7 (hardback)
ISBN 978-1-907322-98-3 (paperback)
ISSN (Bithell Series of Dissertations) 0266–7932
ISSN (MHRA Texts and Dissertations) 0957–0322

CONTENTS

	Preface	vii
	Introduction	1
1.	Spatial Representation and the Boundaries of the Literary Text: *Die Grafschaft Ruppin*	20
2.	Spatial Representation as a Strategy of Relativization: *Vor dem Sturm*	46
3.	The Spatial Representation of Awareness: *Schach von Wuthenow* and *Graf Petöfy*	71
4.	Spatial Representation and 'die künstlerische Betrachtung des Lebens': *Irrungen Wirrungen* and *Unwiederbringlich*	99
5.	The Spatial Representation of a *poetische Weltanschauung*: *Der Stechlin*	127
	Conclusion	163
	Bibliography	175
	Index	189

PREFACE

This book was originally presented as a doctoral thesis at the University of St Andrews and is the outcome of research undertaken both there and at the Albrecht-Ludwigs-Universität, Freiburg im Breisgau. I am indebted to the staff of both these institutions, especially, however, to Professor Helen Chambers. The title of PhD supervisor does no justice to the intellectual rigour, personal interest, and patient support that she brought to this project. I am also grateful to Dr Patricia Howe and Dr Michael Gratzke. Many aspects of the study's argumentation benefited directly from their judicious comments. I should like to thank the University of St Andrews and the Baden-Württemburg Stiftung for supporting the research financially. The Fontane-Archiv staff, and those involved with the publication of this volume at the Modern Humanities Research Association, Professor Ritchie Robertson, Dr Graham Nelson, and Dr John Walker all deserve my thanks. Finally, this book could not have been written without the constant support of my family, especially Frank Buck, my parents, my grandfather, and my wife, Margaret, who has endured years of Fontane anecdotes with extraordinary patience.

Where possible, references to Fontane's writings are to the *Werke, Schriften und Briefe* [originally *Sämtliche Werke*], ed. by Walter Keitel and Helmuth Nürnberger, 20 vols in 4 sections (Hanser: Munich, 1962–97), 'Hanser Ausgabe'. Reference to the section, volume, and page will be given in the following form: HA I, 1, 100.

M.J.W., September 2011

INTRODUCTION

~

> Es ist etwas Eigentümliches um die bloße Macht des Raumes!
> THEODOR FONTANE, *Ein Sommer in London*[1]

Space and Fontane

Theodor Fontane (1819-98) had an acute sensitivity to the pregnancy of space. In his autobiographical work *Von Zwanzig bis Dreißig* (1898) he relates how, as an apprentice apothecary, he would visit the Stehely café to read the newspapers and journals there. Unfortunately, these had often been hidden away by other regular customers. Nevertheless, for the young poet, the visit to the Stehely café was worthwhile in itself: 'Aber selbst wenn alles ausblieb, so verließ ich das Lokal mit dem Gefühl, mich, eine Stunde lang, an einer geweihten Stätte befunden zu haben'.[2] This apparently insignificant episode from Fontane's youth demonstrates his awareness of the emotional significance of environment, a defining aspect of his work, and observable in his writings throughout his career, in terms of both form and subject matter. Fontane is the wanderer of the *Wanderungen durch die Mark Brandenburg*, the writer of travel literature such as *Jenseit des Tweed*, a war reporter, and, above all, the author of novels in which setting and description play a key role. He is the creator of Berlin novels, such as *Frau Jenny Treibel*, the master manipulator of local geography in *Unwiederbringlich*. His literary testament is a novel whose title conflates ideas of place and value: *Der Stechlin*.

The purpose of this study is to explore the importance of space in Fontane's works in terms of how spatial representation functions to create symbolic depth in his literary texts, and of how Fontane reflects on the nature of spatial experience itself, the potential meanings of the external world and its objects to individuals. We will see that space, as both a formal and thematic focus of analysis, is a productive lens through which Fontane's art may be studied.

Approaching the issue of space in literature is complicated by the varied range of scholarship dealing with it: philosophers and mathematicians discuss space in an abstract sense; astrophysicists are concerned with space beyond our planet; geographers both delineate our world and explore human beings' ways of living in it; architects, sculptors, and painters create artworks which exist and communicate spatially. While space is of interest to a wide range of specialisms, within literary studies, systematic definitions of literary space are hard to find. 'Space' is not a literary term, and standard reference works such as the *Reallexikon der deutschen Literaturwissenschaft*, Gero von Wilpert's *Sachwörterbuch der Literatur*, or the *Princeton Encyclopedia of Poetry and Poetics* do not list articles dealing with literary space as a concept or which might give pointers to relevant scholarship.[3] Instead, reference works typically list terms such as 'description', 'ekphrasis', 'mimesis', 'Realism', or *'couleur locale'*. Bibliographical periodicals, however, attest to the scholarly interest in space: for 2008 *Germanistik* lists sixty-one entries under 'Raum' and related terms, and the *Bibliographie der deutschen Sprach- und Literaturwissenschaft* lists thirty-three entries.[4]

Criticism ostensibly discussing 'l'espace littéraire' is however often unhelpful, because in many instances 'space' is a convenient metaphorical vehicle for the discussion of literature, rather than an object of inquiry itself.[5] Elsewhere space in literature can become a focus for the discussion of non-chronological tendencies or simultaneity in texts. Here space is conceived of in the negative, it is anti-time, and has little to do with the world a text creates in the imagination.[6] There is thus a plethora of potential starting points for a discussion of space in literature, and an all-encompassing study is as unrealizable as it is undesirable. The limitations and basic premises of this study are therefore stated here.

In this book, a pragmatic definition of space will be used. Space is the world beyond the subject and includes the objects in it; the individual's relationship to that world, his perception of it, movements within it, and the language used to describe it are also potential objects of spatial analysis. In a text, this translates as descriptive passages, described objects and their potential symbolism, journeys, directional and relational terms such as 'right' and 'left', or 'up' and 'down', in short all textual references to the represented world, both those which present it ostensibly objectively and also those which convey the way it is experienced by its inhabitants. To indicate this scope of interest, the broad term 'space' is used rather than other, potentially more restrictive terms such as 'topography', 'place', or 'landscape'. Specific areas of literary study relevant to space are indeed brought into consideration, such as description, or symbolism; a spatial study includes, but goes beyond these narrower terms and foci.

Furthermore, this discussion is concerned with space as a literary phenomenon, and makes no attempt to examine the text as a cultural artefact or as indicative of wider social practices to do with space.[7] For this reason, while there is a brief consideration of how space acquires its special symbolic potential outside the text in this introduction, this study does not draw on theories of socially constructed spaces, or spatial performativity. Rather, the terms of reference of more specifically literary criticism have been favoured. In addition, this study frequently asks how space and literariness are linked, what the relationship between space and the literary text as a symbolic art form is, and how an analysis under the general heading of 'space' leads to fresh insights into the individual text.

It could be argued that so broad a term as space is not conducive to a focused scholarly investigation of a range of texts. The opposite has proved to be the case. The fact that the notion of space allows on the one hand a degree of focus, while on the other encompassing a wide range of potential lines of analysis, has proved a particularly fruitful way of allowing the specificity of each text to emerge. The concern to analyse each of the selected texts individually has been a critical assumption underpinning this project from the outset, and it has been a consistent aim, while attempting to highlight similarities and persistent trends, to provide a critical interpretation of each work in its own right. Like J. Hillis Miller, 'I have allowed the text to dictate the paths to be followed in raising and answering one or another set of my topographical questions'.[8] An overview and discussion of general trends will be given in the conclusion. In what follows, methodological approaches to the analysis of space in the literary text will be reviewed, and the project then situated within the context of relevant Fontane scholarship.

Methodological Approaches to Space in Literature

A literary work is at once a linguistic entity, a text in a narrow sense, and a world of human life and emotion created and experienced in the imagination, expressed and received through the medium of language. Both language and human experience, in so far as they can ever be separated, contribute to the way spaces and spatial locutions acquire significance outside the literary text. A brief analysis of how the semantics of space are constructed discursively and empirically is then appropriate before addressing literary theories of space.

In terms of language, spatial metaphors are a commonplace of both literary and non-literary discourses. As Jurij Lotman writes: 'the language of spatial relations turns out to be one of the basic means for comprehending reality'.[9] Space is a means of mental organization and, as a result, spatial language is used to describe the widest range of ideas, concepts and social structures: 'The most general social, religious, political and ethnical models of the world, with whose help man comprehends the world around him at various stages in his spiritual development, are invariably invested with spatial characteristics'.[10] Gérard Genette offers the following explanation for this linguistic tendency:

> On a remarqué bien souvent que le langage semblait comme naturellement plus apte à 'exprimer' les relations spatiales que toute autre espèce de relation (et donc de la réalité), ce qui le conduit à utiliser les premières comme symboles ou métaphores des secondes, donc à traiter de toutes choses en termes d'espace, et donc encore à spatialiser toutes choses.[11]

> [It has often been remarked that language seems as if naturally more suited to 'expressing' spatial relationships than any other kind of relationship (and therefore of reality), which leads it to use the former as symbols or metaphors for the latter, thus to treat all things in terms of space, and thus further to spatialize all things.]¹²

Here Genette suggests that 'spatialization' is an inherently efficient means of linguistic expression; language has a range of spatial terms at its disposal, and space is thus a suitable means for the symbolic mapping of all kinds of relations. As Genette comments elsewhere, however, it is not only the case that language manipulates a stable spatial semantics as a figurative means of expression; metaphorical spatial discourses actually create spatial meaning, resulting in a 'connoted space':

> Les métaphores spatiales constituent donc un discours, à portée presque universelle, puisqu'on y parle de tout, littérature, politique, musique, et dont l'espace constitue la forme, puisqu'il fournit les termes mêmes de son langage. Il y a bien ici un signifié, qui est l'objet variable du discours, et un signifiant, qui est le terme spatial. Mais du seul fait qu'il y a figure, c'est-à-dire transfert d'expression, à l'objet nommément désigné s'ajoute un second objet (l'espace), dont la présence est peut-être involontaire, en tout cas étrangère au propos initial, et introduite par la seule forme du discours. Il s'agit donc ici d'un espace *connoté*, manifesté plutôt que désigné, parlant plutôt que parlé, qui se trahit dans la métaphore comme l'inconscient se livre dans un rêve ou dans un lapsus.¹³

> [Spatial metaphors therefore constitute a discourse of an almost universal extent, since all things are discussed through it, literature, politics, music; and space constitutes its form, since it provides the very terms of its language. There is here a signified, which is the variable object of the discourse, and a signifier, which is the spatial term. But by the simple fact that there is figurative usage, that is to say transference of expression, a second object (space) is added to the nominally designated object; its presence is perhaps involuntary, in any case it is alien to the initial subject, and is introduced by the form of discourse alone. There is here thus a *connoted* space, manifested rather than designated, speaking rather than spoken, which betrays itself in metaphor just as the unconscious gives itself up in a dream or a lapse.]

This is why spatial terms acquire a powerful connotative aspect; their use recalls layers of associated meanings. These discourses are, of course, variable and subject to historical and cultural change. As Lotman observes, 'historical and ethnical linguistic models of space become the basis of a "picture of the world" — an integral conceptual model inherent to a given type of culture'.¹⁴

Other thinkers have seen space more in terms of mankind's experience of it: space is rendered significant in the first instance because it is interpreted by a subject who thinks and feels; it is symbolic because a subject attempts to understand the world and attributes meaning to it on his own terms. For the phenomenologist Maurice Merleau-Ponty, for example, physical space is conceived in relation to an 'embodied subject'. Physical space is 'my body and things, their concrete relationship expressed in such terms as top and bottom, right and left, near and far'.[15] Thinking about how space acquires meaning in language thus involves considering how objects in the physical world acquire meaning with reference to 'the pragmatic preconceptions of the perceiving subject'.[16]

The subjective experience of physical space is not confined to the present, however. For Gaston Bachelard, the significance of space lies in the role of places and objects in the memory and imagination. Space is, according to Bachelard, a structuring element of memory:

> C'est par l'espace, c'est dans l'espace que nous trouvons les beaux fossiles de durée concretisés par de longs séjours. L'inconscient séjourne. Les souvenirs sont immobiles, d'autant plus solides qu'ils sont mieux spatialisés.[17]
>
> [The finest specimens of fossilized duration concretized as a result of long sojourns, are to be found in and through space. The unconscious abides. Memories are motionless, and the more securely they are fixed in space, the sounder they are.][18]

Put more succinctly: 'space contains compressed time'.[19] Bachelard is not only concerned with space in memory, but also the process by which the imagination and memory affect the way in which individuals interact with external reality:

> L'espace saisi par l'imagination ne peut rester l'espace indifférent livré à la mesure et à la réflexion du géomètre. Il est vécu. Et il est vécu non pas dans sa positivité, mais avec toutes les impartialités de l'imagination.[20]
>
> [Space that has been seized upon by the imagination cannot remain indifferent space subject to the measures and estimates of the surveyor. It has been lived in, not in its positivity, but with all the partiality of the imagination.][21]

For Bachelard, the world can only be understood in terms of this interaction: both in real life, and in memory and imagination. The individual's environment is not detached, separate, 'indifferent'; each individual creates an emotional landscape, a topography of remembrances, dreams, and experiences which inform his continuing existence in that world.

Turning now to address theoretical approaches to literary space, these may be considered with reference to those ideas outlined above about how space acquires significance outside a literary text: in terms of interaction with it, and in terms of a linguistic framework of analogy. Literary theories of space may be divided into two main groups, or seen as representing a continuum between two poles. The first type of approach analyses individual descriptions, in which the most important factor is the influence of the figure describing or seeing the location in question, that is, the perspective or focalization. These descriptions of space are perceived by theorists as being largely independent of each other. The second approach places less emphasis on the relationship between the description and describer or viewer, and stresses rather the relationship between the various places represented in the text, that is, the structure. The represented locations are seen as constituting a meaningful network of alternatives and it could be argued that it is the relative position of the character within that network that carries the most significance. Space acquires meaning outside the text in terms of language and experience; space functions within the text as an organizing structure and marker of subjectivity.

Narratologists have provided significant insights into the structure and function of individual descriptions in the narrative text. For these scholars, description in a narrative text is a problem which needs to be explained, given that the primary function of a narrative, such as a novel, is to relate a story, and descriptive passages impede the progress of that narration. To shed light on this issue, Philippe Hamon analyses how descriptive passages are introduced into a text.[22] He concludes that representations of space are typically presented by a focalizer, an individual who is seeing, and that these descriptions must be motivated.[23] Spatial representation 'stems from the ability of the character to whom vision has been delegated',[24] and the focalizer must be able to know how to and want to see.[25] What is described is thus a subjective representation of the world seen through the filter of a human mind in the text. Hamon's findings are significant for an analysis of literary space, particularly in Realist works as will be the case in this study, because they establish a link between the character and ongoing action and the setting. The latter is no longer a separate backdrop, not objectively described scenery as might be expected of a Realist text, but directly linked to the voices and thoughts which permeate the text, as it is mediated through them. Hamon's focalizer provides an analytical tool for the discussion of subjectively rendered representation. The notion of focalization facilitates the analysis of spatial experience as described by Merleau-Ponty and Bachelard within the text's world.

Another critical approach which focuses on single images in a text is Bachelard's *La poétique de l'espace*, perhaps the best-known critical text on literary space, although in fact literary analysis is not the goal for the phenomenologist Bachelard, who is ultimately concerned with the human imagination. Bachelard contemplates each image in a text in isolation,[26] disregarding information outside the text such as biographical details, and not attempting to consider the relationship between the image in question and other images in the text.[27]

In his own terms, the method Bachelard employs to investigate the represented image is not reduction, which he claims is the psychoanalytical approach, but rather exaggeration.[28] Thus in his analysis of literary representations of the house, he considers a vertical axis running through the house: the cellar represents dark and irrational depths, while the attic is rational and intellectual, as well as a sheltering space under the roof.[29] The real difference may only be a matter of yards, but the imagination develops its significance: 'l'imagination augmente les valeurs de la réalité'.[30] While today it could certainly be claimed that much of Bachelard's work assumes foreknowledge of the western cultural tradition, and that the resulting contingency of many of his analyses goes without saying, Bachelard does restrict his survey of literary examples to western writers, and in this study of a nineteenth-century German novelist his approach is, for the same reason, unproblematic. Bachelard's particular contribution is that he demonstrates the potential significance that even apparently minor spatial references can have, because of their powerfully associative qualities.

Jurij Lotman's chapter on 'The Problem of Artistic Space' is, despite its brevity, the clearest and most thorough introduction to the analysis of space in a literary text. The basis of Lotman's argument is the observation that spatial metaphors are used to describe nearly all aspects of reality, and as such spatial descriptors acquire a wide range of cultural connotations.[31] Lotman goes on to observe that 'individual spatial models created by a text become meaningful against the background of these [cultural] constructions'.[32] An author uses the existing spatial framework and attaches his own thematic connotations, to the dichotomy high/low, for example. Space functions in the text thus as an 'organizing element around which its [the text's] non-spatial features are also constructed'.[33] Significantly, Lotman observes that this additional spatial model created by the text 'represents not only a variant of the general system, but also conflicts in some way with the system by de-automatizing its language'.[34] What Bachelard had termed the need to exaggerate the image, Lotman explains in different terms: because the author creates an alternative model of connotations attached to various spatial markers, the use of the vocabulary of spatial representation acquires a new significance and warrants investigation.

Unlike Bachelard, however, Lotman does not consider a single description in isolation, but rather sees the world represented in the text as constituting a whole.[35] He argues that the represented world is divided into spheres by the author in a 'spatial polyphony'.[36] Individual characters belong to particular zones, which have their own characteristics.[37] In this context, boundaries such as walls, rivers, and forests have special importance.[38] According to Lotman, spheres may only be considered separate if the boundary between them is impenetrable.[39] Michel Butor's analysis of space in the novel is a helpful supplement to this part of Lotman's discussion.[40] He too considers the space represented in the text as a whole, but while Lotman emphasizes division and separateness, Butor stresses the relationship between the constructed spheres:

> L'espace vécu n'est nullement l'espace euclidien dont les parties sont exclusives les unes des autres. Tout lieu est le foyer d'autres lieux, le point d'origine d'une série de parcours possibles passant par d'autres régions plus ou moins déterminées.[41]
>
> [Lived space is by no means Euclidean space, whose parts are exclusive of each other. Every place is the centre of other places, the point of origin of a series of possible journeys via other, more or less determined regions.]

It is from this relationship that the spaces acquire their relative meanings.

Thus Lotman's analysis, and to a certain extent Butor's, are representative of the second type of approach to space: the topography of the text as a framework which is to be studied alongside plot and character relationships. At the same time, the limitations of the division suggested in this discussion of spatial theories become clear: to arrive at an understanding of the overall topography and the properties of each location, an analysis of the descriptions of individual locations is presupposed. In addition, Lotman's analysis of space also necessitates an interpretation of the text as a whole, the investigation of relationships between characters, for example. Having begun thus with individual descriptions, and ended with the total space of the text, the varied possibilities of a spatial investigation become apparent. On the one hand, there is the potential to gain insights into individual characters and their world experience as represented in the text, and on the other, a spatial investigation provides an analytical framework for discussing a text as an integrated entity.

There are, however, limits to spatial poetics. If we consider developments of the positions taken by Hamon and Lotman by other theoreticians for example, these demonstrate a tendency towards over-complication, and occasionally an application of a theoretically defensible deduction which contradicts the evidence may be observed. Schlomith Rimmon-Kenan's *Narrative Fiction* seems to contain examples of the latter problem, which arise out of an over-emphasis on oppositional pairs.[42] Rimmon-Kenan elaborates various types of focalizer, including a narrating focalizer, and considers the different aspects, motivations, and properties of each kind of focalization. She deduces that an external focalizer, which is close to a narrating agent, is objective, while an internal focalizer is subjective.[43] The conclusion that the narrating agent is objective is a generalization which runs the risk of cancelling out the original value of focalization as a source of insight into narrative function. Similarly, Rimmon-Kenan's identification of panoramic views with an external focalizer, and limited observation with an internal focalizer, is potentially problematic, certainly for an author such as Fontane, where panoramic views are frequent and often linked to the subjective outlook of an individual character.[44]

Gabriel Zoran's and Ruth Ronen's theories of space in narrative from the mid-1980s illustrate the difficulties in elaborating and combining the various earlier theories of space in literature.[45] Both identify levels of textual space and seek to analyse these in a structured way. However, in so doing, their arguments become too complex: they go beyond what is necessary to assist practical textual criticism, without significantly contributing to it, partly because they both attempt to provide a model for details in the text where endless variation is possible. Similarly, if Mieke Bal's 'integrated descriptive model' appears to provide a more succesful account of descriptive functions, this is precisely because it addresses non-spatial elements, such as rhythm.[46] In this study, then, no new overarching theory of space in literature is proposed; of the two main types of approaches to space in literature, structural and focalization-based, neither will be given priority. What is required is flexibility and the readiness to respond to the individual text.

Literary Space and Fontane's Poetics

At first glance, the above theories and questions appear to be solely concerned with the presentation of space within the text, with how it works as a structure to communicate meaning to a reader. However, narratological theories of the focalizer introduce a subjective element, in which the subject's experience of his spatial environment within the text is prioritized. Focalization is a way of discussing the presence of subjective perception in description, and it is possible for this perception itself to become a major thematic focus of a text. In Fontane's texts, this has the potential to become a reflexive discourse on the literary process, because aesthetic perception and representation of an empirically real world by an artist or observing subject is the keystone of Realist, and of Fontane's own, poetics.

The central term in Fontane's poetics, and arguably in German Realism in general, is *Verklärung*.[47] This attribute is what distinguishes art from non-art, the artistically created object from real life. The Realist art work is mimetic, but in the work of art the reality which is its source is formed and shaped; its 'Modelung'[48] creates 'Intensität, Klarheit, Übersichtlichkeit, und Abrundung'.[49] *Verklärung* is thus not only an attribute, but a process. It is the 'Läuterung',[50] the rendering and treatment of life into art, the 'Durchgangsprozeß' responsible for 'die künstlerische Wirkung'.[51] This process describes the act of composition, the '*künstlerische Wiedergabe* (nicht das bloße Abschreiben) *des Lebens*',[52] but it may also describe the way in which an object, person, or scene becomes beautiful in real life as a result of light, perspective, or other circumstance.

In Fontane's view, Realist art must be beautiful. Presenting beauty is not synonymous with decorating or falsifying reality, however, as beauty is part of life: 'Der *echte* Realismus wird auch immer schönheitsvoll sein; denn das Schöne, Gott sei Dank, gehört dem Leben gerade so gut an wie das Häßliche'.[53]

The presentations of beauty and reality are not mutually exclusive; rather, the presence of beauty in the artwork is the product of a specific approach to the source: 'Die Schönheit ist *da*, man muß nur ein Auge dafür haben'.[54] Aesthetic perception, 'die künstlerische Betrachtung des Lebens', is at the centre of Fontane's way of thinking and describing his art,[55] and the capacity to perceive defines a poet for him: 'Das Leben ist doch immer nur der Marmorsteinbruch, der den Stoff zu unendlichen Bildwerken in sich trägt; sie schlummern darin, aber nur dem Auge des Geweihten sichtbar'.[56] This concept of artistic perception, of a way of looking at the world and life, is not synonymous with aesthetic theories of detached and disinterested observation. In fact, Fontane consistently underlines the inevitability of subjectivity. In *Vor dem Sturm*, Berndt von Vitzewitz comments: 'ein jeder sieht, was er zu sehen wünscht',[57] and in *Schach von Wuthenow*, Victoire observes: 'das Allerpersönlichste bestimmt immer unser Urteil'.[58] Fontane often argues that engaged and personal interaction with the object is the best way of appreciating the object's value. Particularly in the *Wanderungen*, he stresses the need to look at a landscape, apparently lacking in beauty, with favourable, loving eyes.[59] The viewer must be predisposed to see beauty in the world, and this often means that he must come to the object with knowledge which will draw out a significance not immediately apparent. In *Jenseit des Tweed*, Fontane writes of 'Das Land der "Lady of the Lake"': 'Um dieses Land zu verstehen und zu genießen, ist es nötig, mit dem Inhalt der gleichnamigen Dichtung einigermaßen vertraut zu sein'.[60]

There is no space here to develop a more detailed analysis of Fontane's aesthetics, although there is scope within current research for a more thorough treatment of the theme of aesthetic perception in Fontane's work. From the above outline, however, it should be clear that, because of the close ties Fontane sees between real-world perception and artistic perception, and the key role that viewing and observing plays in Fontane's critical discourse, the representation of observers and of interaction with environment has the potential to become a complex, critical reflection on the artistic process itself.

In its most simple form, then, a spatial analysis is one in which the focus of investigation is on the world represented in the text, the way it is constructed, the way characters interact with it and its meaning for them, rather than the characters themselves or their relationships which might ordinarily be privileged. Considering the spatial theories outlined above, it is clear that a spatial analysis can never be one-sided; a number of interpretative options or questions are available to the analyst of literary space. The representation of the textual world as a whole must be considered. Is it a map which charts developments in the plot or evolutions in emotion? Directions and relationships must be observed carefully: are these used metaphorically to refer to other potential developments? Individual descriptions must be analysed. Who is relating this information to the reader, the narrator or a character? Do these descriptions represent the inner workings of a character's mind, or is an omniscient narrator providing the reader with information relevant to later events? It will become evident in the course of this study that Fontane's texts respond variously to these questions. Each text works differently, even if many of the techniques are similar. Alongside those questions above about the represented spatial world, the more general question must be posed: what is this text about? What is the main issue, and how does space in the text relate to it? In Fontane's texts, these questions often lead to complex and revealing explorations of the function and nature of literature.

Literature Review

Scholars have been examining space in Fontane's works since the beginning of Fontane research in the early twentieth century. Max Tau's 1928 monograph, *Der assoziative Faktor in der Landschafts- und Ortsdarstellung Theodor Fontanes*, has had a lasting effect on how Fontane's spatial representation is perceived.[61] Tau seeks to establish whether Fontane creates coherent, living worlds in his texts, and assesses him largely negatively. According to Tau, the texts do not create convincing impressions of autumn, for example, but typically state that it is autumn, and then list generally accepted signs of that season, such as yellowed leaves.[62] Fontane's worlds are stage scenery against which events unfold, rather than living entities themselves. This negative judgement leads, however, to a more positive contribution to Fontane studies, and one which continues to be relevant: according to Tau, spatial representation in Fontane's texts serves primarily to provide a series of symbolic indicators. Tau lists a number of emblematic symbolic objects, for example, which he argues convincingly have a fixed allegorical value.[63] Tau argues that Fontane's symbolism is not created by the text itself, but draws on the reader's cultural knowledge. The readers associate the object represented with its commonly known meaning, which then informs their reading of the text.

Wolfgang Rost's study, *Örtlichkeit und Schauplatz in Fontanes Werken* (1930), is still useful today, as it is based on a range of manuscripts, some of which have been lost. Rost seeks to give an account of how Fontane's texts represent space, in journalism, ballad, and prose narrative.[64] Positivistic in style, Rost's work includes many precise observations, but makes no attempt at interpretative analysis. Unlike Tau, Rost does not seek to uncover a layer of symbolism in Fontane's work, but rather to elucidate the process by which Fontane creates realistic literary settings based on real places. Bruno Hillebrand's *Mensch und Raum im Roman* (1971) does not develop the views of Tau or Rost substantially, but does provide interesting analyses of individual details, in particular for *Vor dem Sturm*.⁶⁵ Hillebrand's text does, however, provide a bridge between the early phase of spatial scholarship in Fontane studies and the beginning of the modern, productive phase in the 1980s.

In 1981 Gotthard Wunberg produced a topographical analysis of *Der Stechlin*, in which he sees the description of the garden and 'Poetensteig' as an 'implizierte Poetik' and ultimately a representation of Fontane's *Weltanschauung*.⁶⁶ Though at times too neat for such a multifaceted and paradoxical novel, Wunberg's reading shows the potential of a spatial analysis for uncovering unknown layers of meaning, and the connection between spatial representation and poetics is an important precedent for this project. In the same year Gisela Wilhelm's monograph *Die Dramaturgie des epischen Raumes bei Fontane* appeared, and may be contrasted with Wunberg's essay in terms of approach.⁶⁷ While Wunberg had focused on one text, Wilhelm attempts to generalize as to the function of specific types of situations in Fontane's novels, and while some of her insights are valuable, overall the outcomes are too vague.

Klaus Haberkamm's 1986 structuralist analysis of the directional and local terms east/west and left/right in *Effi Briest* can be regarded as a highpoint in spatial research into Fontane's art, and in Fontane scholarship more generally.⁶⁸ Haberkamm exhaustively demonstrates the extent to which the investigation of seemingly insignificant spatial markers, in this case left and right, may uncover a network of meaning in the text. In the same year, Karla Müller published an interpretation of three of Fontane's novels also using a structuralist spatial methodology.⁶⁹ In *Schloßgeschichten: Eine Studie zum Romanwerk Theodor Fontanes*, she produces topographical models for *Graf Petöfy*, *Unwiederbringlich*, and *Der Stechlin*. She considers the spatial world in terms of binary pairs which serve as a template for a wider interpretation of the novels, but her argument also focuses on the representation of the castle in these texts. Through the paradigm of the castle, which she sees linked to sickness, Müller seeks to weave the analyses of the novels together, though the socio-historical reasoning for this, which is presented after the textual readings at the end, seems extraneous to the three interpretations. Michael Andermatt's comparative study addresses *Effi Briest* in his *Haus und Zimmer im Roman* (1988), this time from a narratological perspective.⁷⁰

Space remains a current concern in Fontane studies. In an essay published in 2000, Klaus Scherpe argues that the straying of individual characters from their natural milieus is what precipitates disaster in Fontane's texts,⁷¹ while Haberkamm in a 2006 article provides a convincingly argued demonstration of a symbolic left–right dichotomy in *Irrungen Wirrungen*.⁷² The *Fontane-Blätter* in 2008 published a series of articles related to the representation of interior spaces, topography, and garden landscapes.⁷³

Reviewing publications to date, it appears that the most illuminating spatial analyses have been those which have either focused on an individual text, or, as in Müller's case for example, have allowed for semi-independent analyses of particular works. This insight has informed the structure of this study, which favours the treatment of each text largely separately, drawing out the variety and specificity of Fontane's spatial symbolism.

With this review of criticism which treats space explicitly, the secondary literature relevant to this thesis is by no means exhausted. It is in the nature of spatial studies that work relating to space in literature is conducted under a number of different headings. Research into Fontane's Realism is one particularly valuable source of relevant scholarship. As with the literature on space in Fontane's texts, the story of the critical understanding of his Realism is one of the progressive uncovering of the poetic quality of Fontane's writing. There is a move away from a desire to portray Fontane as the creator of realistic worlds, observable in Rost, to scholarship which poses the question: what does the represented world signify?

For Peter Demetz, whose 1964 monograph is still standard reading, the function of spatial description in Fontane's texts is primarily to provide a suitable situation for conversation.[74] Landscape is, for Demetz, unimportant.[75] Yet earlier works, such as Derek Barlow's study of *Der Stechlin*, had begun to interpret the deeply symbolic worlds Fontane creates.[76] Interest in Fontane's symbolism gained ground in the 1960s, firstly in Vincent Günther's 1967 investigation which aimed at a categorizaion of various types of symbolism in Fontane's work,[77] and then in Ohl's influential work, *Bild und Wirklichkeit: Studien zur Romankunst Raabes und Fontanes* (1968).[78] Here Ohl argues for a particular kind of symbolism, which is contained and created within and by the text alone. He indicates the importance of the panoramic view in Fontane's work, in which the relationships between the individual components of the image, and the image and the viewing character, determine the significance of a description. In a 1971 essay, Dietrich Brüggemann follows Ohl's argument that object and textual meaning are separate in Fontane's texts, but suggests that allegory is a more suitable analytical term than symbolism.[79] Brüggemann's article betrays the lasting influence of Tau, however, and his emphasis on a single, inflexible term ignores Günther's earlier attempt at a more differentiated view of Fontane's symbolic art.

The increasing move towards viewing Fontane's texts as less real and more poetic is not simply the product of the influence of critical theory at the time, but also derives concrete, historical credibility from work by Richard Brinkmann in 1967 and Hugo Aust in 1974 on Fontane's poetics.[80] Both discuss *Verklärung*, the creation of difference between the symbolic textual world and the real world which lies at the heart of Fontane's conception of Realist art.

Research in the 1980s further pursued the dimensions of poetry and imagination in the work of the Realist Fontane. Helen Chambers's 1980 monograph systematically demonstrates the significance of supernatural and irrational elements in Fontane's oeuvre,[81] while Alan Bance's 1982 study explores the relationship between poetic and prosaic elements in Fontane's novels.[82] In 1985, Patricia Howe and Ronald Speirs both published important articles in this vein, focusing on the imagination in *Irrungen Wirrungen*.[83] It is possible to see Lieselotte Voß's monograph, *Literarische Präfigurationen dargestellter Wirklichkeit bei Fontane* (1985), in this context as she suggests intertextual reference rather than the empirical world alone as a source of inspiration for Fontane's represented worlds.[84] The product of these labours has been a more intensive, close analysis of Fontane's texts, in which every detail is seen as meaningful. An example of this kind of close reading is Gunther Hertling's study of *Irrungen Wirrungen*, in which he argues that the whole narrative is prefigured in the first page of text.[85]

There has been, in addition, a range of studies on specific elements in Fontane's texts and their symbolic meanings. Examples of this kind of interpretation of objects in the represented world are Helen Chambers's article on moon and stars in 1984,[86] Klaus Dieter Post's analysis of the heliotrope in *Effi Briest* in 1990,[87] and Hauke Stcoszeck's recent contribution on swallows.[88] Berlin and its specific importance for Fontane's oeuvre have also been the subject of research. Albrecht Kloepper's 1992 systematic analysis of the representation of Berlin, in which he divides the city into a series of zones, is particularly valuable.[89]

A further significant development in recent years which is of relevance to a spatial investigation is the research conducted into the *Wanderungen durch die Mark Brandenburg* in the context of travel literature. This adds to the general tendency of research away from questions about 'realistic' representation, towards seeking to investigate and evaluate the potential literary function of description. In 1995 Hubertus Fischer published an article which examines the cultural historical context in which Fontane's *Wanderungen* emerged, with a view to uncovering their artistry.[90] Stefan Neuhaus's 1998 discussion of Fontane's journalism can perhaps best be described as an appeal to scholars to study it as literature,[91] an appeal which has been answered in part in the recently published *'Geschichte und Geschichten aus Mark Brandenburg': Fontanes Wanderungen durch die Mark Brandenburg im Kontext der europäischen Reiseliteratur*, a collection of conference papers on the *Wanderungen* in the context of travel literature.[92] This volume is evidence that the debate about the represented world in Fontane's oeuvre is ongoing and relevant to today's scholarship, and capable of opening new avenues into the workings of his texts.

INTRODUCTION 15

Summary and Aims

This introduction to the subject of space in Fontane has sought to demonstrate that the analysis of spatial representation is an appropriate methodological approach to the study of Fontane's texts, in order to gain a clearer sense of Fontane's own spatial sensibility and of the Realist awareness of space as a carrier of poetic meaning, and also because space has proved a productive analytical tool in previous studies and continues to be a fruitful focus of scholarly debate.

It has been shown that there are two main approaches to analysing the function of space in literary texts, one focusing on topography, the other on figural focalization. This discussion draws on both methodologies, adopting a flexible methodological approach which responds to the individual text. In addition to general theories of literary space, it also draws on Fontane's own aesthetics, as documented in his writings and scholarly research.

This study seeks both to build on existing scholarship and, more importantly, to break fresh ground by dealing with a wider range of texts, incorporating more primary material than many of the more recent works on space in Fontane have done. In line with current research, the project incorporates the *Wanderungen* together with a range of novels. The novels have been selected to provide a balanced picture of Fontane's narrative output: early and less well-known works have been analysed alongside later, more canonical novels. This investigation thus addresses a more diverse selection of texts from the oeuvre than scholarship on space hitherto. While tracing correspondences, it provides a series of coherent interpretations based on spatial insights which can stand independently in their own right.

In addition, most spatial interpretations focus entirely on spatial representation in the text as an aspect of the literary text's formal composition. As Lotman argues, however, the view that a literary text is defined primarily by its formal qualities is erroneous; it is the semantic aspect of literature, the layers of meaning, which create the difference between an aesthetically functioning text and other text forms.[93] Viewed in this light, space in the text is not only form but also content. This study uncovers the extent to which space and spatial experience can at times become the object of literary exploration in Fontane's works, and argues that through this Fontane creates a complex, reflexive discourse on his art and its place in our lives.

Notes to the Introduction

1. HA III, 3/I, 12.
2. HA III, 4, 186.
3. *Reallexikon der deutschen Literaturwissenschaft: Neubearbeitung des Reallexikons der deutschen Literaturgeschichte*, ed. by Jan-Dirk Müller and others (Berlin: de Gruyter, 2007); Gero von Wilpert, *Sachwörterbuch der Literatur* (Stuttgart: Kröner, 1969); *The New Princeton Encyclopedia of Poetry and Poetics*, ed. by Alex Preminger and others (Princeton: Princeton University Press, 1993).
4. *Germanistik: Internationales Referatenorgan mit bibliographischen Hinweisen*, ed. by Wilfried Barner and others (Tübingen: Niemeyer, 1960–); *Bibliographie der deutschen Sprach- und Literaturwissenschaft*, ed. by Wilhelm R. Schmidt (Frankfurt a. M.: Klostermann, 1970–).
5. See Maurice Blanchot, *L'espace littéraire* (Paris: Gallimard, 1955).
6. See Joseph Frank, 'Spatial Form in Modern Literature', in Joseph Frank, *The Widening Gyre: Crisis and Masters in Modern Literature* (Brunswick, NJ: Rutgers University Press, 1963), pp. 3–62, throughout, but especially pp. 13, 56, 60.
7. See Sigrid Weigel, ' "On the Topographical Turn": Concepts of Space in Cultural Studies and *Kulturwissenschaften*. A Cartographic Feud', *European Review*, 17 (2009), 187–201.
8. J. Hillis Miller, *Topographies* (Stanford, CA: Stanford University Press, 1995), p. 5.
9. Jurij Lotman, 'The Problem of Artistic Space', in Jurij Lotman, *The Structure of the Artistic Text*, trans. by Ronald Vroon (Ann Arbor: University of Michigan, 1977), pp. 217–31 (p. 218).
10. Ibid.
11. Gérard Genette, 'La littérature et l'espace', in Gérard Genette, *Figures II* (Paris: Seuil, 1969), pp. 43–49 (p. 44).
12. Translations unless otherwise stated are my own, M. W.
13. Gérard Genette, 'Espace et langage', in Gérard Genette, *Figures, essais* (Paris: Seuil, 1969), pp. 101–08 (p. 103). Genette's emphasis.
14. Lotman, 'Artistic Space', p. 218.
15. Stephen Priest, *Merleau-Ponty* (London: Routledge, 1998), p. 103. Merleau-Ponty distinguishes between 'physical space', which is conceived as objects in relation to each other, and 'geometrical space', which consists of positions not dependent on the existence of things.
16. From Merleau-Ponty's introduction to *Phénoménologie de la perception*, cited in Priest, *Merleau-Ponty*, p. 5.
17. Gaston Bachelard, *La poétique de l'espace* (Paris: Presses Universitaires de France, 1967), p. 28.
18. Gaston Bachelard, *The Poetics of Space*, trans. by Maria Jolas (Boston: Beacon Press, 1994), p. 9.
19. Ibid., p. 8.
20. Bachelard, *Poétique*, p. 17.
21. Bachelard/Jolas, *Poetics*, p. xxxvi.
22. Philippe Hamon, 'Introduction à l'analyse du descriptif (1981)', in Philippe Hamon, *La Description littéraire. De l'antiquité à Roland Barthes: une anthologie* (Paris: Macula, 1991), pp. 264–73 (p. 264).
23. Ibid.
24. Ibid.
25. Ibid.
26. Bachelard, *Poétique*, p. 8.

27. Roch C. Smith, *Gaston Bachelard* (Boston, MA: Twayne, 1982), p. 118.
28. Ibid., p. 118.
29. Bachelard/Jolas, *Poetics*, p. 5.
30. Bachelard, *Poétique*, p. 23.
31. Lotman, 'Artistic Space', p. 216.
32. Ibid., p. 218.
33. Ibid., p. 229.
34. Ibid.
35. Ibid., pp. 229–31.
36. Ibid., p. 231.
37. Ibid.
38. Ibid., pp. 229–30.
39. Ibid., p. 230.
40. Michel Butor, 'L'espace du roman', in Michel Butor, *Essais sur le roman* (Paris: Gallimard, 1969), pp. 48–58.
41. Ibid., p. 56.
42. Schlomith Rimmon-Kenan, *Narrative Fiction, Contemporary Poetics*, 4th edn (London: Routledge, 1993).
43. Ibid., p. 80.
44. Ibid., p. 77.
45. Gabriel Zoran, 'Towards a Theory of Space in Narrative', *Poetics Today*, 5 (1984), 309–35; Ruth Ronen, 'Space in Fiction', *Poetics Today*, 7 (1986), 421–38.
46. Mieke Bal, *On Story-Telling* (Sonoma, CA: Polebridge Press, 1991), pp. 132–45.
47. For Fontane specifically, see Hugo Aust, *Theodor Fontane: 'Verklärung'. Eine Untersuchung zum Ideengehalt seiner Werke*, (Bonn: Bouvier, 1974); for Realism in general, see Hugo Aust, *Literatur des Realismus* (Stuttgart: Metzler, 2000), pp. 53–55.
48. *Theaterkritiken* (1890), 'Holz/Schlaf: *Die Familie Selicke*', HA III, 2, 847.
49. Essay on Paul Lindau, 'Fassung aus dem Nachlaß' (1886), HA III, 1, 569.
50. 'Unsere lyrische und epische Poesie seit 1848' (1853), HA III, 1, 241.
51. HA III, 2, 847.
52. 'Emile Zola' (1883), HA III, 1, 540. Fontane's emphasis.
53. To Emilie Fontane, 14 June 1883, in Theodor Fontane, *Briefe*, ed. by Gotthard Erler, 2nd edn, 2 vols (Munich: Nymphenburger Verlagshandlung, 1981), II, 103. Fontane's emphasis.
54. Ibid.
55. To Martha Fontane, 22 August 1895, HA IV, 4, 472.
56. HA III, 1, 241.
57. HA, I, 1, 176.
58. HA I, 1, 616.
59. See HA, II, 1, 12.
60. HA IV, 3, 289.
61. Max Tau, *Der assoziative Faktor in der Landschafts- und Ortsdarstellung Theodor Fontanes* (Kiel: Schwartz, 1928).
62. Ibid., p. 22.
63. Ibid., pp. 24–31.
64. Wolfgang E. Rost, *Örtlichkeit und Schauplatz in Fontanes Werken* (Berlin: de Gruyter, 1930).
65. Bruno Hillebrand, *Mensch und Raum im Roman: Studien zu Keller, Stifter und Fontane* (Munich: Winkler, 1971).
66. Gotthard Wunberg, 'Rondell und Poetensteig: Topographie und implizierte Poetik

in Fontanes "Stechlin"', in *Literaturwissenschaft und Geistesgeschichte: Festschrift für Richard Brinkmann*, ed. by Jürgen Brummach and others (Tübingen: Niemeyer, 1981), pp. 458–73.
67. Gisela Wilhelm, *Die Dramaturgie des epischen Raumes bei Fontane* (Frankfurt a. M.: Fischer, 1981).
68. Klaus Haberkamm, '"Links und rechts umlauert": Zu einem symbolischen Schema in Fontanes *Effi Briest*', *MLN*, 101 (1986), 553–91.
69. Karla Müller, *Schloßgeschichten: Eine Studie zum Romanwerk Theodor Fontanes* (Munich: Fink, 1986).
70. Michael Andermatt, *Haus und Zimmer im Roman: Die Genese des erzählten Raums bei Eugenie Marlitt, Theodor Fontane und Franz Kafka* (Berne: Lang, 1988).
71. Klaus R. Scherpe, 'Ort oder Raum? Fontanes literarische Topographie', in *Theodor Fontane am Ende des Jahrhunderts: Internationales Symposium des Theodor-Fontane-Archivs zum 100. Todestag Theodor Fontanes 13.–17. September 1998 in Potsdam*, ed. by Hanna Delf von Wolzogen and Helmuth Nürnberger, 3 vols (Würzburg: Königshausen & Neumann, 2000), III, 161–69.
72. Klaus Haberkamm, '"Nein, nein, die Linke, die kommt von Herzen." Zur Rechts-Links-Dichotomie in Fontanes *Irrungen, Wirrungen*', *FBl*, 82 (2006), 82–109.
73. *FBl*, 85 (2008): Uta Schürmann, 'Tickende Gehäuseuhr, gefährliches Sofa: Interieurbeschreibungen in Fontanes Romanen', 115–31; Constantin Stroop, 'Raum und Erzählen in *Vor dem Sturm*: Eine Mikroanalyse', 103–14; Jana Kittelmann, '". . . die ganze Welt ein Idyll"? Gartenbeschreibungen bei Theodor Fontane und Hermann von Pückler-Muskau', 132–49.
74. Peter Demetz, *Formen des Realismus: Theodor Fontane. Kritische Untersuchungen* (Munich: Hanser, 1964), pp. 116–18.
75. Ibid., p. 121.
76. Derek Barlow, 'Symbolism in Fontane's *Der Stechlin*', *German Life and Letters*, 12 (1958–59), 282–86.
77. Vincent J. Günther, *Das Symbol im erzählerischen Werk Fontanes* (Bonn: Bouvier, 1967).
78. Hubert Ohl, *Bild und Wirklichkeit: Studien zur Romankunst Raabes und Fontanes* (Heidelberg: Stiehm, 1968).
79. Dietrich Brüggemann, 'Fontane's Allegorien', *Neue Rundschau*, 82 (1971), 290–310 and 486–505.
80. Richard Brinkmann, *Theodor Fontane: Über die Verbindlichkeit des Unverbindlichen* (Munich: Piper, 1967); Aust, *Verklärung*.
81. Helen E. Chambers, *Supernatural and Irrational Elements in the Works of Theodor Fontane* (Stuttgart: Heinz, 1980).
82. Alan Bance, *Theodor Fontane: The Major Novels* (Cambridge: Cambridge University Press, 1982).
83. Patricia Howe, 'Reality and Imagination in Fontane's *Irrungen, Wirrungen*', *German Life and Letters*, 38 (1985), 346–56; Ronald Speirs, '"Un schlimm is eigentlich man bloß das Einbilden": Zur Rolle der Phantasie in *Irrungen, Wirrungen*', *FBl*, 39 (1985), 67–78.
84. Lieselotte Voß, *Literarische Präfiguration dargestellter Wirklichkeit bei Fontane: Zur Zitatstruktur seines Romanwerks* (Munich: Fink, 1985).
85. Gunther H. Hertling, *Theodor Fontanes 'Irrungen, Wirrungen': Die erste Seite als Schlüssel zum Werk* (New York: Lang, 1985).
86. Helen E. Chambers, 'Mond und Sterne in Fontanes Werken', *FBl*, 37 (1984), 457–76.
87. Klaus Dieter Post, '"Das eigentliche Parfüm des Wortes": Zum Doppelbild des Heliotrop in Theodor Fontanes Roman *Effi Briest*', *FBl*, 49 (1990), 32–39.

88. Hauke Stcoszeck, 'Schwalben: Ein Nachtrag zu Fontanes poetischer Avi fauna', in *FBl*, 70 (2000), 76–92.
89. Albrecht Kloepper, 'Fontanes Berlin: Funktion und Darstellung der Stadt in seinen Zeit-Romanen', *Germanisch-Romanische Monatschrift*, 42 (1992), 67–86.
90. Hubertus Fischer, 'Märkische Bilder: Ein Versuch über Fontanes *Wanderungen durch die Mark Brandenburg*, ihre Bilder und ihre Bildlichkeit', *FBl*, 60 (1995), 117–42.
91. Stefan Neuhaus, 'Und nichts als die Wahrheit? Wie der Journalist Fontane Erlebtes wiedergab', *FBl*, 65–66 (1998), 188–213.
92. *'Geschichte und Geschichten aus Mark Brandenburg': Fontanes 'Wanderungen durch die Mark Brandenburg' im Kontext der europäischen Reiseliteratur. Internationales Symposium des Theodor-Fontane-Archivs in Zusammenarbeit mit der Theodor Fontane Gesellschaft 18.–22. September 2002 in Potsdam*, ed. by Hanna Delf von Wolzogen (Würzburg: Königshausen & Neumann, 2003).
93. Yury M. [sic.] Lotman, 'The Content and the Structure of Literature', in *Twentieth-Century Literary Theory: A Reader*, ed. by K. M. Newton (London: Macmillan, 1988), pp. 176–80 (p. 177).

CHAPTER 1

~

Spatial Representation and the Boundaries of the Literary Text: *Die Grafschaft Ruppin*

Abhandlungen haben ihr Gesetz und die Dichtung auch.
Letter to Emilie, 24 June 1881[1]

Introduction

To modern readers, Fontane is above all known as the author of social novels, such as *Frau Jenny Treibel* (1892), or *Effi Briest* (1895). For his contemporary readership however, Fontane's identity as a novelist was a later addition to his already established reputation as the writer of a series of travel feuilletons about the local area and its history, the *Wanderungen durch die Mark Brandenburg*, which the author began in 1859 following his return from Britain, wrote over a period of twenty years, and edited until into the 1890s.[2] Twentieth-century Fontane scholarship has consisted, in part at least, in revising the perception of Fontane as wanderer, Prussian conservative, and balladeer in favour of a novelist of a subtle but highly refined art with a critical, liberal disposition. Accordingly, the *Wanderungen* have been viewed by modern scholars as subordinate to Fontane's novelistic output, either as incomplete,[3] or as a training ground and collection of motifs and settings to be employed in the fiction of his later years.[4]

From the 1990s onwards however, primarily in the wake of new interest in travel literature,[5] but also as a result of shifting attitudes to Fontane's journalism,[6] and indeed journalism more generally, a new consensus seems to be emerging that the *Wanderungen* should be treated as a work of poetic literature.[7] The recent publication *'Geschichte und Geschichten aus Mark Brandenburg.' Fontanes 'Wanderungen durch die Mark Brandenburg' im Kontext der europäischen Reiseliteratur* is dominated by articles which argue for such a reading.[8] In this chapter, we will consider what a spatial analysis can bring to the debate. We will begin in this introduction by addressing some of the problems with seeing the *Wanderungen* as poetic literature, before proposing that the *Wanderungen*'s texts may be classed into three groups according to their various types of spatial representation. These groups will then be discussed in turn.

Considering the *Wanderungen* as literature in the narrow sense raises major issues. The first problem concerns the text's apparent lack of unity, arising from its extended genesis and overall length. Many commentators have highlighted the evolution in Fontane's political views during the *Wanderungen* years, from conservatism to liberalism and a more critical stance towards the establishment.[9] Fontane's aims and ambitions for his text also evolved. While the earliest diary entries which refer to a *Wanderungen* project suggest a reference work, written for the purposes of collecting material for future poets,[10] the first written chapters are impressionistic travelogues, closer to the type of travel writing Fontane praised in related, contemporary works.[11] In addition, once the *Wanderungen* were being produced, Fontane acknowledged further changes in style. Writing to Wilhelm Hertz in 1861, he comments:

> Dennoch denk' ich es ist richtig, daß ich diesen Touristen-, diesen gemüthlichen Wandrer-Ton [...] aufgegeben und statt dessen mehr eine Erzählungsweise angenommen habe, die von dem Erzähler selbst möglichst abstrahirt und den *Stoff* giebt wie er sich findet, sei er nun historisch oder landschaftlich.[12]

The outcome of these shifting aims and methods of writing is further complicated by the author's editorial practices. It is not simply the case that the earliest chapters are located at the beginning of the text, and the later ones at the end. Fontane was constantly adding to and changing the text, as it grew into its four volumes, and the final collection *Spreewald* (1882) contains in fact many of the oldest compositions. The product is thus a complex and multifaceted text, which challenges, even at a superficial level of analysis, 'quite possibly *the* fundamental [...] aesthetic criterion', unity.[13]

Nevertheless, despite these difficulties, scholars have been able to deal with the issue of unity by acknowledging the variety of the text, and admitting a looser sense of coherence,[14] or by ascribing significance to discord. Pierre Bange for example sees it as a formal representation of relativism and scepticism.[15] Perhaps, however, Peter Wruck's view is the most persuasive. He argues that the *Wanderungen* is composed of individual chapters within an open, cumulative macrostructure, and that consequently it is a work which it is difficult to approach with traditional aesthetic models.[16]

Yet it is not primarily the matter of unity which occupies scholars most when arguing that the *Wanderungen* ought to be considered as a literary text. Commentators stress rather the subjectivity and self-sufficiency of the *Wanderungen* text. Stefan Neuhaus puts the argument clearly. He states that 'die Geschlossenheit, Stimmigkeit, und Ausrichtigkeit des Textes auf eine

Aussage hin war Fontane wichtiger als die Authentizität', and that accordingly the *Wanderungen* deserve literary interpretation.[17] Neuhaus is arguing here that the *Wanderungen* texts are independent, that they work as an integrated, organic whole, and that their relationship to reality is of secondary importance. These are standard descriptions of a literary text's qualities. Gero von Wilpert's *Sachwörterbuch der Literatur*, for example, describes 'Dichtung' thus: 'Dichtung schafft eine in sich geschlossene Eigenwelt von größter Höhe, Reinheit und Einstimmigkeit mit eigenen Gesetzen'.[18] To use a term more appropriate to a spatial investigation of literature, the poetic text is another world, it is a heterocosm.[19]

These types of arguments about the other-worldliness of literature rest essentially on the direction of reference that the signifiers in an aesthetically functioning text make. As Paul de Man puts it, the literary text is free from 'referential constraints'.[20] A text which refers primarily to external reality (and is thus tied to it) is deemed non-poetic or non-literary, whereas referring to itself to construct meaning is typical of a poetic text. It is through its self-reference that the text, as a web of meaning, constitutes an organic whole, and it is unified through its symbolism, the layers of meaning that each textual element acquires, when considered alongside the other parts.

The argument of textual autonomy is also historically defensible here. The Realist poetics Fontane advocated are based on the widespread concept of *Verklärung*, the process of selecting, organizing, and representing reality in a way appropriate to art, which should be beautiful. The independent organicism which Neuhaus and others appear to argue the *Wanderungen* text creates, accords thus not only with generally accepted models of literary theory, but also with Fontane's own.

The purpose of reiterating and explaining some of these, perhaps well-known, arguments is to show that the *Wanderungen* are being accepted as a poetic text not because of a revised view of literature *per se*, but because qualities are being recognized in the text which fit already accepted criteria. The question this chapter will address is, is this new consensus right? Is the *Wanderungen* text a heterocosm?

Again there are immediately visible problems, perhaps most obviously the presence of non-literary elements in the *Wanderungen* such as lists or diagrams. Fontane often adds pages of third-party diary entries or historical documents. How are these texts to be integrated into a literary reading? How can a catalogue of paintings be said to constitute 'eine in sich geschlossene Eigenwelt'? Further, faced with such problems, how is it that scholars have managed to produce persuasive arguments and analyses in favour of a poetic reading? There must be evidence. There are indeed poetic elements in the *Wanderungen*, even fictional, or quasi-fictional, episodes, and the image of the wanderer is in many cases quite clearly metaphorical rather than real.[21] Another, this time methodological, aspect to be considered, however, is that, because the complete text is long, most scholars engaging in detailed analysis do so only with a limited number of extracts. Each of the chapters in the volume '*Geschichte und Geschichten aus Mark Brandenburg*' can necessarily cover only one small part of the *Wanderungen*, and yet from that, many of the authors draw conclusions about the whole four-volume work and its essence. It will be the purpose of this chapter to produce a more precise, nuanced reading, incorporating the range of different text types in the *Wanderungen*.

This analysis will draw only on the first volume of the *Wanderungen*, *Die Grafschaft Ruppin*. This is a manageable amount of text, permitting a thorough analysis, and yet it is representative of the major problems that the *Wanderungen* pose. *Die Grafschaft Ruppin* contains texts from the early and late phases of writing, unlike *Das Oderland*, for example, which is more uniform, and *Die Grafschaft Ruppin* has passages which range from verse and poetic prose to lists. Using the function of spatial representation in the text as a focus and methodological approach in order to produce a textual interpretation, the discussion will pose the following types of questions: does the text refer inwardly as a heterocosmic text, or is it dependent on its real-world context? Is the function of space symbolic in these texts as would be expected in a poetic text? Do objects and places in the represented world carry significance beyond themselves within 'the work itself as a structure of meaning?'[22] If not, how may spatial representation in the text be best described? What alternatives might there be to describing the text as poetic?

Three different functions of space will be distinguished. In the first of these, the text is closest to journalistic or essayistic writing. That is not to say that these texts are objective or simple. The narrator may be observed to organize reality, creating a clarified schema or view; this may serve a purely textual or stylistic need, to orientate the reader for example, or it may serve to support a particular bias or message that the author wishes to convey. This type of spatial representation will be termed *rhetorical*. At the second level it will be demonstrated that the narrator discusses or reacts to the empirical world as if it were an artwork, by attributing symbolic potential to real objects, or by seeing poetic significance in exterior reality. The key characteristic of this kind of spatial representation is the distance between the narrator's comments and the reality to which he refers. This kind of spatial representation will be termed *interpretative*. In the final group of texts a type of spatial representation may be observed which will be described as *poetic*. Spatial representation in these texts assumes a symbolic function. This is not the result of an ironic comment issuing forth from the narrator, but rather reveals itself within the context of the text. Whereas in the other text types, it is primarily the external reality described which is of interest and importance, in the last group of texts, the textual world achieves independence and creates its own internal web of meaning.

It goes without saying that the boundaries between the various types of texts described above are fluid and overlap and within a single chapter more than one approach may be employed. Nor should these identified forms and functions of representation be seen as any kind of hierarchy: 'Classification [...] should be distinguished from evaluation'.[23] What this study hopes to achieve, is to highlight an experimental element in these texts that is perhaps not feasible in the later novels; how Fontane, in a reflective way, explores the boundaries and potentialities of his writing.

Rhetorical Representation

Die Grafschaft Ruppin begins with a description of the land around the Ruppiner See, at the beginning of the 'Wustrau' chapter. The lake is the central point around which the following chapters are to be organized, coming under the general heading 'Am Ruppiner See'. The description is as follows:

> Der Ruppiner See, der fast die Form eines halben Mondes hat, scheidet sich seinen Ufern nach in zwei sehr verschiedene Hälften. Die nördliche Hälfte ist sandig und unfruchtbar, und die freundlich gelegenen Städte Alt- und Neu-Ruppin abgerechnet ohne allen malerischen Reiz, die Südhälfte aber ist teils angebaut, teils bewaldet und seit alten Zeiten her von vier hübschen Dörfern eingefaßt. (18)

The landscape represented here has been divided in a systematic way by the narrator. He gives the lake an easily recognizable form, a half moon. This shape which gives a vertical axis is then divided across a horizontal axis into two zones, whose difference is stressed: the north is aesthetically unappealing, as well as unproductive in terms of agriculture, whereas the south is characterized by woods and farms, and contains four pretty villages. This is more than an objective description of reality; it is a stylistic simplification. The narrator describes a world which is too ordered, too clearly defined to be an accurate description of the empirical world. He creates a stylized impression which is refined and which serves his own textual needs, namely to give orientation to the reader for the chapters that follow. The narrator establishes an easily imagined grid in which the reader can locate and follow the wanderer on his travels. Furthermore, the grid-like structure may be described as serving a pedagogical function. One of Fontane's principal aims in the *Wanderungen* is to inform his readers: 'so daß [...] in Zukunft jeder Märker, wenn er einen märkischen Orts- oder Geschlechtsnamen hört, sofort ein *bestimmtes Bild* mit diesem Namen verknüpft'.[24] The simplified spatial structure serves not only to orient the reader while reading, but also as an aide-mémoire, designed to facilitate retention.

A further example of Fontane's rhetorical use of spatial representation to structure his text occurs in the chapter devoted to the town Neu-Ruppin. The narrator describes the geographical relationship between the houses occupied by some of the characters, whose lives he has been relating: 'In der Mitte der Stadt, gegenüber dem Häuserviereck darin Schinkel und Günther und auch der Held unseres letzten Kapitels: Michel Protzen, das Licht der Welt erblickten, erhebt sich ein kleines, nur drei Fenster breites Häuschen' (134). This continues in the following section: 'Fast unmittelbar neben dem *Michel Protzschen* Hause, dem *Gustav Kühnschen* schräg gegenüber, lag das *Gentzsche Haus*' (137).[25] Again, spatial representation functions here primarily to give structure to the text. The reason for this topographical orientation becomes clear if the beginning of the chapter is brought into consideration. Here the narrator gives details about the history of the Counts of Ruppin (58–64), of the town until the Thirty Years War (64–71), on Andreas Fromm (71–81) and then finally on the years Frederick the Great (1712–86) spent in Neu-Ruppin (81–98). With General Günther, who died in 1803 (104), the narration has reached the nineteenth century, and relates the lives of several contemporaries. Fontane moves thus from a chronological succession of names to a topographical organization, enabling him to create the effect of simultaneity.

In the examples above, the representation of space serves as a rhetorical tool, helping Fontane to construct his text, allowing him to present facts about the real world to his readership in a clear way. However, an organized text is not necessarily a literary one. Fontane's presentation of the world is not symbolic; it has no further meaning. Returning to the initial description of the county at the beginning of the 'Wustrau' chapter, for example, the idea of a moon-shaped lake is neither developed nor integrated into the text, nor does the narrator's comment on the north–south divide reflect other trends or themes.

The number of instances where spatial representation functions purely as orientation are few, however; more frequently, the representation of space does convey a particular message. As Fontane outlines in the foreword to the first edition, he began the *Wanderungen* in the shadow of a tour of Scotland, a land for him steeped in history and literary resonances. The *Wanderungen* project was from the first an attempt to revise the Mark's poor public image by highlighting and disseminating the riches to be found there. The Mark's famous Prussian military heroes constitute one valuable source of interest, and are represented in a specific light in the following examples.

Die Grafschaft Ruppin begins with a chapter about Wustrau, home to one of Prussia's most famous heroes of the Frederician age, Hans Joachim von Zieten (1699–1786). In the description of the manor house in 'Wustrau' the theme of modesty is stressed several times. From the exterior, the house is typical of many buildings from the latter half of the eighteenth century (20), and thus an unremarkable residence for the 'volkstümlichster aller Preußenhelden'.[26] The building is without ornament, except the coat of arms or name plate, but even this arguably demonstrates pride in the family rather than the self (20). Inside the house, the small 'durchaus schmucklos' rooms upstairs are presented as unlikely settings for significant events, yet the narrator relates how in one of the rooms the last of the Zietens died, and in another, Frederick William IV (1795–1861) stayed on a visit to the area (21). The narrator draws particular attention to Zieten's sword (22). It is a 'gewöhnlicher Husarensäbel' kept in an 'einfache[m] Schrein', and the narrator emphasizes that it was drawn only once during the Seven Years War. The story behind the sword thus links the concept of modesty demonstrated so far in the appearance of the building to moderation in action: not what might be expected of a popular war hero or hussar (22–23).

The function of this particular emphasis on 'wie schlicht und anspruchslos der Landadel früher lebte' might be considered to be a critique of the contemporary aristocracy (19). However, at this early stage in the *Wanderungen* project when Fontane was arguably more sympathetic to conservatism, and particularly given the prominent position of Zieten's sword in the text, it seems most likely that the simplicity which is displayed in Zieten's home functions rather to create an implied contrast with the great deeds accomplished by Zieten himself, acts considered too well known to warrant further mention. Fontane thus presents a subjective image of the home of a Prussian hero, which complies with the Prussian ideology of Spartan values, and yet confronts and denies the image of Prussian military heroes as sabre-rattling: 'Man erkennt schließlich hinter all' diesem Schreckensapparat die wohlbekannten märkisch-pommerschen Gesichter, die nur von *Dienst wegen* das Martialische bis fast zum Diabolischen gesteigert haben' (23)[27] Fontane shows the surprisingly modest home of Zieten, and in doing so humanizes him. This serves to increase respect for the service, bravery, and sacrifice of Prussia's men.[28]

The treatment of the house belonging to another well-known Prussian hero, Karl Friedrich von dem Knesebeck (1768–1848), in 'Carwe' is similar in style. Knesebeck's biography, as related by Fontane, is one of relative rags to relative riches under Frederick William I (1688–1740), the *Soldatenkönig*. Knesebeck is presented as a man who has earned his position and his privilege, and the description of the house mirrors his story. The building was financed with the aid of the king as a reward for service (32). While it is a 'Flügelbau', it remains 'kleiner und ärmer an Rokokoschmuck' than its Berlin equivalents (31), and the park has an 'einfach edlen Stil[e]' (31). Knesebeck, a hardworking man who, in Fontane's version of events, master-minded the defeat of Napoleon in Russia, is identified with old Prussia and her values: the library does not contain the usual 'Goldschnittsliteratur', but rather volumes to be read (33), and the family room contains one of the tables from the Soldier King's 'Tabakkollegium', 'billig und derb' and 'nicht salonfähig' (34). The modesty of Knesebeck's home serves thus not in the first instance as a contrast to his greatness, as in 'Wustrau', but precisely as an expression of those characteristics that made him great.

Historical military figures are not the only subject of interest to be found in the Mark, however. The works of art to be found in the Grafschaft Ruppin and the aesthetic quality of the landscape are issues to which Fontane returns with frequency, as he attempts to recreate some of the romance of foreign lands such as Italy or Scotland, and seeks to make his readers aware of treasures closer to home.[29] This tendency may be observed in the 'Radensleben' chapters.

The description of Radensleben begins thus:

> Das Ruppiner Land ist überhaupt eins von den stillen in unsrer Provinz, die Eisenbahn streift es kaum und die großen Fahrstraßen laufen nur eben an seiner Grenze hin; aber die stillste Stelle dieses stillen Landes ist doch das *Ostufer* des schönen Sees, der den Mittelpunkt unserer Grafschaft bildet und von ihr den Namen trägt. *Durchreisende gibt es hier nicht.* (44)[30]

The image created of the Grafschaft Ruppin is one of separation, isolation, and stillness, and the representation of Radensleben underscores its limited size: it is contained within the county, and then within the province. Isolation and closedness are its defining factors: '*Durchreisende gibt es hier nicht*'. This small compass is analogous to both the modesty that defines Wustrau and Carwe and arguably also a representation in spatial terms of perceived limitations in other areas, such as aesthetic beauty.[31]

Most significantly, the limitation, the defined borders and parameters expressed may be seen to recall the characteristics of *Heimat* in general, specifically within the literary tradition.[32] The nineteenth-century *Bildungsroman* alters the genre's earlier spatial model of discovery, learning and experience from an outward exploration of the new and distant, to include awareness of close, familiar space by incorporating a final 'Rückkehr in die Heimat'.[33] Similarly, in 'Radensleben', knowledge is not sought without, but within. The narrator enters an unassuming house, and discovers unexpected qualities:

> Und im selben Augenblick wo wir eintreten erkennen wir auch, daß das Haus nach gut märkischer Art tüchtiger ist als es von außen her erschien und daß seine Fachwerkwände nur eine Hülle sind, hinter der ein massiver älterer Bau verbirgt. (45)

What the house contains is perhaps more surprising: 'Kunst, echte Kunst überall. Das gut Märkische schwindet und der Zauber *italischer* Ferne steigt vor uns auf' (45).[34] Fontane emphasizes strongly the opposition between outward appearances and inner worth already dealt with in 'Wustrau' and 'Carwe', but here this familiar characteristic of the Mark's men takes on a wider significance. The journey into a limited place, within the narrowness of home, in and under a modest exterior uncovers a world of art. Furthermore, these artworks are, like the Correggio in Carwe, links to distant places: one can broaden one's horizons even within a narrow geographical sphere. Reflecting upon another collection of objects, the Zieten Museum in the Gymnasium in Neu-Ruppin, the narrator observes that it is precisely because these items are discovered near to home that they become especially interesting:

> [Es] liegt auch hier, in dieser Kollektion von Altertümern, etwas Anregendes *darin*, daß alles Beste was die Sammlung bietet, entweder in dem immerhin engen Kreise der heimatlichen Provinz oder sogar in dem allerengsten der *Grafschaft selbst* gefunden ist. Eine Streitaxt, wie die vorstehend geschilderte, ist allerorten interessant, aber sie ist es doppelt und dreifach, wenn sie auf dem Acker meines Gutsnachbarn ausgegraben wurde. Genau *dies* ist es, was die sonst tote Landschaft, den Elsengrund und das Torfmoor belebt, und auch in den ödesten Heidestrich eine Welt voll Leben zaubert. (197–98)[35]

In an inversion of traditional spatial metaphors of exploration and discovery, a deeper investigation of the limited province produces the same journey into the wide world and the knowledge (of art) that it brings. The material existence of these objects remains paramount, however: the chapter 'Radensleben II' catalogues the artworks which are to found in the house, proving and fixing their empirical existence outside the text. The section treating the Zieten Museum also lists and describes the various artefacts it contains: the principal aim of the text is to indicate the real existence of this place and the objects found there.

It is not, finally, only through its collection of objects of aesthetic beauty that isolated Radensleben, the 'stillste Stelle dieses stillen Landes', is compared to foreign locations; the land itself is ascribed a romantic atmosphere, a poetic quality: 'Aber was *unser* Interesse weckt, das ist ein andres, ist die poetische, beinah absolute Stille, die ihren Zauberkreis um dies Stück Erde zieht' (44)[36]

Reality is so presented as to support the author's view that a journey in the Mark Brandenburg can be just as rich in experiences as travel abroad, as he outlines in the foreword: 'War jener Tag minder schön, als du im Flachboot über den Rheinsberger See fuhrst, die Schöpfungen und die Erinnerungen einer großen Zeit um dich her? Und ich antwortete: *nein*' (10–11)[37]

In summary, Fontane's representation of space in the *Die Grafschaft Ruppin* often takes the form of a simplified schema serving to orientate the reader. More often, however, Fontane selects and defines reality to make clear a specific message, be it about the heroes of the Mark, or the reasons for considering the Mark worthy of interest: spatial representation serves a rhetorical purpose. It is nevertheless important to note that, however selective or even subjective, the representation of space functions here to communicate information about the real world, and refers primarily outside itself, the most obvious example being the cataloguing of artefacts or artworks. The texts considered do not create 'eine in sich geschlossene Eigenwelt' as a poetic text does.[38] Rather than being considered a failing however, this strategy should be viewed within the context of Fontane's aim in the *Wanderungen*, namely to make his readers aware of the treasures their region possesses in reality: 'Erst die Fremde lehrt uns, was wir an der Heimat *besitzen*' (9).[39] That this property or quality is art or poetry leads on to the next section of the analysis, interpretation.

Interpretative Representation

'The fundamental method of literature is to present a subject concretely — not abstractly. It depends heavily upon implication rather than explicit statement'.[40] In the interpretative form of spatial representation, space, the world represented and the objects in it, is seen and described by the narrator in terms of a wider significance he attributes to it. This is a step further towards poeticization than the rhetorical form of spatial representation, in that reality acquires a further layer of potential meaning, but this remains an 'explicit statement'. The narrator adds opinion and comment in the text, but this is separate and distanced from the world represented.

In 'Wusterhausen a. D.', the narrator, who has been largely absent from the description of town, church, and hospital, relates how he, after being given a tour by the 'esprit fort' of the hospital, sat alone and contemplated the courtyard (430). He is present as an observer: 'ich [...] sah mich mußevoll um'. The narrator comments on two images which have known symbolic connotations: an apple tree (430) and a stork (431). He describes the garden as divided into two halves with an apple tree in the middle, its branches outstretched over both halves (430). One half of the garden contains flowerbeds, the other a dung heap. Playing on the literary associations of the apple tree as the Tree of Life in the Garden of Eden, the narrator describes how the tree's branches extend over 'Gerechte und Ungerechte' (430). He calls the stork 'ein sonderbarer Genosse hier' (431). This remark only makes sense if the stork's connotations of childbirth are born in mind, which has nothing to do with the real birds themselves. The narrator ascribes in a humorous way the connotations of literary or cultural emblems to their real-life counterparts. The humour in the tone signals the narrator's self-awareness, his knowledge that what he is implying is only play.

This kind of interpretative spatial representation may be further observed in 'Lindow'. Having wandered out of the convent, the narrator finds himself in a garden which he identifies as no longer belonging to the convent but rather to a modern, middle-class owner (487). What the narrator notices is that there is no dividing line between the garden and the convent. This he considers to be no accident: 'Diese Scheidelinie fehlte, weil der Trennungsstrich auch in den Herzen nicht vorhanden ist und der Besitzer des Gartens Frieden und Freundschaft hält mit den Klosterfrauen von drüben' (487). The narrator identifies the absence of a physical line with the metaphorical lack of a division in the hearts of the owners, attributing thus a symbolic significance to the world. A further example is the description of the graveyard, the narrator comments as follows: 'Von dem richtigen Gefühl ausgehend, daß Leben und Tod Geschwister sind, die sich nicht ängstlich meiden sollen, hat man hier die *Spiel-* und *Begräbnisplätze* dicht nebeneinander gelegt und dieselben Blumen blühen über beide hin' (486). Here it is evident that Fontane identifies the spatial proximity of the graveyard and playground with the relationship between life and death. He sees the flowers which bloom in both places as a link both between the two physical locations and the concepts he perceives symbolized. This is important because it illustrates in a concrete way the extent to which the author Fontane was aware of the potential significance such a description in a text might have. In this extract and in these interpreting passages generally, the reader is made aware of a stage between reporting reality and poetic creation. Other cases are more ambiguous. In the 'Gantzer' chapter, the narrator, walking from garden to cemetery, notes: 'Es summen Bienen drüber hin und träumerisch die Steige verfolgend, stehen wir plötzlich statt zwischen Beeten zwischen Gräbern. Unwissentlich haben wir den Tritt aus Leben in Tod getan' (460). This passage is perhaps less clear than the others because the author not only compares the space around him to another idea, here the relationship between life and death, but in fact uses a spatial metaphor: life and death become places into which the wanderer can step. Nevertheless, as in the other example, the chapter 'Gantzer' is about real places, and describing those, drawing attention to their existence is what the text is about. Ultimately, though metaphorical, the author's observation of a step into a realm of death does not affect the world he is describing, it functions merely to provide a link to the paragraph treating the church (460), which again assumes a factual style, the narrator indicating objects of historical interest.

The separation between interpretation and object is clearer in the following extract from 'Wustrau'. In front of the last Zieten's tomb, the narrator observes: 'Hinter sich die lange Gräberreihe der Bauern und Büdner, macht dies Grab den Eindruck, als habe der letzte Zieten noch im Tode den Platz behaupten wollen, der ihm gebührte, den Platz an der Front seiner Wustrauer' (27). Here the separation between comment and object is evident: it is an 'als ob' situation indicated by the subjunctive 'als habe'. The materiality of the real-world context and the subjectivity of the narrator's comment are placed in the foreground. The idea of a symbolically meaningful world is itself the fiction.

It is clear that in these texts spatial representation is different from what it is in those texts examined under the rhetorical heading. In the interpretative representation of space, the narrator introduces a level of significance by analogy or external cultural reference which gives objects and places in the world meaning beyond themselves. What differentiates this treatment from poeticization is that in a poetic or literary text, the author creates an independent world which produces its own meaning through its existence as an organic whole. It is not 'as if' the world were symbolic, it *is* symbolic. In the interpretative mode, places and objects in the world which the text describes are said to be potentially significant by the narrator. The significance remains an added, often humorous commentary; it is evident that the significance the narrator ascribes to these objects lies outside them, in his mind, rather than being a part of the objects or places themselves. The world the text describes is thus neither symbolic nor independent. Like the rhetorical form of representation, the world the interpreting narrator describes only makes sense if it is understood as reality. In a poetic text, a stork *could* indicate childbirth; in these texts humour is found precisely in the irreconcilability of the literary connotation with reality.

'Die Ruppiner Schweiz'

The boundaries between the three forms of spatial representation are naturally fluid, and this study does not claim absolute validity or exclusivity for the three terms used. They highlight key points on a continuum, rather than clearly delineated genres. In the 'Ruppiner Schweiz' chapter, which will now be examined, it appears, however, that Fontane was aware of formal variety in the work, and that accordingly this needs to be acknowledged.

The 'Ruppiner Schweiz' group is composed of four short chapters of a few pages each. Rather than historical essays or lists of artworks, these brief texts are a series of word-pictures. More particularly, the texts tend to present a description of a particular moment in time, be it the point at which the wandering narrator stops to consider a particular situation, or a memory from his past, as is the case with the 'Zwischen Zermützel- und Tornow-See'. This series of chapters presents on the one hand a case which may be said to be on the border between the highly stylized essay and the literary presentation of milieu. Yet on the other hand, as will be demonstrated, it is possible to distinguish between poetic passages and more factual passages, and significantly the author at times makes this transition evident visually, stylistically, and in terms of content. There is thus a strong case for differentiation.

The introductory chapter to the 'Ruppiner Schweiz' group of chapters is divided into two sections, which are separated by a break in the text (331). The first is composed of a piece of prose; the second contains a short paragraph of prose followed by a poem, which had been previously cited as the motto at the beginning of the chapter. The visual partition underscores a stylistic and functional difference. The form of spatial representation in the first part of the text in question is interpretative, in the second it is poetic.

The first section begins with a humorous comment: 'Die Schweize werden immer kleiner' (330). This humour establishes distance. The chapter revolves around a question of central importance to the *Wanderungen* project, the relative aesthetic qualities of landscapes, in this case, which place in the Ruppiner Schweiz is the most picturesque, an apparently unsolvable question. Thus from the beginning of this chapter the emphasis is on aesthetic appreciation and evaluation: 'Und so gibt es [...] auch eine *Ruppiner* Schweiz, der es übrigens, wenn man ein freundlich-aufmerksames Auge mitbringt, weder an Schönheit noch an unterscheidenden Zügen fehlt' (330).[41] The narrator describes the process of looking at and assessing the landscape; he goes on to discuss the relative beauty of different places within the area, and whether these places are poetic or prosaic.[42] The prosaic lot of the river Rhin is to carry the peat barges, while its poetic beginnings are accompanied by forests and watermills. The aesthetic ambiguity of the Ruppiner Schweiz area is explained in the following statement: 'Die Frage nach der größeren Schönheit [ist] eine bloße Frage der Beleuchtung, der Stimmung, des zufälligen Schmuckes' (331). Fontane's text may be understood thus as a critique of absolute aesthetic values, in favour of a less prejudiced relativism, and a greater understanding of how places come to appear beautiful. The above quotation describes *Verklärung*, being perceived in favourable light, which is seen here to define beauty.[43] In sum, it is evident that the world is being considered and represented in aesthetic terms. An evaluative consciousness underlines the division between subject and object which defines the interpretative form of spatial representation. The text discusses, rather than creates, beauty.

In the second section of text (331), a change in tone is immediately obvious. The first sentence is strikingly complex. The first word, 'ausgestreckt', is revealing: it describes the position of the daydreamer. No longer is the Ruppiner Schweiz itself in the centre ground, under observation, but rather the 'du' of this passage, the emotional and psychological effect that the landscape has on the individual, is now the primary focus of the reader's attention. There are three attributive phrases which precede the 'so träumst du hier'. This anastrophe indicates immediately that the world presented is being seen through less functional eyes than was previously the case. The waiting, slow rhythm produced by this beginning replicates the contemplative state which is being described, and this pattern is repeated in the second sentence, 'mit angespannten Sinnen lauschest du'. This grammatical waiting reproduces moreover the 'wachsende Stille'; in other words there is a correlation between what is occurring temporally in the narration and in the rhythm of the sentence: by the time the reader reads the word 'bis die wachsende Stille dich erschreckt' he is at the end of the sentence. The reader has been led from the timelessness at the beginning of the passage to a specific moment, an effect achieved both in terms of the content of the sentence and by its structure. There is thus a greater level of linguistic sophistication at work here than in the first section.

The described landscape has three key features: the hill, the wood, and the lake. The relationship between these elements is constructed around the central, dreaming figure: the woodland is at his head, the lake at his feet, and he lies outstretched on the edge of the hill. The importance of the individual, suggested by the initial position of the adjective 'ausgestreckt' at the beginning of the paragraph, is now made evident by the ordering of nature around and with reference to that individual. What is being represented is communion with, rather than evaluation of, nature.

The subject lies dreaming. Once he has been shocked by the increasing silence, which is itself a product of his surroundings, he listens 'mit angespannten Sinnen'. This is a description of poetic *Erlebnis*. The central figure listens with heightened sensitivity and becomes aware of the 'Rätselmusik der Einsamkeit', a phrase of Romantic heritage, recalling a text such as Tieck's *Der blonde Eckbert*.[44] What follows, however, is a more Fontane-specific image, the lake. 'Es ruft aus ihm'; there is a message from the lake. Hermann Fricke in his 1936 essay 'Das Auge der Landschaft. Mit Fontane an märkischen Seen' describes the function of lakes in Fontane's writings in the following way: 'Tief sein und in die Ewigkeit weisen, ist des Dichters Gebot. In ihrer mystischen Erscheinung werden die märkischen Seen dem Dichter zur geheimnisvollen Eingangspforte zum Ewigen'.[45] Considering the silence that surrounds the lakes in Fontane's writing, Fricke observes the following: 'In dieser Stille läßt Fontane für den Leser miterlebbar das dichterische Urerlebnis aufklingen, hinauszuhorchen in die Ewigkeit und teilzunehmen an ihrem Geheimnis als dem Quell dichterischer Schau'.[46] Sensibility is at the heart of this short text, evident even from Fontane's few pregnant sentences. This is an image of the poetic experience and its mystery. Mystery is an essential part of the experience, and remains unexplained: 'Ist es Täuschung, oder ist es mehr?' (332) It is 'Rätselmusik' (331), and the events themselves are presented in the *tempus irrealis* 'als würden Geigen gestrichen' (332).

It must of course be noted that the otherworldly experience is brought to an abrupt end by the rather more prosaic sound of the mill, and the saw is taken up again after what has been only a lunchtime interlude. This is Fontane's typical irony, but it does not detract from the fact that, as has been illustrated, Fontane distinguishes between the essayistic text at the beginning and the poetic text at the end visually; they are separated. The landscape discussed in the first section is *described as* poetic, it is evaluated; in the second text however, space takes on a significance, a life of its own in interaction with the individual.

In sum, it has been demonstrated that the interpretative representation of space is to be distinguished from the poetic representation of space. In the former, the representation takes the form of observations and comments about the empirical world as if it were an artwork. Aesthetic criteria and an awareness of potential symbolism characterize the interpretative representation of space. The poetic representation of space has been so far distinguished in terms of linguistic refinement, close interweaving of subject matter and form, and the emotional experience of the individual. This will be more thoroughly discussed in the following section.

Poetic Representation

Fontane's *Wanderungen*, and even the first volume under consideration here, *Die Grafschaft Ruppin*, are as much a tour around the concept of literature as a journey through the Mark. They contain letters, lists of objects, reports, subjective descriptions of locations and events, and lyrical passages of elegance and real beauty. The chapter with which this discussion of poeticized elements in *Die Grafschaft Ruppin* begins is one such lyrical episode, 'Am Wall' (200–01). A short chapter of two pages, 'Am Wall', occurs at the end of the 'Neu-Ruppin' group of chapters. The history of the 'Wall' and its transformation from a defensive rampart to a park have already been discussed at an earlier stage in the text (85). The content of the chapter is thus not historical or factual; rather, the focus here is on the subjective, on the experience of the wanderer. The narrator describes how he walks in the Park am Wall and gradually realizes he has come to a graveyard (200–01). He describes the process by which he becomes aware of his surroundings and the beauty he sees. The themes of this passage are thus life and death, the process of becoming aware, and beauty.

The wall itself is described as an 'Überrest mittelalterlicher Befestigungen' (200). The wall, the dividing line between two zones, the town and the fields outside, is then itself a symbol of two different times, the past and the present. It is important too that the wall is just the remnants of a previous wall: it has lost its original function, its practicality, and serves now simply to be decorative, much like the piece of writing itself. This is mirrored in the park and the plants in it, which are ornamental, such as the plane trees, in contrast to the productive vegetable garden beyond the wall. It is in this unproductive place, a space that is no longer functional, that the narrator is able to sit and contemplate the important relationship between life and death, the old and the new. The text can thus be read as a defence of or apology for poetry, and more specifically for poetic elements within the *Wanderungen*.

The converging of two worlds, times, and spaces is an appropriate and common metaphor for the relationship between life and death; and it is notable that here, although there are many references to barriers, to separations of space into distinct spheres, that these barriers remain fluid, and permeable: the wall itself is a ruin, and the park gate allows the wanderer a view of the fields (200–01). The idea of crossing a threshold is explored at the beginning of the passage. The narrating character walks from a space where the light cannot pierce the trees, because the leaves are still too thick on the branches, to an area which is light (200). Recalling biblical poetics of inversion, the narrator moves into a cemetery, from life into death, but is accompanied by the move from darkness into light. It is at this point of the description that the wanderer's first-person plural ('uns', 200) changes into the first-person singular: 'saug ich das Licht ein' (201). This metaphorical communion with the light which occurs in the lyrical 'ich' form underscores that the description is far from an objective report, but rather a focalized representation of subjective experience and poetic reflection.

From this point onwards the language used becomes far more literary: the undeclined adjective in the phrase 'entzückend Bild' is another announcement of the shift to poetic prose (201). Fontane's language has here an elegant rhythm, and above all it is the use of anadiplosis, alliteration, and repetition, as well as polysyndeton, that characterize the prose:

> Entzückend Bild! Aus dem Rasengrunde vor mir wachsen allerlei Hagebuttensträucher auf, kahl und windzerfahren. In diesem friedlichen Augenblick aber hängen die roten Früchte still am Gezweig und zwischen den Ästen spannen sich Spinneweben aus und schillern in allen Farben des Regenbogens. Hinter dem Buschwerk eine Mauer und hinter der Mauer Gemüsegärten mit Dill und Dolden in langen Reihen, und dann Stoppelfelder weit, weit, und am Horizont ein duftiges Blau und in dem Blau der schwarze Schindelturm einer Dorfkirche. (201)

These poetic devices are especially evident in the last phrase of the quotation. They all build upon the basic idea of repetition, be it of sounds, words, or whole phrases, and the effect is to create movement towards a climax at the end. Here, the viewer's eye rests on the church in the distance. Fontane guides the reader's gaze naturally from the graveyard, the earth, out into the fields, and using a prose which has a rising, intensifying effect, he comes to rest on a physical symbol of ascension, the link between the earth and heaven, a spire. The paragraph which begins 'aus dem Rasengrunde' thus leads the reader out of the lawn and up to heaven at a linguistic, content, and symbolic level.

The link between heaven and earth, the covenant, is repeated in many symbolic elements throughout the passage, the most obvious of these being the rainbow in the paragraph just discussed (201). That these elements are indeed symbolic is underlined by the narrator's ironic, self-referential comment: 'Und *nicht* der Zufall warf ihn [den Stein] hierher' (201).[47] This suggests that these objects may or may not exist in reality, but have certainly been placed in text by a knowing creator. The narrator describes the process by which he recognizes objects in this place which indicate that he is in a graveyard: 'Erst kaum erkennbar in dem Moose das ihn umkleidet, erkenn' ich jetzt seine scharf behauene Kante. *Die* sagt, was es ist' (201).[48] The walk in the park is a symbolic journey in which the world unveils itself in poetic *Erlebnis*. The narrator does not add symbolic meaning; truth is revealed to the narrating character. Yet the comment just quoted underlines the fact that the narrator is of course already aware of the symbolism and meaning of these objects; they were placed there by him. The passage is thus a knowing fiction of the processes of realization and creation, a spatial representation of reading and writing, a depiction of hermeneutics.

Many of these elements recognized by the narrator and which indicate that he is in a graveyard are half hidden: 'Unter den Bäumen hin und nur halb in ihrem Blätterschatten geborgen, erheben sich die Wahrzeichen solcher Stätten' (201). Similarly the butterfly and torch motifs on the headstones are 'halb erblindet' (201). It is in the light of the evening sun that these become visible once again. The process of recognition is thus linked with perceiving what is half hidden, thus that which is not immediately evident. This theme, principally in its representation of the partially concealed graves behind the trees, recalls the permeable, partial barriers discussed earlier. In this way, a link is suggested between recognition, in this context particularly poetic insight, and transcendence. The fact that it is the descending sun that provides the light which permits the narrator to see the torch and butterfly motifs is itself significant. Not only is the process of one of realization, of knowledge linked to transcendence, to life and death; but also the passage of time, age, and dying here are processes which facilitate that insight.

This rendering visible may be seen more specifically as a representation of Fontane's own poetics, which revolves around the central concept of *Verklärung*: beauty is a 'Frage der Beleuchtung' (331), and requires a 'Transparentmachen'.[49] Here it is the specific light of evening that draws attention to the emblems on the gravestones, and, what is more, in an aesthetically pleasing way: 'die sich neigende Sonne goldet es wieder auf' (201). The image here may thus be considered self-referential. As suggested in the introduction, the focalized representation initiates a reflexive exploration of the aesthetic process. The *image* of *Verklärung* in this text may be contrasted with the explicit discussion of the 'Frage der Schönheit' in the 'Ruppiner Schweiz' section (331).

The representation of space as demonstrated in the 'Am Wall' chapter is a sophisticated process. Here, the represented space functions as a metaphorical tapestry, in which life and death, transcendence and poetic creation are explored and interwoven. As we have seen, 'Am Wall' deals to a large extent with the theme of recognition; the form of poeticized spatial representation which occurs in that text thus centres on readily identifiable symbols or emblems, such as the spire, light, and cypress trees, the use of which has been identified by research as constituting an integral part of Fontane's style.[50] The kinds of structuralist spatial symbolism identified and researched by later scholars such as Klaus Haberkamm or Karla Müller may also be observed in *Die Grafschaft Ruppin*, notably in the 'Rheinsberg' chapter.

This chapter may be considered to have a central importance in the *Wanderungen* project, as it was upon remembering a day at Rheinsberg, a memory relived during the trip to Scotland in 1858, that, according to Fontane in his foreword, the idea for a work dealing with the history and geography of the Mark Brandenburg was born (9).[51] Rheinsberg was also a post on the first of Fontane's journeys around the Mark in 1859, although the other houses listed in the 'Rheinsberg' group of chapters were first visited in 1861.[52] The central theme in the chapter is historical and *menschlich*, in keeping with Fontane's aim of telling the personal side of history, giving 'Einblicke in das private Leben' of the great men of Prussia.[53] It presents the relationship between Frederick the Great and his brother Henry.

The beginning of the chapter creates a feeling of distance between Rheinsberg and Berlin (262). As becomes clear later in the chapter, this reflects the cool relationship between the court at Rheinsberg around Prince Henry, and the government and his brother the king in Berlin (262–63). Rheinsberg is not easily accessible from Berlin, the nearest railway station is six miles away (262), and although the narrator remarks that Rheinsberg is more easily reached from Neu-Ruppin, this still involves a journey through a landscape which seems to be a foreign wilderness, a 'Sandwüste' populated by French 'colonists' (262). The narrator even comments that he is unsure whether to address them in German or French, although this should be considered an ironic, humorous comment. Moreover, the beginning of the text lists what must be one of the few instances in the *Wanderungen* where Frederick the Great is shown to be fallible: a road he decreed not requiring repair is described by the narrator as badly in need of improvement (263). These details create a sense of detachment from Berlin. This is underlined by the first glimpses of the town Rheinsberg, which is perceived as a 'hinter reichem Laubholz versteckt[es], immer noch rätselhaft[es] Etwas' (263). Once again, this is a journey of discovery and uncovering.

Unable to proceed directly to the palace because the warden is sleeping, the narrator instead visits the church. This is an excellent example of how Fontane describes reality in such a way that it both reflects, and more importantly provides a commentary on, the themes under discussion. As the 'Rheinsberg' chapter as a whole is based upon the opposition between Frederick and Henry, so the Rheinsberg church description reflects two eras in Rheinsberg, one under the Bredows, the other under Prince Henry. The narrator relates how these two times are 'völlig entgegengestezte Epochen' (265). The church is the only place in Rheinsberg where these two ages meet, and where one 'diesen Gegensatz als solche empfindet' (265): this is a place of concentrated, representative value.

Entering the church, the narrator describes the headstones in the 'Vorbau' (265). On the left is a monument to a violinist from the time of Prince Henry, to the right are six Bredow family graves (266). The brick monument to the violinist contains a French inscription, a poem, which the narrator judges laconically: 'so reimte man damals in Rheinsberg'. The Bredows' headstones were, as the narrator points out, previously in the church proper. The personification of the headstones, as they gaze 'ernst verwundert', adds a mildly humorous tone to what is clearly criticism of a lack of respect for historical forebears and the home culture. The fact that the Bredows cannot speak French identifies the Prince Henry era newcomers as outsiders.

This short description of the entrance to the church is an introduction to the type of description that typifies the whole chapter. If in the 'Am Wall' section it was the symbolic qualities of individual elements (plants, or other emblems) and a poetic language that carried meaning, then here it is much more the structure, the relationship between individual elements of the description which are assigned qualities by the narrator that is important. For example, in the 'Am Wall' chapter the church spire has a symbolic significance which the author uses, but did not create. Here in this section, the gravestones of the Bredows do not symbolize anything inherently, but placed next to the grandiose, brick monument to the violinist with its poor French poetry, they assume the attributes of modesty, durability (they are stone), of that which is native, of true or real poetry, and of course, of nobility. Fontane's use of these two different methods of producing symbolic effects reflects the subject matter: here he is dealing with themes for which there is not a set of ready-made emblems to hand, as is the case with death and the afterlife discussed in 'Am Wall'. Furthermore, the discussion of two different epochs, and two different social worlds, favours, it could be argued, the structural, oppositional approach.

This method of structural presentation is best illustrated by the description of Rheinsberg palace itself (270–78). Significantly, the section detailing Rheinsberg palace begins with the narrator leaving dry land: he approaches from the lake (271). There is no real practical necessity for this, as the wanderer had reached the back of the castle on foot and has to pass the courtyard to take a boat onto the lake: he goes out of his way. The reason this is done is to allow a view of the castle from the front. More importantly, however, the initial description from the lake serves as an organizing point from which that of the building and the rooms within it are oriented: left and right refer not to the narrator, not to an ever-changing perspective, but to a set and determined point of view. For example: 'Dieser Konzerthall befindet sich (immer von der Seefront aus) im *linken* Flügel des Schlosses' (273).[54] The fact that the narrator describes the approach from the water, then refers to this as a central point of reference, and then finally gives a visual stress to the adjective 'linken' in the above quotation signals the significance that such terms acquire in the representation of the palace.

The palace is composed of a central *corps de logis* and two wings which occupy a forward position (272). The courtyard is closed by a colonnade between the two wings. Looking firstly at the description of Crown Prince Frederick's rooms,[55] these consist of the concert hall in the left-hand wing of the castle, and the study in the right-hand wing (273). The concert hall is large, forty feet long and deep, and it is richly decorated with mirrors, gold frames, and paintings. Furthermore, the painted ceiling by Antoine Pesne (1683–1757) shows ' "die aufgehende Sonne vertreibt die Schatten der Finsternis" oder wie einige es ausgelegt haben "der junge Leuchtprinz vertreibt den König Griesegram" ' (273). The study on the right-hand side of the building is small; again, Fontane gives approximate measurements, putting the size at twelve feet square (274). It has a view out over the wood and the lake (274), which can be seen from the window seats (275). Here too there is a picture by Pesne, but this time small in size, and illustrating peaceful study (275).

The image of these two contrasting rooms is a description in spatial terms of Frederick's character, and the reception of that character by the following generations, the myth of Frederick the Great. The left-hand side represents his artistic side and the conflict with his father, the serious Soldier King.[56] That side of the building is richly ornamented, that is, the side of his character which might be associated with the French, compared to the Prussian austerity of Frederick William I. The other side of the building shows the more serious, contemplative, and hard-working side of the Frederick's nature. Here it might be argued the Frederick has adopted the more restrained nature of his father, because of the limited dimensions of the room. This is the image of the modest Frederick. The view from this room is natural, in contrast with the artificial scene in the mirrored concert hall.

Considering this parallel structure, which balances artistry and arguably French influence on the left, with modesty on the right, it is striking to look back at the descriptions of the entry into the town and the church. Upon entering the town, it is noted that there is a park to the left, and a mill to the right (263). In the entrance to the church, as has already been discussed, the violinist's monument, with its French inscription, is situated on the left, while the small Bredow headstones are on the right (265). Thus there is established a set of parallel images throughout the text, which oppose on the one hand the rather negative values of 'Frenchness', of artificiality on the left-hand side, and rather more positive values of naturalness, hard work, and 'Prussianness' on the right. The opposition is less clear cut in the rooms of the Crown Prince than in the church, however. The busts of Voltaire on the right-hand side are testimony to the French influence (275), and there are paintings in both rooms by the French artist Pesne, even if the ornamentation and sun image in the concert hall might be considered a clear identification with Versailles (273). This ambiguity is of course an aspect of the character of Frederick himself: he unites these two elements, which are so opposed.

Similar topographical or structural constructions may be said to comment implicitly on Henry. His rooms are situated in the *corps de logis* (276). This is partly because it is in the nature of the building that the prince's rooms should be here: this is the main, central location, and the name *corps de logis* itself refers to the fact that lodgings are to be found here. However, returning to the point of reference, the lake, it may be observed that the *corps de logis* is situated at the back of the house, while the wings of the house assume a forward position. This mirrors the relationship between the two brothers: 'An derselben Stelle, wo er durch fast zwei Menschenalter hin gelebt und geherrscht, geschaffen und gestiftet hat, ist er ein halb vergessener, bloß weil der Stern seiners Bruders *vor* ihm ebendaselbst geleuchtet' (279).[57] The perspective from the lake creates a situation in which the *corps de logis* assumes the attribute of being located behind the wings. The text manipulates the palace's layout to mirror the relationship between the two brothers, which the narrator sees as an injustice.

There is a further parallel to be drawn between the schema of the house as a whole and Prince Henry's rooms. The prince's 'Sterbezimmer' is described as being divided into two halves by 'ein Paar Säulen' (276). Henry's deathbed is located in the dark, behind these columns, but the narrator notes with surprise that it is not an unpleasant place (276). The position of the bed reflects the general structure of the castle: the *corps de logis* is perceived from the lake as behind the colonnade that links the two wings (272). Furthermore, in the same way as the forward position of Frederick's rooms replicates the brothers' relationship, which the text highlights in a phrase describing that relationship (the 'vor' quoted above), so here the light before the columns and the dark behind them are manipulated in the following comment on the fate of Prince Henry's memory: 'Das harte Los, das dem Prinzen bei Lebzeiten fiel, das Geschick "durch ein helleres Licht verdunkelt zu werden", verfolgt ihn auch im Tode noch' (278). That such a parallel, between the description of the castle and the narrator's assessment of the brothers' relationship, should happen once might be put down to chance; for it to happen twice is surely significant. To the question of what that significance might be, it could be argued that the text itself provides the answer: 'Dem Prinzen hat der Dichter bis zu dieser Stunde gefehlt' (279). As in 'Am Wall', the poet announces himself here subtly as the creator of a meaningful world. This poeticized description of Rheinsberg is a literary rehabilitation for Henry.

It cannot be maintained that 'Rheinsberg' demonstrates the linguistic or stylistic lyricism of 'Am Wall', and it must be noted that the narrator relates information about real objects and places, later describing an obelisk in the park in great detail. Nevertheless, the section of text examined employs two of Fontane's typical poetic devices: on the one hand, his ability to allow things to speak for themselves, as Thomas Mann observed.[58] Fontane's description is made up of elements which do indeed exist in empirical reality, but through his treatment of them, in this case his carefully constructed description around a central perspective, through the process of transfiguration, they acquire additional, symbolic significance.[59] On the other hand, and complementary to this first aspect, there is Fontane's irony, his knowing manipulation of quotations, be they from his own text or from other texts, as has been extensively researched by Bettina Plett and Lieselotte Voß.[60] In this instance it is the parallel between the precise words of the narrator's judgements on Henry and Frederick and the corresponding description which fit this aspect of his poetics. With this level of textual sophistication, it is clear that in terms of spatial representation the *Wanderungen* move here beyond the realm of a carefully constructed essay and into the literary treatment of a subject. That the narrator draws attention to the lack of poetic reception of Prince Henry 'bis zu dieser Stunde' may be considered a further ironic twist (279).

To summarize this section: spatial representation, its nature, and its function have been analysed in the chapters 'Am Wall' and 'Rheinsberg' under the rubric 'poeticization'. What this means in practice is that the textual worlds described are independent, self-referential, and symbolic. The symbolic meaning of space, its meaning for the text, which it acquires through and with reference to the text, is more important than the relationship to reality, affording the text the independence essential to literature. In 'Am Wall' it was observed that the narrator made use of emblematic imagery and highly stylized language in a representation of a graveyard which explored the creative, poetic process. In 'Rheinsberg' the description of the Rheinsberg church highlighted the spatial opposition between graves belonging to the Prince Henry era and the Bredows era. The spatial structure functioned as a means of depicting the opposition between these two epochs. Spatial structure took on a more complex form in the description of the Rheinsberg palace. This was described with reference to a particular perspective from the lake. This enabled the narrator to fix the relative terms left and right, which were used to highlight the complex personality of Frederick the Great, as well as the relationship between the two brothers, in which the spatial structure both mirrored and provided a critical commentary on that relationship.

Conclusion

In this discussion, we have sought to provide an answer to a question posed by many scholars recently about the *Wanderungen*. Is this text, are the *Wanderungen*, a poetic text? How are they to be read? Our discussion focused on the notions of independence, symbolism, and integration as markers of a poetic text. The questions were asked: is the *Wanderungen* text a separate world, or dependent and referential in the first instance to its real-world context? Do its various texts create symbolic meaning? If not, how can space be described in the *Wanderungen,* and by extension, what kinds of texts, what kind of text is the *Wanderungen*?

The *Wanderungen* is a collection of different types of texts, and as such a single notion, 'poetic' or 'journalistic', does the text no justice. What is required is greater specificity in analysis and acknowledgement of diversity. In an attempt to get nearer to a proper understanding of how the texts work, this chapter looked at the first volume, *Die Grafschaft Ruppin*, and identified three tendencies of spatial representation within its varied texts. The first of these was termed rhetorical: here space is manipulated to structure the text; spatial representation is selective and often biased. However, subjectivity alone does not make a poetic text. In this form of spatial representation, the text refers primarily outside itself. Here the text is concerned with the real world, points to it, and is bound to its existence. Many of the more problematical texts such as lists may be grouped under this first type. The second form of spatial representation is more complex, involving an interpretation of the real world by the narrator. Symbolic potential is introduced into the text, but the text distinguishes between the narrator's comments and the real world, which has no poetic significance. This form of spatial representation is in many ways the most intriguing, as here the texts are often borderline, allowing insight into a stage between a journalistic text and a poetic text. The third group were examined as poetic texts, and it was shown that in these texts, the represented world takes on a level of meaning and complexity which is absent in the others. Here, it is not the narrator who interprets the world, but the reader who interprets the text. The textual world is now the symbolic, meaningful object. In these texts, it is not important whether the places described are real: space achieves its significance within the text as a structure of meaning.

It is thus clear that at times the texts in *Die Grafschaft Ruppin* achieve the heterocosmic independence, organic unity, and symbolic depth of a poetic text. This is, however, relatively rare. *Die Grafschaft Ruppin* also contains many other, non-poetic texts. How does this new knowledge affect our understanding of the *Wanderungen*? In the light of this research, it seems that to claim that the *Wanderungen* are valuable because they are a poetic text is misleading. The value of the *Wanderungen*, in terms of literary history, is that at a time when the poetics of literary genres such as the novel, in which Fontane would later excel, were highly normative, the *Wanderungen* presents a collection of texts which cannot be classified easily. Here Fontane explores the boundaries of his art, in that he constantly oscillates between a reporting, factual style, then a type of writing which admits the potential pregnancy and meaning of a still-real world, and then truly poetic texts. Fontane moves across thresholds. This makes the *Wanderungen* valuable for readers too. If we call the *Wanderungen* poetic, we do them an injustice. It is precisely the borderline cases, the difficulties of this text, which cause us as readers to reflect more deeply on what a poetic text might be, about where the cross-over from fact to fiction might lie. This is perhaps why, at the beginning of the twenty-first century, after years of advancement in critical theory, this study has found itself addressing basic questions which remain unresolved by research. What is this text? Is it poetic, independent, symbolic? The most literary quality of the *Wanderungen* is that they cause us to reflect on the nature of literature itself.

Notes to Chapter 1

1. HA IV, 3, 148.
2. HA II, 3, 812–13.
3. Conrad Wandrey, *Theodor Fontane* (Munich: Beck, 1919), p. 92.
4. Among others: Anselm Hahn, *Theodor Fontanes 'Wanderungen durch die Mark Brandenburg' und ihre Bedeutung für das Romanwerk des Dichters* (Breslau: Friedrich-Wilhelms-Universität, 1935).
5. See Fischer.
6. See Neuhaus, 'Und nichts als die Wahrheit?'. John Osborne's research into the *Kriegsbücher* is a good example of Fontane's journalism being re-examined. See *Fontane-Handbuch*, ed. by Christian Grawe and Helmuth Nürnberger (Stuttgart: Kröner, 2000), pp. 850–68, especially p. 850.
7. The schema given is of course simplified. In the 1960s Ernst Howald described the *Wanderungen* as 'dem Romanwerk Ebenbürtiges' (Ernst Howald, 'Fontanes *Wanderungen durch die Mark Brandenburg*', in Ernst Howald, *Deutsch-Französisches Mosaik* (Zurich and Stuttgart: Artemis, 1962), pp. 269–89 (p. 289)), while in the relatively recent *Fontane-Handbuch*, the *Wanderungen* continue to be listed under 'Das journalistische Werk' (Grawe, *Fontane-Handbuch*, p. 818).
8. Stefan Neuhaus describes the *Wanderungen* as a 'Novellenzyklus', Stefan Neuhaus, 'Archäologie der Poesie: Überlegungen zum Kompositionsprinzip von Fontanes *Wanderungen*', in Delf von Wolzogen, *Geschichte und Geschichten*, pp. 398–415; Gabriele Radecke makes a text-genetic argument for a literary reading, Gabriele Radecke, 'Von Reisen zum Schreiben: Eine textgenetische Betrachtung der *Wanderungen* am Beispiel des "Pfaueninsel"-Kapitels', in Delf von Wolzogen, *Geschichte und Geschichten*, pp. 231–52.
9. Gotthard Erler, 'Fontanes *Wanderungen* heute', *FBl*, 21 (1975), 353–68 (p. 360).
10. Helmuth Nürnberger, 'Nachwort', in Theodor Fontane, *Wanderungen durch die Mark Brandenburg*, ed. by Helmuth Nürnberger, 3 vols (Munich: Deutscher Taschenbuch Verlag, 2006), III, 1329–1360, (p. 1331). It is beyond the scope of this chapter to detail the

complex genesis of the *Wanderungen*. Information is available in all of the standard editions, as well as in Jutta Fürstenau, *Fontane und die märkische Heimat*, Germanische Studien 232 (Berlin: Ebering, 1941).
11. HA II, 3, 813.
12. To Wilhelm Hertz, 26 February 1861, HA IV, 2, 25. Fontane's emphasis.
13. Preminger, *Princeton Encyclopedia of Poetry and Poetics*, entry 'Unity'.
14. Compare Neuhaus, who describes the *Wanderungen* as a 'Novellenzyklus', in Neuhaus, 'Archäologie der Poesie', p. 398.
15. Pierre Bange, 'Zwischen Mythos und Kritik: Eine Skizze über Fontanes Entwicklung bis zu den Romanen', in *Fontane aus heutiger Sicht*, ed. by Hugo Aust (Munich: Nymphenburger Verlagshandlung, 1980), pp. 17–55, (p. 44).
16. Peter Wruck, 'Fontane als Erfolgsautor: Zur Schlüsselstellung der Makrostruktur in der ungewöhnlichen Produktions- und Rezeptionsgeschichte der *Wanderungen durch die Mark Brandenburg*', in Delf von Wolzogen, *Geschichte und Geschichten*, pp. 373–96.
17. Neuhaus, 'Und nichts als die Wahrheit', p. 198. Neuhaus is careful to deny that the *Wanderungen* present a fiction (p. 197), although the question of fictionality might arguably be considered a secondary concern in a Realist text in any case.
18. Wilpert, *Sachwörterbuch der Literatur*, entry 'Dichtung'.
19. The term is taken from Kenneth Knowles Ruthven's *Critical Assumptions* (Cambridge: Cambridge University Press, 1979), p. 1. The term originates with Baumgarten. See *Alexander Gottlieb Baumgarten's 'Reflections on Poetry'*, trans. by Karl Aschenbrenner and William B. Holther (Berkeley and Los Angeles: University of California Press, 1954), § 51.
20. Paul de Man, 'The Resistance to Theory', *Yale French Studies*, 63 (1982), 2–20 (p. 10).
21. See HA II, 1, 55. Page numbers in brackets throughout this chapter refer to this volume.
22. Cleanth Brooks, *The Well Wrought Urn, Studies in the Structure of Poetry* (London: Methuen, 1968), p. xi.
23. René Wellek and Austin Warren, *Theory of Literature* (Harmondsworth: Penguin, 1976), p. 26.
24. To Ernst von Pfuel, 18 January 1864, HA IV, 2, 115. Fontane's emphasis.
25. Fontane's emphasis.
26. HA III, 3/I, 274.
27. Fontane's emphasis.
28. Compare Michael Gratzke's interpretation. Gratzke sees the sword, and indeed the 1862 *Wanderungen* collection, as a peacetime warning not to confuse warmongering or military pomp with the seriousness of war. Michael Gratzke, '"Das Opfer war Gebot, war Leidenschaft": Männlichkeit und Heldentum in Fontanes *Wanderungen durch die Mark Brandenburg*', in *Masculinities in German Culture*, ed. by Sarah Colvin and Peter Davies, Edinburgh German Yearbook, II (Rochester, NY: Camden House, 2008), pp. 65–80 (p. 69).
29. See letter to Wilhelm Hertz, 26 February 1861, HA IV, 2, 25.
30. Fontane's emphasis.
31. 'Vorwort zur zweiten Auflage' (12).
32. The dichotomy 'Heimat/Welt' forms the basis of Hans-Heinrich Reuter's analysis of the *Wanderungen* and has more recently been examined by Michael Ewert, see Hans-Heinrich Reuter, *Fontane*, 2 vols (Munich: Nymphenburger Verlagshandlung, 1968), I, 340–67; Michael Ewert, 'Heimat und Welt: Fontanes Wanderungen durch die Mark', in *Fontane und die Fremde: Fontane und Europa*, ed. by Konrad Ehlich (Würzburg: Königshausen und Neumann, 2002), pp. 167–77.

33. Sabina Becker, *Bürgerlicher Realismus: Literatur und Kultur im bürgerlichen Zeitalter 1840–1900* (Tübingen: Francke, 2003), pp. 165–66.
34. Fontane's emphasis.
35. Fontane's emphasis.
36. Fontane's emphasis.
37. Fontane's emphasis.
38. Wilpert, *Sachwörterbuch der Literatur*, entry 'Dichtung'.
39. My emphasis, M.W.
40. Cleanth Brooks and Robert Penn Warren, *Understanding Poetry* (New York: Holt, Rinehart, and Winston, 1960), p. 551.
41. Fontane's emphasis.
42. This is a key dichotomy in Fontane's work. See Bance, *The Major Novels*.
43. See Brinkmann, *Theodor Fontane*, esp. p. 40.
44. Compare 'Waldeinsamkeit' in Ludwig Tieck's *Der blonde Eckbert* (1796), in Ludwig Tieck, *Werke in vier Bänden*, ed. by Marianne Thalmann (Darmstadt: Wissenschaftliche Buchgesellschaft, 1973), III, 9–26, at p. 20.
45. Hermann Fricke, 'Das Auge der Landschaft: Mit Fontane am märkischen Seen', *Brandenburgische Jahrbücher*, 3 (1936), 41–47 (p. 47).
46. Ibid., p. 46.
47. Compare Goethe's poem 'Der Wandrer': 'Diese Steine hast du nicht gefügt, | Reichhinstreuende Natur!', in *Goethes Werke*, ed. by Erich Trunz, 15 vols (Hamburg: Wegner, 1952), I, 36–42 (p. 37).
48. Fontane's emphasis.
49. Brinkmann, *Theodor Fontane*, p. 40.
50. See Tau.
51. This genesis story was challenged by research at an early stage. See Charlotte Jolles's reprinted dissertation: *Fontane und die Politik: Ein Beitrag zur Wesensbestimmung Theodor Fontanes* (Berlin and Weimar: Aufbau, 1983), p. 146.
52. HA II, 3, 859. See also Jutta Fürstenau's table, in Fürstenau, *Fontane*, pp. 191–96.
53. To William Hertz, 31 October 1861, in *Briefe*, ed. by Gotthard Erler, 2nd edn, 2 vols (Munich: Nymphenburger Verlagshandlung, 1981), I, 283.
54. Fontane's emphasis. Wolfgang Rost (p. 40) refers to this, but does not draw any meaningful conclusion from it.
55. The Crown Prince Frederick, later Frederick the Great, lived in Rheinsberg before his ascension to the throne.
56. For an account of the relationship between father and son, see the 'Katte-Tragödie' in *Das Oderland* (831–70).
57. Fontane's emphasis.
58. 'Die Sache ist die, daß der Künstler zwar nicht selber redet, sondern die Dinge reden läßt', Thomas Mann, 'Der alte Fontane', in *Theodor Fontane*, ed. by Wolfgang Preisendanz, Wege der Forschung, CCCLXXXI (Darmstadt: Wissenschaftliche Buchgesellschaft, 1973), pp. 1–24 (p. 13).
59. In the later novel *Graf Petöfy*, Fontane once again uses a house with two wings to represent schematic division, this time between the characters of the two Petöfy siblings, Adam and Judith.
60. See Voß, and Bettina Plett, *Die Kunst der Allusion: Formen literarischer Anspiegelungen in den Romanen Theodor Fontanes* (Cologne and Vienna: Böhlau, 1986).

CHAPTER 2

∼

Spatial Representation as a Strategy of Relativization: *Vor dem Sturm*

TEMPELHERR: Daß doch in der Welt
Ein jedes Ding so manche Seiten hat! —
Von denen oft sich gar nicht denken läßt,
Wie sie zusammenpassen!
SALADIN: Halte dich
Nur immer an die best', und preise Gott!
Der weiß, wie sie zusammenpassen.

LESSING, *Nathan der Weise*, IV. 4[1]

Introduction

In this chapter we turn our attention from the formally varied *Wanderungen* to a work in which multiplicity is a central idea, Fontane's first novel, *Vor dem Sturm: Roman aus dem Winter 1812 auf 13* (1878). The analysis will begin by addressing the issue of diversity in the text: a correspondence will be drawn between the novel's variety and Fontane's concern as an essayist and historian to accommodate conflicting accounts within his own prose. It will be argued that the spatial structures in *Vor dem Sturm* function similarly to balance and offset multiple viewpoints, experiences, and ideologies, a process which, by implication, acknowledges their individual values. As the mature Fontane would later write to Georg Friedlaender, 'alles hat sein Gewicht und Bedeutung, auch das Kleinste'.[2] The examination of the represented world in *Vor dem Sturm* will then focus on three aspects: the presentation of characters through milieu, spatial polyphony, and spatial continuity.

The Genesis of a 'Vielheits-Roman'

Vor dem Sturm is set in occupied Prussia towards the end of the Napoleonic Wars. It relates the development and failure of an uprising against a French garrison in Frankfurt on the Oder organized by an old Mark nobleman, Berndt von Vitzewitz, and the coming of age and love interests of his son, Lewin. Along the way, the reader is introduced to a panoply of characters and places, and within an overarching central narrative strengthened by a complex symbolic framework, Fontane's text incorporates numerous anecdotal episodes and *Genrebilder*. As a result, the issue of unity and diversity in the text has become a central concern for commentators from 1879 to the modern era. Many have criticized the text's lack of integration,[3] some have attempted to show that the text does possess a form of unity,[4] while others have seen a potential strength in its 'polycentrism'.[5]

Like the multifaceted *Wanderungen*, *Vor dem Sturm*'s peculiarities are in part the result of an extended genesis. Fontane's first thoughts about a novel set in the Napoleonic Wars can be traced back to the mid-1850s, and while most of the intensive work took place from 1876 to 1878, some chapters date from the winter of 1863-64.[6] Research is divided about whether to see the text primarily as a product of the later years, or as a conglomerate of parts written at different stages. Hans-Friedrich Rosenfeld and Walter Hettche point to important differences between early drafts and the later work,[7] whereas Wolfgang Rost has argued that the basic plans for the topography of the novel remained unchanged;[8] and Fontane, writing to Ernst Gründler in 1896, comments that *Vor dem Sturm*'s first chapters were the oldest and remained the best, discrediting the idea that early work was significantly overhauled.

The long genesis poses further problems of interpretation, because it is often argued that Fontane's political views evolved considerably during that time. As Gotthard Erler comments: 'Als Fontane den Roman zu schreiben begann, übernahm er den "englischen Artikel" bei der "Kreuzzeitung"; als das Buch erschien, bekundete der Autor seinen "Haß" gegen die Devise ebenjenes Blattes: Mit Gott für König und Vaterland'.[9] Erler notes furthermore that: 'der Reifeprozeß von "Vor dem Sturm" war der Werdeprozeß des Erzählers Fontane'.[10] The novel's lack of unity thus also appears the product of the author's evolution as a writer. These biographical and text-genetic considerations have led some scholars to see *Vor dem Sturm* primarily as a 'Bindeglied', as a document of literary historical interest, which shows Fontane's progression from wanderer to novelist, from conservative to critic.[11]

There is evidence, however, that Fontane saw variety in his text as performing a literary function. In a letter to Paul Heyse, Fontane asks:

> Meinst Du nicht auch, daß neben Romanen, wie beispielsweise Copperfield, in denen wir ein Menschenleben von seinem Anbeginn an betrachten, auch solche berechtigt sind, die statt des Individuums einen vielgestaltigen Zeitabschnitt unter die Loupe nehmen? Kann in solchem Falle nicht auch eine Vielheit zur Einheit werden? [...] auch der Vielheits-Roman, mit all seinen Breiten und Hindernissen, mit seinen Portraitmassen und

> Episoden, wird sich dem Einheits-Roman ebenbürtig — nicht an Wirkung aber an Kunst — an die Seite stellen können, wenn er nur nicht willkürlich verfährt, vielmehr immer nur solche Retardirungen bringt, die während sie momentan den Gesammtzweck zu vergessen scheinen, diesem recht eigentlich dienen. [...] andre haben mir gesagt, daß der Roman schwach in der Composition sei; ich glaube ganz aufrichtig, daß umgekehrt seine Stärke nach dieser Seite hin liegt.[12]

While it must be acknowledged that Fontane is writing to a famous contemporary author in defence of a completed work here, it is still evident that Fontane saw the novel's multiplicity as justified: it provides a different kind of unity and has a formally representative function. Diversity can, he argues, be an appropriate expression of the idea, or material, behind a novel. Here Fontane suggests that the novel's form reflects a desire to depict society during an historical period, rather than to follow the course of a single life.[13] This argument echoes Fontane's earlier wish to call the novel a 'Zeit- und Sittenbild'.[14]

Yet in *Vor dem Sturm* Fontane breaks with formal tradition not only because the novel is representative of an idea, but because it is expressive of a mentality. Fontane wrote to Wilhelm Hertz: 'der Schwerpunkt liegt vielmehr in der *Gesinnung*, aus der das Buch erwuchs'.[15] In an earlier letter, Fontane admits that the novel's form and content is an expression of his own self, his personality and individuality: it is '[eine] Arbeit *ganz nach mir selbst*, nach meiner Neigung und Individualität'.[16] The novel's polyphony and multifaceted character may thus be seen as the product of Fontane's own inner complexity, his capacity for pointed criticism on the one hand, and admiration or acceptance of the same object on the other. As he writes in *Aus den Tagen der Okkupation* (1871):

> Gesunde Sinne haben auch dem Bewundernswerten gegenüber ein Recht, die Dinge zu vergleichen, zu prüfen, zu unterscheiden. Das aber *ist* Kritik. Bei diesem ganzen Prozeß offen und ehrlich auf der einen Seite, demutsvoll auf der andern zu sein, — darauf kommt es an.[17]

In Fontane's narrative prose, this is reflected in their *Vielstimmigkeit*, a tendency to permit a range of voices and perspectives to be heard in novels characterized by dialogue and ambivalence.[18] This approach does, however, precede the novels in Fontane's non-fiction writings. Fontane's career as an essayist began in England in the early 1850s, and it is significant that the first ideas for an historical novel were also formed at that time.[19] These early essays too are characterized by a rhetorical strategy which relies on the inclusion of competing voices and opinions, as Charlotte Jolles observes: 'Er sucht die Wahrheit [...] "im Zusammenhang" und "im Widerstreit mit anderen Meinungen."'[20]

If the earliest thoughts for the novel can be traced to the 1850s, much of the material for the novel dates from the *Wanderungen* years. Certainly, it can be argued that initially Fontane's *Wanderungen* texts were one-sided. Nevertheless, he quickly re-adopted his more balanced style, evident in *Das Oderland* (1863). In this second volume, Fontane published his essay on Marwitz,[21] the principal source for Berndt von Vitzewitz.[22] The essay has been criticized as laudatory,[23] but in fact a balanced, critical judgement of Marwitz is presented. He is deemed to have been trapped in class prejudices, for example.[24]

A further aspect of *Vor dem Sturm*'s diversity may be followed back to Fontane's early years as an essayist: his historical awareness. 'Geschichtlich sehen' is something Fontane again learnt in England;[25] he attained a historical perspective.[26] History is not a simple, singular idea in *Vor dem Sturm*. Rather, diverse historical views and narratives coexist. There is what Müller-Seidel calls a 'Pluralität der Geschichtsbegriffe': 'Historisches wird nicht einseitig gesehen, sondern in der Vielheit seiner Erscheinung'.[27] This historical novel thus also questions the capacity of a single historical narrative to account for society's experience of the past.

In short, *Vor dem Sturm*'s lack of focus may be seen as the negative result of an extended creative phase and ideological about-turns; rather than viewing the novel as the product of change, however, it is useful to consider the text in the context of certain constants: textual structures which allow scope for divergent and antithetical perspectives, and historical awareness which places events and accounts of these in relief. Like Fontane's essays, *Vor dem Sturm* employs strategies of what we will term relativization. This active pluralism is not to be confused with "relativistische Beliebigkeit", as Norbert Mecklenburg observes.[28] Rather, space functions variously to express the need and 'Recht, die Dinge zu vergleichen, zu prüfen, zu unterscheiden'. Beginning with the text's presentation of individual characters, and then considering structural aspects of spatial representation in the novel, it will be demonstrated that in *Vor dem Sturm* Fontane constantly undermines simple or limited perspectives in favour of a less well-defined but therefore truer image of the times.

The Characterization of Multifaceted Figures

It has been frequently observed that in *Vor dem Sturm*, the historical setting becomes a foil and the focus of the novel rests upon the depiction of more human, personal conflicts.[29] The principal characters in *Vor dem Sturm* are not types, such as 'the student', 'the pastor', 'the noble', although Fontane does show a cross section of society; rather human nature is shown to be naturally divided, complex, and at times hypocritical. Konrektor Othegraven, discussing his intended proposal to Marie Kniehase with Pastor Seidentopf, remarks: 'Wir sollten vielleicht vor solchen Widersprüchen, in die auch ein gläubig Herz geraten kann, weniger erschrecken, als wir gewöhnlich tun. [...] Was starr ist, ist tot'.[30] This view of human nature is represented spatially in the text, in that, as in all of Fontane's novels, description plays an important role in characterization, and in *Vor dem Sturm* this spatial characterization underlines the inconsistency and foibles of men and women.

The most obvious example is the representation of Prediger Seidentopf's house. The pastor and amateur archaeologist has attempted to organize the space in his study so as to bring 'Amt und Neigung in ein gewisses Gleichgewicht' (85). The study has two windows, between which Seidentopf has erected a partition wall going into the middle of the room. This creates two work spaces called the 'camera archaeologica' and the 'camera theologica'. On one desk is Luther's translation of the Bible, while on the other is 'Bekmann's historische Beschreibung der Kurmark Brandenburg, Berlin 1751 bis 53'. The narrator goes so far as to say that the two spaces in the study belong to two people of the same name, one a priest, the other a collector; and Seidentopf has not only two occupations, but also completely different personalities. As a pastor, he is lenient and tolerant, emphasizing an all-embracing Christianity. He buries Hoppenmarieken in the church graveyard for example (699), despite the fact that she read cards and is generally considered a witch. As an archaeologist however, Seidentopf is a pedant and prejudiced, denying the existence of Wend culture and insisting that Mark Brandenburg has always been German territory (86). Seidentopf not only has two interests, but his approach and behaviour is the opposite in each: 'Innerhalb der Kirche, wie Uhlenhorst sagte, ein Halber, ein Lauwarmer, hatte er, sobald es sich um Urnen und Totentöpfe handelte, die Dogmenstrenge eines Großinquisitors'. (86). This imbalance in enthusiasm is also represented in the description of his house. While the modest collection of books in the camera theologica is dusty and underused (86), the collection of antiquities fills the corridor and dominates the study, making it into a 'heidenisches Museum' (85). The highpoint of the collection is the 'Arcus triumphalis', a cabinet around the study doorway which houses Seidentopf's most treasured items. The boastful connotations of the name 'Arcus triumphalis' contrast with the humble exterior of the parsonage: the house is a simple wattle-and-daub structure with a thatched roof, unlike the prosperous peasants' houses (83). The difference reflects the inconsistency in Seidentopf's nature. In the representation of Seidentopf's house the narrator adopts a humorous tone, however: he comments on the inviting sound of the doorbell (84), and the serious names 'camera theologica' and 'camera archaeologica' are, after all, simply the old man's two desks (85). The narrator's light-heartedness reflects the loving acceptance of the man's shortcomings and strengths, both by the Vitzewitz household and by the village population.[31]

Similarly, Tante Amelie's home also represents the contradictory nature of her character. Firstly, as Henry Garland has highlighted, Guse is a purchased property, and not hereditary,[32] which seems to conflict with the countess's aristocratic prejudices. Secondly, the representation of the salon at Guse reveals through subtle irony Amelie's political hypocrisies. The room, though predominantly decorated in the 'Bleu-de-France' (159), reflecting the Francophile tendencies of the countess, is in fact decorated in red, white, and blue, the revolutionary *Tricolor*: the carpet is red, the marble busts are white, and everything else is blue (158). Amelie has unwittingly decorated her salon, a place where she wished to assemble high society (142), and a monument to her days at the Rheinsberg court of Prince Henry (158), in the colours in the revolution. This reflects the fact that Amelie, the character most associated with a past world and with aristocratic prejudice, projects herself as an enlightened soul, acquainted with the works of Montesquieu, Voltaire, and Rousseau, whom she frequently quotes (122), ignoring the fact that it was their intellectual inheritance that was responsible in large part for the revolution itself. The room's colours provide thus an ironic commentary on Amelie's superficial acceptance of Enlightenment ideals: 'Humanitätstiraden und dahinter die alte eingeborene Natur' in Lewin's words (123).

Finally, during Lewin and Renate's visit, which is the motivation for the description of the salon, the narrator relates that the countess descends a spiral staircase into the room (158). It is not until later that it is explained why the staircase is there: namely so that the would-be enlightened sceptic Amelie does not have to go through the hall of mirrors to get to the main staircase when going to bed; she fears the 'schwarze Frau' in her house (185). Worst of all for Amelie, she wonders whether she is simply seeing her own reflection in the mirror when she passes in her night clothes. The spiral staircase leads from the salon to Amelie's bedroom located above it. The staircase thus represents the intrusion of the irrational, of dreams, nightmares, and night into the salon, the place *par excellence* of rationalist, enlightened conversation. Lewin's judgement, 'so erweist sich alles als leere, pomphafte Redewendung, als bloße Maske, hinter sich der alte Dünkel birgt' (122-23), though meant as a comment on Amelie's aristocratic prejudices, is also true of her superstition in spite of herself.

The representation of Berndt von Vitzewitz's study and 'Amts- und Gerichtsstube' is of particular importance (212). The description of the study (32) follows the short biography (28-32) given by the narrator, which not only explains Berndt's past and character, but also his primary motivation for his hatred of the French occupation: it cost him his wife's life. This is the cause of an unhealthy obsession: 'Berndts Charakter hatte sich unter diesen Schlägen aus dem Ernsten völlig ins Finstere gewandelt' (30). Napoleon becomes for him the '*Böseste* auf Erden' (31). Yet it is this hatred that gives him an aim in life, hope for the future — to expel the French — and has brought him out of his brooding over his lost wife (30). Furthermore, the narrator stresses Berndt's love for his children (31), and although it is not mentioned explicitly in the biography, there can be no doubt of Berndt's feeling of loyalty to the king and above all to his homeland, which is discussed several times throughout the novel.³³ Berndt's character is thus divided, albeit more subtly than Amelie's or Seidentopf's: on the one hand he has the positive qualities of love, loyalty, modesty, earnestness, and of being a man of action, while on the other events in his life have made him obsessed and gloomy.

This is reflected in the description of his study (32). Berndt's down-to-earth, hard-working character is displayed: there is no luxury in the room, but rather comfort and a certain lack of tidiness. It is a practical room catering for 'jenes Alles-zur-Hand-Haben geistig beschäftigter Männer, denen nichts unerträglicher ist als erst holen, suchen oder gar warten zu müssen' (32). The maps of Russia recall Fontane's positive description of Knesebeck in *Die Grafschaft Ruppin*, the general who, in Fontane's view, masterminded the defeat of Napoleon in Russia.³⁴ This is ironic, given Berndt's later failed uprising in Frankfurt, and its limited, provincial, and amateurish character.³⁵ The portrait of his wife signals his devotion to her, and the useless, sooted mirror illustrates disinterest in his own appearance, if also a lack of intellectual reflection (83), while the contrast with Amelie's hall of mirrors and superficial character is evident. The conscientious, impatient aspect is the positive part of Berndt's character, but also that part which has led to the negative obsession with chasing the French out of Prussia as quickly as possible, and his inability to wait for the king's command.

Thus, as well as indicating potentially positive elements of Berndt's personality, the lugubrious room, darkened from its original yellow to grey by tobacco smoke, the sooted mirror, and the darkened portrait all underline the perverted nature of Berndt's character. Even the disorder of the maps, attached to the wall 'je nachdem es sich am bequemsten gemacht hatte' (32), while on the one hand showing indifference to external appearance and modesty, a typically Fredericzian quality, also shows here the provincial man and amateur. Comfort and ease have nothing to do with the rigour of military planning. The first signs of the failure of Frankfurt are illustrated here. It is a lack of professionalism that characterizes the enterprise: the decision to go ahead is made in the comfort of Drosselstein's gallery (586); the plan is sketched out on an inn table (611); the ground surveyed at a leisurely pace. In the first discussion, in Berndt's study, between Lewin and his father, it is Lewin who sits upright, while Berndt relaxes with his feet up (33). The image is not one of competence, but at best of well-meaning armchair politics gone too far.

This is further illustrated in the representation of Berndt's office and court room (213). Here, in the room where Berndt should act in his official capacity, a similar combination of positive values with unprofessionalism is apparent. On the one hand, the room, which lacks beauty, betrays Berndt's lack of concern for outward appearances, while the papers and books are testimony to hard work. This Spartan diligence reflects the example of Frederick the Great and the portrait of him on the wall establishes the link with the past king clearly. Yet in this official room, the Prussian order embodied by the Pole Ladalinski (328) is sorely lacking. Berndt's files are 'in chaotischem Durcheinander. [...] Man sah deutlich, es fehlte der Schönheits- und Ordnungssinn. Es hatte sich zusammengefunden; weiter nichts' (213). This raises questions about Berndt's competence as a leader, and it is worthwhile considering this within the historical context. Following the Treaties of Tilsit (1807), the Prussian government under the ministers Stein, Hardenberg, and Scharnhorst embarked on a series of wide-ranging reforms of a social and military system largely unchanged since the days of Frederick II. Berndt, a man of the older generation, is a symbol of the now redundant Frederician era, an inherited but unsatisfactory system of government.

Berndt's two rooms, the study and the office, are near equivalents to Seidentopf's two camerae, but whereas Seidentopf separates his two spaces and his two selves, Berndt treats his office simply as a cooler room in which he prefers to work in the summer (213). The private and the official are not distinguished as at the parsonage. This has its consequences: while the maps of Russia, the portrait of the wife, and the first conversation about the coming conflict are located in the study (32–33), that is to say the personal grounds for the uprising have their roots in a personal space, when Berndt receives Schulze Kniehase to discuss the planned uprising with him, he has him come to his office (214). He meets him in his official persona. Here, within this 'Amts- und Gerichtsstube' (212), Kniehase's objection 'es geht nicht ohne den König' has special resonance (216). Berndt has transferred arguments from the personal sphere into his official work, which leads him to overstep the boundaries of his duty. The picture of Berndt is thus mixed. On the one hand, he shares many traits with other Prussian heroes: modesty, a disregard for the superficial, hard work, and loyalty. On the other, his motivations and actions are criticized: he has strong personal reasons for his hatred of the French, and allows these ultimately to spill over into his official, public role. This may be read as a critique of the feudal system Berndt embodies.

In these characterizations, spatial representation mirrors a human nature which is at times contradictory and divided. This is accepted as inevitable and often taken with good humour. With the description of Berndt's study and chamber of justice, however, this becomes a means of relativizing a story of patriotic fervour. Fontane examines and criticizes the motives for what appears to be patriotism, that is, a human emotion, by focusing on the complexity of human beings. This is a psychological study. The contrast between the various, even contradictory aspects of an individual's personality, and the fact that they must be considered as a whole, constituting the character of a person, lies at the heart of the dichotomy *Vielheit/Einheit* in *Vor dem Sturm*. In the next two sections, it will be shown how the text is structured according to these two poles, multiplicity and unity, and how they both function as a means of expressing Fontane's critical attitude.

Relativization through Spatial Polyphony

Vielstimmigkeit has become a key term in Fontane scholarship to describe the impartiality of his novels and the role of the objective, distant narrator.[36] In *Vor dem Sturm* the assembly of several perspectives on a single subject is a structuring principal which may be observed in many guises. Demetz has highlighted the structure of the novel around several groups of characters.[37] Reuter has explored the two versions of Romanticism in the novel represented by the characters Faulstich and Hansen-Grell,[38] while Müller-Seidel[39] and Erler[40] have stressed the positive role the critical voices Bninski and Hirschfeld play in undermining any historical jingoism. The strategy is the same: for each opinion there is an alternative. Everything may be, and ought to be, seen from various perspectives.[41] As Berndt comments: 'ein Sprichwort ist des andern wert' (560).

This polyphony is mirrored in the spatial structure of the represented world in which the events in *Vor dem Sturm* take place. This can be observed in the representation of Hohen-Vietz. Wolfgang Rost has argued that the village is described from the perspective of the manor house, and that from there all later topographical developments are organized. Thus, when the narrator refers to the left- and right-hand side of the road in Hohen-Vietz, he means as seen from the manor house: left is east, right is west from the view of the house.[42] The observation needs qualification, however. The village is indeed seen from the house perspective predominantly, but not exclusively; in fact, the text sets up a pair of opposing perspectives. The rooms of both Lewin in the manor house and Marie in the village overlook the park and the church. While on the one hand this is an evident prefiguration of their marriage, it is on the other the spatial construction of a different point of view. Seen from the manor house, the church lies to the east (35), that is, to the left according to Rost. For Marie however, the church is on the right (82). There is thus in this novel no consistent correspondence between the spatial markers 'left' and 'right' and specific moral or thematic attributes, as has been observed in *Irrungen Wirrungen* and *Effi Briest*.[43] Rather, in *Vor dem Sturm* that level of unity is deliberately deconstructed. This pattern may also be observed in the use of the spatial markers 'west' and 'east'. At the beginning of the novel the wind is blowing from the east. The east may be said to represent freedom and salvation:

Russia and Napoleon's defeat lie to the east, and the original Hohen-Vietz castle had a 'freie[r] Blick nach Osten' (14). The freedom which appears to lie to the east is also linked to spiritual salvation, in that the Hohen-Vietz church faces in that direction. Yet General Bamme comments on the inevitability and the positive effects of the changes brought about by the 'Westwind', the influence of the French Revolution (706). Both west and east thus signify positive change. Fontane avoids creating a unified structure based upon geographical direction in the text, and instead sets up a balance.

Returning to the representation of Hohen-Vietz, the village public house and the men's discussions there about local news and the political situation constitute a counterpoint to the castle, where the same issues are discussed.[44] Not only does this reflect the intention to portray a social panorama, but it also serves to create a dialectic in the text, as the debates in the two spaces, the manor house and the public house, produce different answers. In the tavern, the peasants want a legal, regular war: 'Gib uns Gott einen ehrlichen Krieg' (59), while a note of pragmatism is also noted: 'die Welt geht nicht unter und wir auch nicht' (539). This may be considered in contrast to the discourse in the manor house, centred on Berndt's sense of obsessive suffering under the French occupation, and his eventual decision to lead an uprising without royal sanction.

The more general shape of the village appears to be built around clear-cut opposites. The manor house is situated to the north (53), and a tree-lined lane leads to the church (36) at the top of the hill, to the east (35). Both of these buildings have a long, stable history.[45] They have their mirror image in the south of the village, in the 'Forstacker'. Here the residents are transient, poor and the local witch Hoppenmarieken lives here too. Similarly, the mill owned by the non-conformist Mieckley is also located to the south. Social and religious opposites at each end of the village thus face each other, and yet the reflection shows likeness, as well as difference. The mill, a sign of relative wealth, appears to undermine an all too simplistic economic division, and Hoppenmarieken is a regular churchgoer (64). The symmetrical structure of Hohen-Vietz thus contrasts things which are not as different as they may appear: pre-established models have limited validity, because human beings cannot be categorized absolutely. Through Hohen-Vietz the text confronts the reader with a space consisting of contradictory and complementary parallels. This study *en miniature* reflects the wider structure of the novel, which will now be examined.

The world of *Vor dem Sturm* is limited: the main settings are Berlin and the Lebus and Frankfurt area of the Mark Brandenburg. There is what Demetz has called 'die straffste Begrenzung des Ortes'.[46] This corresponds to the author's desire to portray the life of ordinary people, rather than the grand, Europe-wide conflict itself, as Fontane comments in a letter to Friedrich Wilhelm Holtze in 1865: 'Auf Schilderungen des *Kleinlebens* in Dorf und Stadt kommt es mir an; — die großen historischen Momente laß ich ganz beiseite liegen oder berühre sie nur leise'.[47] Yet despite this limited geographical focus, Fontane's aim from the beginning was to create a 'Zeit- und Sittenbild',[48] that is to show a wide social panorama, with attention given to the 'einfache Lebenskreise'.[49] The complementary spheres of the inn and the manor house in Hohen-Vietz have already been mentioned, as has the Francophile zone at Schloß Guse. Rosenfeld has highlighted the distinction between Berlin and the country, arguing that Fontane aimed to show the mood in both the town and the country at the same time.[50] Frau Hulen's flat, and in particular the dinner party she hosts (333–52), is a depiction of the lower middle classes, and the antidote to Amelie and Guse. Jürgaß's apartment is a space of the officer corps and wealthy aristocrats (408–30), while Ladalinki's house is the place of the city aristocracy.[51] The 'Kastalia' evening (374–95) and Lewin's attendance at a lecture by Johann Gottlieb Fichte (1762–1814) (370–74) give a taste of the literary, educated classes' life, while the Windmühlenberg is the Berlin equivalent of the Hohen-Vietz inn.

The multiplicity of these enumerated locations serves the same purpose as the variety of perspectives in the representation of Hohen-Vietz: it provides the reader with knowledge and awareness of other possibilities, enabling comparison and critical evaluation. The 'Bei Frau Hulen' chapter has, for example, been considered a weakness within the novel, as an excursion which is 'almost entirely irrelevant'; but this is precisely the point.[52] Scenes such as this undermine the illusion of action focused around a single hero.[53] This is the argument Fontane himself makes when defending his 'Vielheits-Roman' to Paul Heyse. Space functions here to express the diversity of human experience. Indeed, the movement of narrative focus from one space to another enables the presentation of simultaneously occuring, but unrelated events. The text constructs a 'Synchronie', illustrating that the same period of time may be experienced variously by individuals.[54]

A striking example is the occasion of Tubal's death at Hohen-Vietz: upstairs, Tubal lies dying, while downstairs Doktor Leist and Bamme spend a highly enjoyable afternoon chatting by the fire (682). Later Ladalinski comes to collect his son's body and return it to the family home in Poland. After the description of that scene, the narrator turns to what Bamme had been doing at the same time:

> Um dieselbe Stunde, wo der alte Geheimrat, begleitet von Berndt und Lewin, zu der Kirche hinaufgestiegen war, war auch Bamme, nach Anlegung seines Husarenrocks, aus dem Herrenhause getreten, hatte sich aber nach fast entgegengesetzter Seite hin begeben. Es lag ihm daran, dem Begräbnis Hoppenmariekens [...] beizuwohnen. (697)

The account of the broken father's journey had ended on a sentimental note: 'Scharf und leise klang das Glöckchen, und scharf und leise fielen seine Tränen' (696). The move from the shattered father who leaves the house in one direction, to the rather grotesque figure of Bamme leaving in another, in order to go and see the body of the equally grotesque Hoppenmarieken, breaks sharply with the pathos of Ladalinski's image. That the narrator stresses that these two actions happened at the same time at different sides of the same house emphasizes this contrast, avoiding undue sentiment.

The narrator's indication of diverse, simultaneous action in various spaces is not always so obvious, but is nevertheless a significant and recurrent technique. In the above examples, the narrator indicates both that the actions occurred at the same time, and gives specific descriptions of where they occur. Often, however, this is done more subtly. In Chapter 2, the narrator takes up a chair by the fire in Hohen-Vietz and relates the history of the castle and the family: 'In der Halle schwelen noch einige Brände; schütten wir Tannäpfel auf und plaudern wir, ein paar Sessel an den Kamin rückend, von Hohen-Vietz' (14). At the beginning of the following chapter, a temporal indication is given, while it is implicit that the location has changed: 'An Lewins Seele waren inzwischen unruhige Träume vorübergegangen' (23). The narrator has moved the focus from downstairs by the fire, and relates now what was happening at the same time upstairs, in and around Lewin's bedroom.

It could plausibly be argued that this strategy is a common feature of narrative fiction. The argument here is not, however, that the process of emphasizing the diversity of events in various places is unique to *Vor dem Sturm*, but rather that its frequent employment is a defining characteristic of the text. It takes on within the wider context of *Vor dem Sturm* the function of relativization, the textual integration of varied individual experiences, perspectives, and ideologies. So far the examples discussed have taken place within two contiguous spaces, but the text also highlights simultaneity in spaces further apart.

The day after Amelie's dinner party at Guse, the friends Tubal and Lewin visit Doktor Faulstich in Kirch-Göritz, in Chapters 27-29. The following chapter, whose title 'in der Amts- und Gerichtsstube' indicates a change in location, begins by summarizing Berndt's actions and whereabouts during the same time: 'Berndt von Vitzewitz war, während Tubal und Lewin ihren Besuch in Kirch-Göritz machten, nach Hohen-Vietz zurückgekehrt' (212). This seems insignificant at first sight. However, Lewin's visit to Faulstich and his dislike of the disorder he finds there are significant in terms of his psychological development: he sees the negative side of a false Romanticism. Berndt is concerned with other, political matters, managing to persuade Drosselstein of the need to attack the French (212). At the same moment, in two different places, the two characters Berndt and Lewin have completely different concerns. On the one hand, this is a demythification: during the French occupation not everyone spent all his time plotting an uprising. Yet on the other, the reader may ask whether Lewin's private and aesthetic occupations are trivial beside the serious plans and concerns of his father.

Events do not have to occur absolutely simultaneously to achieve a similar effect. In Chapter 37, Berndt arrives in Berlin at six o'clock in the morning. He visits Prince Ferdinand, and the chapter ends at lunch time at the 'Zur Sonne' guest house (301). The following chapter relates a conversation that occurs 'in dem "Wieseckeschen Saal auf dem Windmühlenberge"' in the evening. The next chapter, 39, moves to the house of Geheimrat Ladalinski at ten o'clock in the morning. Chapter 40 gives an account of the party at Frau Hulen's. In a short time frame, the author, though this time proceeding chronologically, depicts the varied and largely unrelated concerns of a wide range of society. Within the limited time frame, the presentation of various locations functions to give value to the diversity of human experience.

The temporal relationship between events is not the only means of highlighting the diversity which space functions to express; represented journeys do this too. This can be observed in Chapter 33, after the robbers who entered Hohen-Vietz have been tracked and caught. The group of friends, except Renate who is ill, decide to go and visit Graf Drosselstein. The narrator describes their journey in the following way: 'Als sie an Miekleys Mühle vorüberkamen, begegnete ihnen Doktor Leist von Lebus, der sich getreulich einstellte, um nach seiner Kranken zu sehen. Nur kurze Grüße wurden gewechselt' (246). The narrator then follows Leist back to Hohen-Vietz, and to Renate. The meeting has several functions. Firstly, the narrator has already said that Tubal, Lewin, Kathinka, and Berndt were going to visit Drosselstein (246). There is thus an implied set of events that will take place at the end of their journey, but this remains unelaborated. At the same time, the narrator implies other events and spaces that had led Doktor Leist to be on the road at the same time. These give him a life and independence of his own. Whereas previously in Berlin the various spheres described were separate and linked temporally, here in a journey, two different stories and groups of characters meet, they are joined spatially. The world is shown not simply as one unique series of events around one character and his journey through space and time; rather it is, as Butor argues, a network, a series of crossing and interrelated journeys.[55] Apparently discrete existences cross over in life and narrative. In avoiding following the others to Drosselstein, where he and Berndt would no doubt discuss the planned uprising, the narrator moves instead to Renate's sick bed. This is again a means of demystification of the period before the wars of liberation. Here the reader learns that people fell ill, as always. As Renate gives her maid love and marriage advice (248–49), the reader is shown that even in the times of great events, the private concerns of ordinary people remain unchanged.

The same technique is used shortly afterwards, at the beginning of Chapter 35. This time old Rysselmann is on his way back to Frankfurt with a letter from Berndt for Justizrat Turgany (272). On his way, he meets and exchanges words with Othegraven, who is coming from Frankfurt (273). Then the narrator follows Othegraven back to Hohen-Vietz, to the parsonage, and eventually to Kniehase's house where he asks Marie to marry him (276-78). Again the journey Rysselmann is making creates the impression of another world, with its own characters and events at the end of it. The narrator once again turns back to Hohen-Vietz however, to the private and intimate, relating Othegraven's discussion with Seidentopf on the subject of marriage (273-76), and his rejected proposal to Marie (277). The journey is an economical way of broadening the spatial scope of the novel, suggesting worlds beyond, yet remaining within the narrow focus, both spatially around Hohen-Vietz, and metaphorically, in terms of private issues and concerns.

If in many ways this crossing of paths serves to evoke another world, without directly representing it, then it could be suggested that it serves a similar function to the anecdote and related story, which is another key feature of *Vor dem Sturm*.[56] With these narratives within the narrative, Fontane creates a much wider scope of spatial comparison, for within the limited boundaries of Brandenburg and Berlin such far-away places as Greenland, Russia, and Spain are discussed. The two war stories 'Borodino' (419-29) and Hirschfeld's memoirs from Spain (387-94) are of particular importance. Both recount tales of battles, and convey the huge European scope of the Napoleonic Wars. This serves as a contrast to the limited and amateurish enterprise undertaken by Berndt. The image given of Europe is as a war-ravaged place. This places in relief the relatively unintrusive French occupation as experienced by the main characters in Hohen-Vietz and Berlin. Fontane's comments to Ludwig Pietsch shed light on his intention here:

> Ob es W[illibald] Alexis aber in dem Zeitton getroffen hat [in *Isegrimm*], ist mir zweifelhaft. Ein jeder wird glauben müssen, 'es sei alles so ernst und düster und fanatisch gewesen', ich *selbst* würd' es glauben, wenn ich ein Fremder wäre; meine Eltern aber und die gesammten Swinemünder Honorationen [...] haben mir immer nur erzählt, wie kreuz fidèl man damals gewesen sei, alles *entente cordiale* mit den lieben, kleinen Franzosen, alles verliebt und alles lüderlich. Was Alexis schildert, existierte auch, aber es war die Ausnahme.[57]

The description of events in these distant locations thus exposes the provincial nature of the events in the main plot of *Vor dem Sturm*, when compared with the scope of the conflict in the rest of Europe. At the same time, they underline the relatively favourable situation in Brandenburg and ultimately undermine Berndt's argument for an uprising.

Relativization through Spatial Continuity

In the previous section the focus of analysis was spatial variety in the text. It was demonstrated that space functions in the text to make the multiplicity of perspectives and experiences evident, deconstructing the 'Einheits-Roman', the conventional narrative unified around a single character or ideology, in favour of a more nuanced view of life. It will now be proposed that the spatial representation is also expressive of temporal continuity. Events are not isolated; they are shown to exist within a wider context of other such events in the past and future, against which they must be measured. Spatial representation functions to make this temporal context visible. There are thematic grounds for such an analysis. A central question in the novel is whether to wait for the government's call for an uprising against Napoleon, or to decide for immediate, independent action. The text revolves around balancing the long term and the momentary, history and the episode, and this is reflected in its structure. Space will be analysed with reference to three stages of temporality: narrative time, historical time, and metaphysical time.

A peculiarity of the text is the frequency with which a single space may be the setting for a number of events, and the way the narrator underlines this. A clear example occurs at the beginning of Chapter 38, 'Auf dem Windmühlenberge':

> In dem 'Wieseckeschen Saal auf dem Windmühlenberge', in dem erst am Abend vorher der große Silvesterball stattgefunden hatte, waren am Neujahrstage wohl an hundert Stammgäste mit ihren Frauen und Kindern versammelt. Alles war wieder an seinem alten Platz, und auf derselben Stelle, wo sich vor kaum vierundzwanzig Stunden die Paare gedreht hatten, standen jetzt, als ob der Ball nie stattgefunden hätte, die grüngestrichenen, etwas wackligen Tische mit den vier Stühlen drum herum. (309)

The description begins with details of what happened in the hall on the previous evening, irrelevant to the immediate concerns of the narrative. The space is thus shown in an ambivalent way: the reader cannot simply identify this location with the men smoking, reading papers, and discussing politics, which is the scene the narrator goes on to represent. Before that setting is described, the text alerts the reader to the changing and fleeting nature of the events which occur within this space, to the contingency of spatial experience.

A similar discursive technique is employed in Chapters 40 and 41. This time the narrator relates two consecutive events which occur in the same place, but which are quite different in character. In Chapter 40, Frau Hulen, Lewin's Berlin landlady holds her New Year party. She has to do so before Lewin returns from Hohen-Vietz, however, as, with his consent, she makes use of his rooms for the evening, too (333). Lewin returns to Berlin at the beginning of the following chapter (353), and finds his rooms prepared for him by Frau Hulen, who has even decorated the house with ivy for his arrival (353–54). As was highlighted earlier, the description of personal space is a primary means of characterization in Fontane's novels. It is thus striking here that the reader's first impression of Lewin's room is in fact as one of Frau Hulen's 'Festräume' (333). Lewin's world is shown without Lewin in it: the world the novel portrays is not focused on a single hero, but rather actively deconstructs the literary convention which concentrates everything around a central protagonist.

The reverse happens with the representation of Geheimrat Ladalinski's study. This is first described towards the beginning of Chapter 39, as Ladalinski enters and reads a letter from Amelie (322–23). Then when Lewin arrives at the Ladalinski house in Chapter 41, he is led by Baron Geertz into a side room. The narrator describes it as follows: 'Er war das uns wohlbekannte Arbeitszimmer des Geheimrats, das aber heute, um es als Gesellschaftsraum mitverwenden zu können, eine vollständige Umgestaltung erfahren hatte' (358). The narrator goes on to describe the furniture that has been moved, and what is found in its place (358–59). The address to the reader in the phrase 'das uns wohlbekannte' has a number of functions. Firstly, unlike in the 'Bei Frau Hulen' and following chapters, it is not immediately obvious that the room that Lewin enters is the Geheimrat's study: the narrator seeks to underline this. More importantly however, the particular use of 'uns' and 'wohlbekannte' signals the importance of knowledge here that the readers possess. They have been made aware of the fact that this room has another guise and use. Underlining the readers' knowledge of this space's other function has the same effect as the 'Bei Frau Hulen' chapter. In both cases, the reader is presented with a use of the space which is different from what Lewin sees, as Lewin was not present either at Frau Hulen's party, nor while the Geheimrat was reading his letters. The lives of the secondary characters, and their living spaces, are thus mobilized to give the reader knowledge of a world outside the principal action.

The process of placing different events in the same location in the text occurs as a matter of course within the limited world of Hohen-Vietz. Particular attention may be drawn to the 'mehr genannte[n] Hügelkirche' (36), or the military review which takes place where Tubal and Lewin had previously rescued Hoppenmarieken from the robbers (618). In Frankfurt, Bamme reflects upon the difference between the initial optimism during the planning, and the bitter feeling of failure, as they pass the 'letzter Heller' for the second time: 'Hier wurde es geplant, und hier geht es zu Ende' (647). Passing the location of their initial hope heightens the sense of defeat here.

It is not only the narrator who indicates that spaces exist beyond the moment of narrative action; spatial markers perform this function too. This may be observed in the representation of Ladalinski's study. When Lewin enters, most of the furnishings are different from when the reader first saw the room, but not all: the portrait of Ladalinski's wife is still on the wall. This portrait, a reminder of Ladalinski's youth and Kathinka's future, serves here too as a marker of time: it is a remnant of the room's earlier form, and testimony to the fact that that space exists beyond the moment of the party. The representation of spaces outside Berlin is similar. When Ladalinski arrives at Bohlsdorf (502), he and Renate enter the church to talk (504). The narrator reminds the reader that it is the same church that Lewin entered on Christmas Eve on his way to Hohen-Vietz (504), but the narrator also notes a small detail: the hymn numbers from the previous Sunday (502). These temporal reminders, provided by the church setting, indicate how quickly events have unfolded, that the historical time frame of the long narrative is in fact relatively short. At the same time however, precisely this process of amplification, of underlining the rapid chain of events that has taken place, has the effect of undermining their long-term importance. Spatial markers refer to times beyond the narrative and in so doing highlight the episodic nature of what is being portrayed. The significance of this aspect of spatial representation is revealed during Lewin's illness, in Chapter 55, when Doktor Leist gives his 'Verhaltungsbefehle' to Renate: 'Wir warten. Das ist überhaupt das Beste, was der Mensch tun kann. Zeit, Zeit. Die Zeit bringt alles. Dem Kranken bringt sie Gesundheit. Wir warten also' (499).

Space serves not only as a marker of narrative time, but also of history. The historical spaces in *Vor dem Sturm* outlive their inhabitants and their worries; they are witnesses to change, and in that they carry the marks of the past, such as the major's blood stain in the Hohen-Vietz church (38), they bear testimony to the challenges faced by, and the eventual survival of, the past generations. The Hohen-Vietz church is the most striking example. The exterior of the building indicates its age. It dates from the times of the first Christian colonizers, and other than a few minor changes, it has remained the same as it was at the time of the Cistercian monks (36–37). The interior, however, bears the scars of history:

> Von den Tagen an, wo die Askanier hier ihre regelmäßig wiederkehrende Fehden mit den Pommerherzögen ausfochten, bis auf die Tage herab, wo der Große König an ebendieser Stelle, bei Zorndorf und Kunersdorf, seine blutigsten Schlachten schlug, war an der Hohen-Vietzer Kirche kein Jahrhundert vorübergegangen, das ihr nicht in ihrer inneren Erscheinung Abbruch oder Vorschub geleistet, ihr nicht das eine oder andere gegeben oder genommen hätte. (37)

The narrator places this description within the wider context of village churches in the Mark Brandenburg as a whole: 'Nur unsere Dorfkirchen stellen sich uns vielfach als die Träger unserer *ganzen* Geschichte dar, und die Berührung der Jahrhunderte untereinander zur Erscheinung bringend, besitzen und äußern sie den Zauber historischer Kontinuität' (37).[58] One small detail which may easily go unnoticed is the yew tree in the graveyard. Because of the extremely slow growth and long life of these trees, it has clear historical connotations. Within a German cultural context, the yew tree is also associated with Christmas, a time of rebirth.[59] It is thus significant, when, during what should be a stirring, nationalistic sermon in Chapter 5, Lewin becomes bored, while his father uses his imagination to make up for Seidentopf's rhetorical failings (41–42). Lewin is instead attracted by the yew tree outside, whose branches tap on the window (41). In a moment of would-be patriotic fervour, a symbol of history and of Christian hope makes itself heard, but it is only Lewin, not his obsessive father who hears it. The voice of history causes the individual to place fleeting, momentary concerns in a greater scheme of events, and leads thus to a truer assessment of current situations.

Yet the novel's primary focus is not the grand narrative of political or military history peopled by great men. Indeed, the title *Before the Storm* indicates the avoidance of the *Befreiungskriege* proper. Instead, Fontane's text details local and family histories, alternative narratives of experience, which function as 'Gegenbild[er] zur vorherrschenden Geschichtsschreibung'.[60] Thus it is not only through the spatial representation of the past that the novel's world places the events of 1813 in context; the spatial representation of alternative histories challenges the validity of the national historical narrative, too.

Like the church, the Hohen-Vietz estate and its inhabitants the Vitzewitz family have a long history, related by the narrator, and this history serves to relativize the severity of French occupation (14–22). The once impregnable Hohen-Vietz castle at the top of the hill was razed in the Thirty Years War (15), and the family, unable to afford to rebuild it, had to settle for a modest 'Fachwerkbau' at the bottom of the hill (16). The modest house was improved by the addition of a 'Bankettsaal' (16), and then a new renaissance building, but the family home remains at the foot of the hill at the time of the narrative, i.e. 1813. The experience and survival of 'Niederlage' is mirrored in the spatial move from the top of the hill to the bottom. The narrator reports that Anselm Vitzewitz had announced in the seventeenth century that the family would ascend again (17), although war and family strife prevent this. According to the narrator's account of the family's history, Anselm believes that the Vitzewitzes simply have to wait for their day to come:

> All Ding, so etwa schloß er, habe seine Zeit, auch Krieg und Kriegsnot, und der Tag werde kommen, wo seine lieben Freunde und Nachbarn wieder auf der Höhe bei ihm zu Gast sein und frei ostwärts mit ihm blicken würden. (17)

Thus, like Prussia in 1812–13, the Vitzewitz family is awaiting a change in its fate and a corresponding ascension. However, the family history and the house's position do not function simply as an allegorical representation of Prussia;

more importantly, an awareness of their history allows comparison with the trials of previous generations. In contrast to its fate in the Thirty Years War, the Vitzewitz family has not suffered greatly during the conflict with the French. The house has not been attacked or occupied. Moreover, if the Vitzewitzes were living at the bottom of the hill from the mid-seventeenth century to the Napoleonic Wars, then they were doing so during the time of Frederick the Great, the glory period of Prussia. For the Vitzewitzes the Frederician epoch was not the highpoint of history, at least not in spatial terms. The history of the family home makes the reader question the severity of the suffering in 1813, and thus the necessity of Berndt's desired uprising on the one hand, and the glory period against which he and most of his comrades compare the French occupation on the other.

Seen in the context of space as a marker of history, the criticized ending is fully in keeping with the rest of the novel.[61] The wanderer-narrator stands and considers Renate's grave (711). This is a spatial testimony to the fact that the family survived and that the evidence is visible in the contemporary world of the reader. This is the concrete expression of a statement made by Bamme about the family's durability: 'Die Franzosen werden nicht ewig im Lande Lebus bleiben, aber die Vitzewitze noch lange' (661). Renate's grave is tangible evidence of survival, just as the Hohen-Vietz church is. At the same time, the fact that the final image is a grave is significant in that it underlines the transience of human existence. The visual, spatial evidence of history and the past places even the most terrible events within a single human life in a wider perspective.

The history of the Vitzewitz family is of further importance in the novel, because it introduces the ideas of fate and destiny into history. Time in the novel has a metaphysical dimension, too. The family is cursed to have only one son per generation (22), because of a duel between the brothers Matthias and Anselm in the seventeenth century (20). According to a prophetic rhyme, however, the family can be saved from its cursed state when 'eine Prinzessin kommt ins Haus' (22). This will permit the family once again to assume its position on the top of the hill: 'und wieder von seinem alten Sitz | Blickt in den Morgen Haus Vitzewitz' (22). The position of the family home is thus the result of destiny; space is a marker of forces beyond the control of the individual. Like history in the novel, the prophecy is linked to concrete things and places within Hohen-Vietz which are visible reminders of the past: the 'Saalanbau', in which the murder took place is next to Renate's bedroom (246); a portrait of Matthias hangs over the fire in the Hohen-Vietz living room (27); and the former division in the household is symbolized by a tree in the churchyard which is split in two (22). The prophecy appears to have specific relevance for Lewin, as he marries Marie, whom he calls his 'Goldsternprinzessin' (703), because of the starry dress she wore as a child. Marie is associated with stars and mystery, and

Lewin's psychological development is marked by a series of dreams and spatial experiences in which stars and mystery play a significant part, prominently Lewin's first visit to the church in Bohlsdorf, where he reads a rhyme linking victory, stars, and a mysterious female character.[62]

Spatial representation also serves to highlight a metaphysical understanding of time with recourse to biblical models and references. At the most basic level, the world in *Vor dem Sturm* is compared on more than one occasion to the biblical world. For example, the land around Guse is, not without a certain degree of irony, compared to Canaan (131), and Tante Schorlemmer compares Frankfurt to Jericho (631). Like the anecdotes, these humorous references widen the spatial parameters of the text's world, while still permitting a focus on life within a limited sphere. Moreover, the places Canaan and Jericho are synonymous with the great events which took place there, and have entered into a mythologized understanding of the past. The antiquity of the events and their importance place, arguably, not only Berndt's actions in relief, but also the whole Napoleonic conflict, undermining its relative significance.

In Fontane's first plans, the novel was set between Christmas and Easter, although in the final version the novel concludes in February.[63] From this initial plan it is clear that Christ's life and ascension were to provide a recognizable allegorical canvas, and a set of readily identifiable symbols for the story of the rise of Prussia and the Vitzewitz family.[64] In Chapter 1, Lewin is collected from his home in Berlin at Christmas by the Hohen-Vietz coachman.[65] The light and dark imagery of these first (and older) chapters is striking. There are constant references to the general state of darkness, and the presence of small lights, be they stars, or street lamps (7), or the partial light in the Bohlsdorf church (11). The narrator links the lights in these descriptions to the biblical metaphor of Christ as light, albeit in mildly ironic way: 'Und der "Heilige Christ", der hier und dort einzuziehen begann, warf seinen Glanz auch in das draußen liegende Dunkel' (7). This is a spatial reference to the light and dark imagery which is common in prophetic scripture read at Christmas, such as Isaiah 9.2: 'The people that walked in darkness have seen a great light: they that dwell in the land of the shadow of death, upon them hath the light shined'.[66] In the Christmas setting, it is clear that the small, isolated lights can be read as symbols of hope here. Fontane skilfully makes the prophecy narrative and its symbols compatible with pre-existing biblical models: the physical symbol linking hope, expectation, and Marie, destined to bear a son for the Vitzewitzes, is a star.

Like the family prophecy, the biblical references in the text widen the historical parameters: the Bible presents a world history spanning from creation to the end of the world, it is an all encompassing time-line.[67] Secondly, history and time become not simply objective concepts, but are governed by fate and destiny. Time in the novel moves towards what can be, in the end, only a positive outcome: salvation. This necessarily positive view of history serves again to underline the criticism of Berndt's actions. The message of hope in Isaiah and John is one of waiting, not of action. Yet even this criticism is balanced. After the failed attempt to take Frankfurt, Lewin is captured and in desperation Berndt begins to question his own motives (648). In the separation of his room in Küstrin, Lewin reads Judges (699), whose last lines read as follows:

> And the children of Israel departed thence at that time, every man to his tribe and to his family, and they went out from thence, every man to his inheritance.
> In those days *there was* no king in Israel: every man did *that which was* right in his own eyes. (Jud. 21, 24–25)

The reference provides a degree of justification for Berndt's mistakes: what Berndt wants is a real war, but the absence of decisive government means that he feels obliged to take matters into his own hands. The end of the novel thus sees a reconciliation between the two views of Lewin and Berndt: neither is condemned, both are understood. It is thus clear that the spatial references to light and dark at the beginning of the text are part of a network of intertextual references which provide a commentary on the events of the text itself: the biblical world, its teleological temporal model, and the scope for critical intertextuality it provides are skilfully exploited by Fontane as a subtle means of expanding the scope of the novel, permitting comparison and evaluation.

Conclusion

Fontane was right to call his first novel a 'Vielheits-Roman'. The novel's polycentric, multifaceted form was perhaps the inevitable outcome of successive creative phases and an evolving artistic and political consciousness. Nevertheless, it is possible to see diversity in *Vor dem Sturm* as essential to an organic form emergent from a creative mind, disposed at all times to balance 'Bewunderung' with 'Kritik', a form appropriate for representing the variety of human life and the complexity of the human soul.[68] Conceived abroad and written during years which saw travels throughout Europe, *Vor dem Sturm*, like *Der Stechlin* twenty years later, is expressive of the need for knowledge of happenings and lives beyond the individual, beyond the province, beyond the present moment. Only through an awareness of the diversity of human experience can we evaluate our own situation and make reasonable decisions in our own lives.

Through description of private milieux, Fontane creates portraits of his characters which balance their favourable qualities with subtle criticism. In this text, human beings are flawed and led astray by their failings, but valued because of their strengths. The all-encompassing view of man is mirrored in the spatial representation of a world which enumerates contrasting perspectives, settings, and locations. The text deconstructs a unified perspective of the world in Hohen-Vietz. This plurality is echoed in the wider spatial structure. The text juxtaposes diverse locations and the events therein. The enumeration of various represented settings is a strategy which permits the comparison of contrasting human experiences. The spatial structure promotes an understanding of human life which balances the concerns of the individual with other potentialities.

Space not only functions to make the reader aware of life adjacent to any given character in a spatial sense; spatial representation in the text also underlines a temporal context. Space is shown to exist across time, which has a narrative, historical and metaphysical dimension. The episodic concerns of an individual are shown firstly not to be unique, secondly when judged against the past, to be less serious than previous struggles which have been overcome, and thirdly, not without hope, when considered against a prophetic and teleological view of events. Lewin's growing pains and Berndt's impatience to oust the occupying French are placed in temporal relief by means of a spatial strategy which consistently reminds the reader of past and future.

Fontane's account of Prussia's occupation thus accommodates a narrative of patriotism, about a significant historic moment and about inevitable victory; it tells that story. Yet at the same time, the motives for patriotic action are examined critically and the adequacy of a single historical narrative to account for the experience of a whole society is questioned. The significance of *Vor dem Sturm* is greater than the critical historical awareness it promotes, however. Its value lies primarily in the specifically *Fontane'sche Weltanschauung* that it depicts: acceptance, admiration, love of an object, person, or narrative must always be balanced with awareness of other possibilities and of alternative realities. The role of spatial representation in this text, written by a wanderer on his way to world literature, is to promote that sovereign view of life's variety.

Notes to Chapter 2

1. Gotthold Ephraim Lessing, *Gesammelte Werke*, ed. by Wolfgang Stammler, 2 vols (Munich: Hanser, 1959), I, 727.
2. 5 June 1886, in Theodor Fontane, *Briefe an Georg Friedlaender*, ed by Kurt Schreinert (Heidelberg: Quelle & Meyer, 1954), p. 40.
3. See Julius Rodenberg's contemporary review, in *Theodor Fontane: Briefe an Julius Rodenberg: Eine Dokumentation*, ed. by Hans-Heinrich Reuter (Berlin and Weimar: Aufbau, 1969), pp. 120–24, especially p. 120. Among later critics, compare Reuter, *Fontane*, II, 536, or Brinkmann, *Theodor Fontane*, p. 63.
4. Walter Wagner, *Die Technik der Vorausdeutung in Fontanes 'Vor dem Sturm' und ihre Bedeutung im Zusammenhang des Werkes* (Marburg: Elwert, 1966), p. 31.
5. Berndt Witte, 'Ein preußisches Wintermärchen: Theodor Fontanes erster Roman *Vor dem Sturm*', in Delf von Wolzogen and Nürnberger, *Theodor Fontane am Ende des Jahrhunderts*, I, 143–55, (p. 148).

6. Charlotte Jolles, *Theodor Fontane*, 4th rev. edn (Stuttgart: Metzler, 1993), pp. 37–38. For a detailed account, see Theodor Fontane, *Romane und Erzählungen*, ed. by Peter Goldammer and others, 8 vols (Berlin and Weimar: Aufbau, 1969), 'Aufbau Ausgabe', I, 325–75. This edition is hereafter cited as 'AA'.
7. Walter Hettche, 'Die Handschriften zu Theodor Fontanes *Vor dem Sturm*: Erste Ergebnisse ihrer Auswertung', *FBl*, 58 (1994), 193–211 (p. 210); Hans-Friedrich Rosenfeld, *Zur Entstehung Fontanescher Romane* (Groningen and The Hague: Wolters, 1926), pp. 11–13.
8. Rost, p. 89.
9. AA I, 330.
10. AA I, 325.
11. Peter Wruck, 'Zum Zeitgeschichtsverständnis in Theodor Fontanes Roman *Vor dem Sturm*', *FBl*, 1 (1965), 1–9 (p. 2).
12. To Paul Heyse, 9 December 1878, HA IV, 2, 639.
13. Helmuth Nürnberger highlights the influence of Karl Gutzkow on the novel's 'kompositorische Nebeneinander' (Helmuth Nürnberger, *Theodor Fontane in Selbstzeugnissen und Bilddokumenten* (Reinbeck bei Hamburg: Rowohlt, 1973), p. 128).
14. To Ludwig Pietsch, 24 April 1880, HA IV, 2, 80.
15. 1 December 1878, HA IV, 2, 637–38.
16. 17 June 1866, HA IV, 2, 163. Fontane's emphasis.
17. Fontane's emphasis. HA III, 2, 708.
18. Jolles, *Theodor Fontane*, pp. 118–19; Norbert Mecklenburg, *Theodor Fontane: Romankunst der Vielstimmigkeit* (Frankfurt a. M.: Suhrkamp, 1998).
19. The phrase is Reuter's. See Hans-Heinrich Reuter, 'Die englische Lehre: Zur Bedeutung und Funktion Englands für Fontanes Schaffen', in *Formen realistischer Erzählkunst: Festschrift für Charlotte Jolles*, ed. by Jörg Thunecke and Eda Sagarra (Nottingham: Sherwood Press, 1979), pp. 282–99.
20. Theodor Fontane, *Sämtliche Werke*, ed. by Edgar Gross and others, 24 vols (Munich: Nymphenburger Verlagshandlung, 1959–75), 'Nymphenburger Ausgabe', XVII, 609, hereafter cited as 'NyA'.
21. HA II, 1, 763–85.
22. Jolles, *Theodor Fontane*, p. 39.
23. Henry Garland, *The Berlin Novels of Theodor Fontane* (Oxford: Clarendon Press, 1980), p. 6.
24. HA II, 1, 783.
25. Helmuth Nürnberger, 'Die England-Erfahrung Theodor Fontanes', *FBl*, 58 (1994), 12–28 (p. 20).
26. Jolles, *Fontane und die Politik*, p. 154.
27. Walter Müller-Seidel, *Theodor Fontane: Soziale Romankunst in Deutschland* (Stuttgart: Metzler, 1975), p. 131.
28. Mecklenburg, p. 51. Mecklenburg uncovers a 'Relativitätsprinzip' in the novels based on his analysis of dialogue (p. 162).
29. Among many others: Jolles, *Fontane und die Politik*, pp. 149–50. The 'Abrücken vom Historischen' is a process which occurs throughout the genesis of the work, as Fontane moves further away from the historical material. See Rosenfeld, p. 8, and also Hettche, 'Handschriften zu *Vor dem Sturm*', throughout, but especially p. 201.
30. HA I, 3, 275–76. Page numbers in brackets throughout this chapter refer to this volume.
31. See p. 59.
32. Garland, p. 13.

33. See pp. 214-22 and pp. 304-09, esp. p. 308.
34. HA II, 1, 36.
35. Principally pp. 72-73.
36. See Fritz Martini, *Deutsche Literatur im bürgerlichen Realismus 1848-1898*, 4th edn (Stuttgart: Metzler, 1981), p. 737.
37. Demetz, p. 54.
38. Reuter, *Fontane*, II, 539-47.
39. Müller-Seidel, *Soziale Romankunst*, p. 117.
40. AA I, 329.
41. Whether this process of allowing many opinions to exist side by side is an expression of democratic, liberal tendencies is however a completely different matter. For the purposes of this discussion, it is a textual strategy, as observed in Fontane's essays, even those treating patriotic subjects.
42. Rost, p. 91.
43. See Haberkamm, '"Nein, nein, die Linke"', and Haberkamm, '"Links und rechts umlauert"'.
44. See Chapter 7, 'Im Kruge', pp. 53-61.
45. For the history of the house, see throughout Chapter 3, pp. 23-28; for the church, see pp. 36-40.
46. Demetz, p. 52.
47. Fontane's emphasis. 6 December 1865, in Erler, *Briefe*, I, 322.
48. To Ludwig Peitsch, 24 April 1880, HA IV, 3, 80.
49. To Wilhelm Hertz, 17 June 1866, HA IV, 2, 163.
50. Rosenfeld, p. 6.
51. For example pp. 356-66.
52. A. Robinson, '"Bei Frau Hulen": An Examination of Chapter 40 in Fontane's Novel *Vor dem Sturm*', in Thunecke and Sagarra, pp. 471-77 (p. 472).
53. See Stroop. Stroop in a recent article suggests that *Vor dem Sturm* operates around a basic topographical opposition between Hohen-Vietz and Berlin. This framework is based around Lewin as the central character, and his experiences. This seems to undervalue the importance of characters such as Berndt, and as will be argued here, the novel's spatial representation serves precisely to undermine focus on a single individual or perspective.
54. Müller-Seidel, *Soziale Romankunst*, p. 130.
55. Butor, p. 56.
56. See Siegfried Hajek, 'Anekdoten in Theodor Fontanes Roman *Vor dem Sturm*', *Jahrbuch der Raabe-Gesellschaft* (1979), 72-93.
57. 24 April 1880, HA IV, 3, 80. Fontane's emphasis.
58. Fontane's emphasis.
59. *Wörterbuch der deutschen Volkskunde*, ed. by Oswald A. Erich and Richard Beith (Stuttgart: Kröner, 1955), entry 'Eibe'.
60. Otfried Keiler, '*Vor dem Sturm*: Das große Gefühl der Befreiung und die kleinen Zwecke der Opposition', in *Interpretationen: Fontanes Novellen und Romane*, ed. by Christian Grawe (Stuttgart: Reclam, 1991), pp. 13-43 (p. 13).
61. See Reuter, Fontane, II, 561-62, who sees the ending as sentimental.
62. The relationship between Marie and Lewin, and the star motif is too complex to be treated here, and has been exhaustively discussed by Hugo Aust (Verklärung, pp. 25-124), among others.
63. See 'Material' quoted by Gotthard Erler, in AA I, 341.
64. Charlotte Jolles has drawn attention to the importance of Fontane's inclination towards

Calvinistic determinism with reference to *Vor dem Sturm*. See Jolles, *Fontane und die Politik*, p. 154.
65. Witte (p. 146) draws attention here to the fact that the coachman's name is Krist. The use of a local short form of the name Christian is here ironic and humorous, and is local colour.
66. References are to the King James Version.
67. Patricia Howe ('Reality and Imagination', p. 349) makes a similar argument about references to religious and folk festivals in *Irrungen Wirrungen*.
68. HA, III, 2, 708.

CHAPTER 3

The Spatial Representation of Awareness: *Schach von Wuthenow* and *Graf Petöfy*

> Ist es Täuschung, oder ist es mehr?
> *Die Grafschaft Ruppin*[1]

Introduction

Schach von Wuthenow (1882) and *Graf Petöfy* (1884) may appear at first to have little in common that would warrant treating them in a single chapter. *Schach von Wuthenow* is generally recognized as a successful *Novelle* which weaves together an 'intim-private Begebenheit' and its causes with the critical portrayal of Prussian society in 1806.[2] Set in Berlin and the Mark, the text's realism has been praised from the earliest reviews, even if most contemporary readers saw the text in the same vein as the *Wanderungen*.[3] *Graf Petöfy* is, however, more commonly considered to be one of Fontane's weaker works.[4] The Hungarian setting has frequently been judged to be unsatisfactory because of a perceived lack of authenticity, and the focus of much Fontane scholarship on the author's social criticism may have diminished interest in this novel in which, on the surface at least, Prussia, the aristocracy, and Christianity (specifically Catholicism) are praised.

There are points of similarity, however, the most obvious being that both texts end with the suicide of the main male character. These men are survived by their wives, who look to the future at the end of both *Erzählung* and *Roman*. The Catholic religion also features prominently in these two narratives of death and survival, and in both works distance is established between the setting and Fontane's contemporary world, betraying a shared ambivalence towards contemporary Prussia, the new Reich and its values. In the historical narrative *Schach von Wuthenow* this remove is achieved primarily temporally, while the contemporary Austro-Hungarian setting creates spatial remoteness in *Graf Petöfy*.

This chapter will examine a further common theme: awareness. In *Schach von Wuthenow*, the protagonist is a naive man, unaware of profound human beauty. Through his relationship with the veiled, pockmarked Victoire, Schach embarks on a journey towards greater understanding of human complexity, though he is ultimately unable to cope with this new knowledge. *Graf Petöfy* explores similar issues, this time focusing on the awareness of illusory states. An old Graf and a young actress marry on the understanding that she will be allowed amorous liberty. Isolated on their Hungarian estate, the Graf eventually believes the fairy tale of their marriage, while his wife, bored and yearning for excitement, falls for the insincere advances of the Graf's nephew. In both texts spatial representation plays a significant role in charting these developments, and the modes of spatial expression employed in the two texts are similar. As in *Vor dem Sturm*, pregnant descriptive passages serve to give insight into complex psychologies and to situate characters within the texts' abstract thematics, while the topographical structures provide subtle indicators of plot progression and inner human states.

Schach von Wuthenow

> L'homme du monde est tout entier dans son masque. N'étant presque jamais en lui-même, il y est toujours étranger, et mal à son aise quand il est forcé d'y rentrer.
>
> JEAN-JACQUES ROUSSEAU, *Émile ou de l'éducation*[5]

Introduction

Schach von Wuthenow, like many of Fontane's works, appears to revolve around the indeterminate nature of people, events, and would-be truths. The *Erzählung aus der Zeit des Regiment Gensdarmes* seems simple: a vain man, Schach von Wuthenow has a brief affair with a pockmarked girl. Her mother insists on marriage, which Schach attempts to avoid because he fears social ridicule. When the king intervenes, Schach agrees to the marriage but commits suicide immediately afterwards.

Schach's individual tale and the historical period which the text depicts are closely interwoven. The narrative is set just before the Prussian defeats of Jena and Auerstädt (1806), battles in which the Frederician army was swept away, leading to the surrender of Prussia, and subsequent, wide-ranging reforms of the state and military. Schach's own regiment, the Gensdarmes, was one of the old regiments disbanded during these reforms. Schach's case thus represents the army and society in the period leading up to this watershed date, showing a Prussia out of touch with its roots, superficial and decadent. Most critical interpretations of the text tend to focus on the importance of the narrative's historical content, and less on the human interest of Schach's character.[6] Schach is seen primarily as 'mehr Repräsentant als individuelle Person', a symbol of the times, his story a representative example of the Prussian malaise, be that purely historical or as a criticism of contemporary Prussia.[7] Considering the text solely from this perspective overlooks, however, the text's significant focus on Schach's psychology. Conrad Wandrey recognized this, arguing that, despite all historical interest, *Schach von Wuthenow* is a novel about 'Menschendarstellung', and 'seelische Analyse'.[8] Another early critic, Kenneth Hayens saw the novel as a representation of 'the weakness of a man who attempts to face life'; like Prussia, Schach is 'brought into contact with living reality'.[9] As will be demonstrated in what follows, examining the represented world in the novel reveals new aspects of this psychological portrait of a man confronted with the unexpected truth of life.

The text closes with two letters which reflect different views of Schach and his actions. In the first, Hans von Bülow interprets Schach's behaviour from the standpoint of a social critic. For him Schach's actions were motivated by a hollow conception of honour, concerned with outward appearances rather than inner realities, and indicative of wider social and military problems. In the final letter, Victoire, provides an assessment based on Schach as an individual. For her, his suicide was not motivated ultimately by her appearance, but by a loner's inability to come to terms with the thought of married life in Wuthenow. Yet Victoire also surrenders to the inevitable obscurity of events. The simple clarity of Bülow's interpretation of Schach's actions is balanced against Victoire's assertion that such puzzles are, in the end, too complex to be solved: 'Wie lösen sich die Rätsel? Nie' (681).[10] The ambivalence created by the text's 'doppelte Optik' at the end may be compared productively with other elements of the text's structure, such as the characterization through dialogue, the presence of two main female characters, and the representation of social authority by people of conflicting standards: Prince Ferdinand, a womanizer, and the king, Frederick William III, a family man.[11] Consistently, 'living reality' in the text is more complex than Schach himself or his apprehension of his world.

Complex realities and simple appearances recur as structural themes throughout the text, specifically with reference to the two main characters, Schach and Victoire. Victoire is symbolic of a rounded, multifaceted humanity. Beautiful once, but left marked by smallpox, Victoire's personality and her appearance are the products of life, change, and survival. Significantly, Victoire is the subject of a discussion of beauty in Chapter 7 (606–09). She is described as possessing an unconventional beauty, which is an expression of humanity and inner qualities, which cannot be categorized easily, and which superficial imperfections do not diminish, but rather enhance. She represents a paradox, *le laid c'est le beau* (608), and paradox is central to her personality: she is 'witzig-elegisch' (607).[12]

'Schöne[r] Schach' appears simple and superficial, though this quality is judged in different ways. Some of Schach's peers see him as characterized by a singular integrity. As Nostitz comments: 'Alles an ihm ist echt, auch seine steife Vornehmheit, so langweilig und so beleidigend ich sie finde. Und *darin* unterscheidet er sich von uns. Er ist immer er selbst' (573).[13] Bülow, however, accuses him of false honour, a slavish deference to society, and sees him as intellectually limited. Indeed, Schach's simplicity is coupled with a certain simple-mindedness, or 'Beschränktheit' (572), and unlike the other characters, Schach is overwhelmingly shown to be without wit in conversation. He is uncritical, easily influenced by society, and his attested faith in the Prussian army (583) is a near word-for-word repetition of Bülow's earlier parody of those same beliefs (572), illustrating Schach's transparency and predictability.

In a discussion based on a reading of space in the novel, it will be shown that through Victoire, Schach becomes aware of a more complex human soul, of necessary contradictions within himself as an imperfect human being. The text elaborates a topographical framework of Schach's evolving awareness as he crosses from a world of superficial beauty, simplicity, and stasis, to an inner realm of complexity, imperfection, and dynamism. The representations of the Carayons' apartment and Sala Tarone in Berlin, the *Landpartie* to Tempelhof, and Schach's home in the Mark, Schloß Wuthenow, chart Schach's growing awareness of those human qualities represented by Victoire, his increasing knowledge about himself.

Berlin: the salon and Sala Tarone

The narrative begins in Berlin, in the salon of Frau von Carayon, a beautiful widow. The salon is Frau von Carayon and her daughter Victoire's favourite room. The salon is where they spend most of their time (574) and it contains a number of items from the Carayons' days in St Petersburg, reminders of their wealth and former prestige there: the malachite clock, the Turkish carpet (574), and a life-sized portrait of the unattractive late Herr von Carayon (575). Of singular importance for Frau von Carayon is her mirror, in which she checks on a daily basis that she is still a beautiful woman (574). The other rooms in the apartment, though mentioned, are not described in detail.

The salon is on the corner of the building, and looks out over the square (574). The view of the street is facilitated by the large windows and the balcony, whose doors, as soon as the weather permits, the Carayons keep open. From this privileged position the ladies can watch the goings-on of the busy Behrenstraße–Charlottenstraße corner, particularly the spring parades with the fine old regiments, above all the Garde du Corps and the Gensdarmes. Significantly, the balcony not only gives them the chance to watch the parades, but also to be seen by the soldiers marching past. The description thus establishes a relationship between the salon and the street. In his discussion of the *Erzählung*, Manfred Dutschke observes that whereas the salon is the place of expression for the bourgeoisie and aristocrats, the street is the space in which the poor can communicate their discontent.[14] Street and salon are thus, in his assessment, opposites. A closer look at the text itself reveals a rather different picture, however.

The salon is a semi-public sphere; it is the place in which Frau von Carayon entertains her guests, and the first elements that are described are the link with the outside world, namely the windows (574). The effect of the large windows and balcony is to render the wall, the barrier between the internal and the external, the private and the public spheres, transparent and permeable. Furthermore, in the salon and the street a common activity takes place: the parade. Describing the furniture, the narrator observes that Frau von Carayon's 'Trumeau' 'paradierte vor allem' (574). Frau von Carayon looks at the mirror and is reminded of her own charms, in the same way that she looks out on the soldiers passing by outside, whose upward, admiring glances have, it could be argued, the same reassuring effect. The differentiation between the street and the salon is thus broken down on the one hand because the physical barrier, the wall, is comprised largely of windows and a balcony, and on the other because what is happening in both spaces is the same. There is a conversation of looking, a narcissistic discussion of external beauty which is communicated visually and publicly.

Transience and the threat of decay are also important features here, as they are throughout the novel. This relationship of observation and appreciation of beauty is based upon what is fleeting: the rococo of the balcony railings is testament to changing fashion, the old regiments parading outside are soon to be swept away at Jena and Auerstädt, while Frau von Carayon needs to reassure herself of her physical beauty only because it is a naturally short-lived quality.

In this context then, the fact that events take place in rooms other than the salon towards the end of the narrative is significant. On Schach and Victoire's wedding day, the guests eat in the previously unseen dining room, an 'unbequemes Anhängsel' at the back of the flat (673), and Frau von Carayon takes Schach into yet another room to apologize for anything she may have said in anger (675). After the wedding Schach returns to the salon only briefly before leaving the party (677). There is thus a move away from the salon, or at least the hegemony it held. Through the marriage to Victoire, Schach and the reader move beyond the superficial realm of the witty salon conversation to less aesthetic but more meaningful places, where even the comic and socially inept Tante Marguerite's comments are well received (674).

After leaving Frau von Carayon's salon at the beginning of the novel, Schach, Sander, Bülow, and Alversleben walk to the corner of Unter den Linden. Here Schach takes his leave, while the others go to the 'Italiener-, Wein- und

Delikatessenhandlung von Sala Tarone' (567). On first appearances, it might be suggested that the purpose of the setting 'Sala Tarone' is to provide another respectable address, as Demetz would suggest, as a backdrop for conversation.[15] Indeed, the reason the gentlemen decide to go there is to talk for an hour, a narrative strategy for further characterization of Schach through discussion, in what Sylvain Guarda calls 'ein prismatisches Schach-Bild aus vier verschiedenen Perspektiven'.[16] What this does not explain is the necessity of describing the difficult entry along the corridor lined with boxes, through which the men have to pass before arriving at the room towards the back of the building.

The door at Sala Tarone is closed when they arrive, because of the late hour, and a head from within, looking through a peephole, verifies the respectability of the men before permitting them to enter. Once inside, the guests have to squeeze down a tight passage lined with boxes, while the dim light is barely enough to see by (567). When these factors are considered alongside the description of Frau von Carayon's salon, it seems clear that Sala Tarone is in many ways the opposite of the beautiful, outwardly oriented salon. While that space was open, light, and at the front of the house, Sala Tarone is hidden, dark and the guests are led to the rear.

It is in this setting that sincerity and falsehood become a theme of discussion, specifically with reference to Schach's personality, and rather than a place of witty salon conversation, Sala Tarone is a place where men can say what they mean. The judgements of Schach's character range from Bülow's damning assessment to Alversleben's observation that Schach is 'immerhin einer unserer Besten' (572). The question of Schach's sincerity is particularly important. Nostitz argues that Schach's behaviour is always an expression of himself, even when one might assume it to be affected, and that this quality distinguishes him from others. Alversleben makes a similar statement, that Schach does not wear a mask (573). The discussion of Schach's personality is thus expressed in terms of exterior appearances and inner realities, and to his peers Schach appears to be at variance with the norm by virtue of his consistency. Consequently, Hugo Aust argues that for Schach there is no difference between the external and the internal; he believes in a harmony which no longer exists.[17] Nostitz's comments suggest rather that Schach is simply unaware of different possibilities, and although Schach's integrity is assessed positively, it seems that he does not understand the relative meaninglessness of these superficial things which constitute his whole self. What is more, whether positively valued or not, Schach's apparent integrity marks him out as in some way limited compared to his colleagues. Schach's personality is thus perhaps better described as naively simple.

With the salon of Frau von Carayon and Sala Tarone, Fontane creates two separate realms which represent on the one hand exterior beauty and superficiality, and on the other inner truthfulness. These two spaces correspond to the major themes in the discussion of beauty and Victoire in Chapter 7. Their separateness is essential so that Schach can be shown to be absent from Sala Tarone, but present in the salon, as a spatial expression of Schach's consciousness. The representation of Berlin becomes a symbolic template of Schach's psychology. It is through the externally shrouded Victoire that he becomes aware of another realm, and the psychological consequences show themselves as 'Schach zieht sich zurück' (618).

Tempelhof

In Chapter 4, the small party comprised of Schach, the Carayons, mother and daughter, and Tante Marguerite make the short journey to Tempelhof, to the south of the city. In the spatial representation of Tempelhof, the text again constructs a world divided into two spheres: the village, an open, social place dominated by display, and the church, an interior, spiritual place. When they arrive at Tempelhof village, Schach and the Carayons go to a guest house, and the narrator comments that the sunshine has attracted a lot of visitors (581). The arrival through an avenue of old lime trees announces an idyllic setting. The purpose of nature here is to decorate: the group sit at a table with a maple tree in its centre, of which the foliage is described as 'Laubschmuck', the living tree is an ornament. On the street, an idealized rural scene is described:

> Equipagen hielten in der Mitte der Dorfstraße, die Stadtkutscher plauderten und Bauern und Knechte, die mit Pflug und Egge vom Felde hereinkamen, zogen an der Wagenreihe vorüber. Zuletzt kam eine Herde, die der Schäferspitz von rechts und links her zusammenhielt. (581)

This idyllic, almost pastoral scene, which the group see from their table, is typical of this space, which is characterized by visibility, where Schach and Frau von Carayon — as a beautiful couple — are themselves conscious of being watched by the other guests. Furthermore, the village road scene in the above quotation is presented as a fixed image, but each of its elements is in fact in the process of moving along a road. The description has captured only a moment. Like the 'Laubschmuck' on a deciduous tree, the beauty and ornament of the Tempelhof description is undermined in the text by references to its transience. The bells in the distance that close the description serve to underline this temporal aspect: not only do they announce in advance the next stage in the *Landpartie*, namely the walk to Tempelhof church itself, but also because they are the 'Betglocke', or vespers, they indicate that it is evening (581). The village thus represents the hollow 'Dressur' of Prussia's army, creating an ironic backdrop to Schach's conversation with Frau von Carayon: Schach confirms his belief in the superiority of the Prussian military (583), articulating the very credo that Bülow had ridiculed earlier (572). The key aspects of the village description (ornament, visibility, the external, transience) recall the salon, while, as will be shown, the section of the text devoted to the church develops those themes represented by Sala Tarone.

The two spaces, village and church, are identified with Frau von Carayon and Victoire respectively, and are strongly differentiated. While the characters are in the village, the narrator focuses on the discussion of Frau von Carayon and Schach. The conversation between Tante Marguerite and Victoire is by contrast given priority as the characters approach the church, shifting the reader's focus of attention to Victoire. While the guest house was situated by the roadside, in this second realm, the church is located at the end of the path. It is a destination, rather than a station on the road; it is distant and isolated on the edge of society; in this way its situation associates the eternal and spiritual aspects with social isolation. The church is identified through the trees in the distance, like the veiled Victoire and her inner beauty. At first, only the red of the church's roof is visible through the twigs and branches of the trees. Red has been shown to represent 'Transzendenz, Aufschwung, Idee, Himmel' elsewhere in Fontane's oeuvre, and thus foreshadows Schach's death here, and is arguably related to the elegiac side of Victoire's character.[18]

Whereas the rural scene represented in the village was idyllic, here the description focuses on less aesthetic aspects: a ploughed field, a field lying fallow, a wasteland (584). This area is marked out by a 'Grasnarbe', recalling Victoire's scars (39). A number of details prefigure events after Schach's affair with Victoire. Within the field around the church, the text describes a pond surrounded by reeds and singing toads. The reeds can be used as nightlights, according to the aunt, indicating Schach's later sleeplessness and night wandering at Wuthenow. The pond is a prefiguration of the lake at Wuthenow, where Schach will eventually be able to rest. The *Unkenruf* is a bad omen, later echoed at Wuthenow where Krist tells Schach he had heard frogs croaking and had known it to be significant (641). The hazelnut bushes in the hedge may also be a reference to Schach's affair with Victoire, as they have been shown to symbolize love and eroticism in German folk culture.[19] As the characters approach the isolated and historic church, the text thus enumerates symbolic indicators of Schach's affair with Victoire, and his consequent experience at Schloß Wuthenow, that other old and lonely place where he would have to spend his days if he and Victoire were married.

It is in the church that Victoire's feelings for Schach become apparent (587) and here the text weaves together subtle prefigurations of their fate. The neglected state of the churchyard is replicated inside the church, which, when the party enters is bathed in the red and purple light of the evening (585). These colours recall the earlier reference to the red roof of the tower, and because of the religious context perhaps also symbolize the Holy Spirit and mourning, or penitence. Entering the space in which Schach and Victoire will be alone for the first time, these prefigurations of mourning and transcendence are especially pregnant given Schach's later suicide (677–78) and the miracle on the altar that saves their child in Rome (683). The light gives the church interior a renewed glory, just as Schach will describe the Templars' fall: 'in einem wiedergewonnenen Glorienschein' (588).

The main feature in the church is the carved image of the Templar knight of local lore (586). According to Sylvain Guarda's analysis, the church is a place where a deep spiritual union between Schach and Victoire is revealed, through the tradition of the Knights Templar.[20] According to the legend related by the verger's daughter, the ghost of the Templar had the locals move his 'Steinbild' from the floor of the church to the wall, to ensure that his image would not be worn away (587). This prefigures Schach's contemplation of his own future image at Wuthenow, as he stands and faces the gallery of his forebears (650). The story of the Templar's ghost drives Frau von Carayon and Tante Marguerite outside, leaving Schach and Victoire alone (587), and thus bringing them together, and in his discussion of the Templar knight, the tone of Schach's words touches Victoire and reveals her vulnerability to his advances (587). Finally, when describing his respect for the Templars, Schach declares 'es lebt etwas in mir, das mich von keinem Gelübde zurückschrecken läßt' (588). In the church with Victoire, Schach announces his readiness to submit to vows — a prefiguration of his later marriage but an ironic comment on his suicide.

It becomes clear that in the *Landpartie* chapter the text constructs a spatial world divided into two spheres: the 'mondäner Ort' of the guest house, and the more isolated sphere of the church.[21] These two incorporate necessarily different ideas: one presents a world of superficial beauty and confidence, but is in fact the product of a fleeting moment; the other has stood for centuries and represents qualities more closely linked to the eternal, the inner self, and spirituality. The former space is associated with Frau von Carayon, while the second is associated with her daughter. A principal line of this enquiry has been to illustrate that the realm associated with Victoire also contains symbolic references to her future and that of Schach, and his contemplation of this at Wuthenow. The constructed realms at Tempelhof complement the spatial model of Berlin. While Schach did not enter Sala Tarone, he does enter the church with Victoire. This signals the beginning of a process of change in Schach's psychology, and that this development is brought about by Victoire.

Wuthenow am See

The third stage in the spatial representation of Schach's psychological development is the description of Schloß Wuthenow and his experiences there. Understanding Wuthenow's function provides essential insight into

Schach's character and psychology. As with Berndt, Seidentopf, and Amelie in *Vor dem Sturm*, Fontane uses spatial representation to lay bare a character's internal divisions. On the one hand, Wuthenow is significant because it shows the reader that there is more to Schach than Berlin society perceives: Wuthenow is the representation of his past; it is the aesthetically unappealing, provincially limited aspect of his life that others do not see, and that he himself has been avoiding. It is his youth, he remains 'der junge Herr', and he has a sense of modesty here, proved by his refusal of his father's title, which is at odds with the 'steife Vornehmheit' criticized by Nostitz (573). On the other hand, Schach's experience of Wuthenow indicates his inability to resolve his disparate identities. In the representation of Wuthenow, the elements which have previously been separate, the internal and the external, come together, as the multifaceted integrity represented by Victoire is perceived by Schach to be part of himself, too.

From the outset, Schach's entry in Schloß Wuthenow involves moving to the opposite side, crossing a boundary, temporally and spatially: he arrives at midnight into Wuthenow, and rides through the village to the manor, which is on the opposite side of the village, built on a hill overlooking the Ruppiner See (640). The castle is described as follows:

> Das Schloß selbst aber war nichts als ein alter, weißgetünchter und von einer schwarzgeteerten Balkenlage durchzogener Fachwerkbau, dem erst Schachs Mutter, die 'verstorbene Gnädige', durch ein Doppeldach, einen Blitzableiter und eine prächtige, nach dem Muster von Sanssouci hergerichtete Terrasse das Ansehen allernüchternster Tagtäglichkeit genommen hatte. Jetzt freilich, unter dem Sternenschein, lag alles da wie das Schloß im Märchen, und Schach hielt öfters an und sah hinauf, augenscheinlich betroffen von der Schönheit des Bildes. (640)

The focalized description is significant because of the analogy between the castle and Schach's perception of it, and Victoire and the evening of his affair with her. The castle is an unappealing 'Fachwerkbau', a type of building which usually has positive historical and moral connotations in Fontane's oeuvre.[22] Schach is momentarily struck by the image of this aesthetically unpretentious building in the moonlight. This recalls his comment to Victoire: 'was allein gilt, ist das ewig Eine, daß sich die Seele den Körper schafft oder ihn durchleuchtet und verklärt' (616), or his argument that there are moments when Victoire's nature covers her with a veil of beauty (607). He considers the castle here a 'Schloß im Märchen', just as he tells Victoire 'alles ist Wunder und Märchen an Ihnen' (617).

The castle also represents complexity, the coexistence of conflicting elements, because it is an historic building which has evolved. Victoire may also be said to represent becoming; her scars are symbols of life. Just as her earlier days of beauty are still occasionally visible, as Schach concedes, so too here Schloß Wuthenow has an older 'Fachwerkbau' base, to which later additions have been made by Schach's mother during the period of Frederick the Great: the 'Doppeldach', the terrace, and a lightning conductor (640). These additions are external and their grandeur stands in contrast with the sobriety of the earlier core. Yet they are still part of the same building, and are seen by Schach as one. So too Victoire's exterior and interior are different, her body and soul to use Schach's terms from the quotation above, but are both part of her person. The spatial representations of the internal and external, which have been shown to be separate in Berlin and Tempelhof, are here united in an image which Schach perceives analogously to Victoire. While Berlin showed Schach's ignorance of a deeper inner sphere, and Tempelhof predicted his affair with Victoire and the psychological changes it brings about, here in this image, which is in part focalized through Schach, these separate elements come together. Schach perceives complexity, variety, and acknowledges its beauty. He has fled Victoire, yet sees a symbol of her in the ancestral home which bears his own name. There can be no escape back to his ignorance, away from his rediscovered, deeper, more complex self.

The representation of his arrival weaves the idea of fate into the recurrent references to Victoire and complexity. Schach ties the reins of his horse to a walnut tree outside the house (641). Apart from being another symbol of age, the walnut tree is traditionally perceived as an oracle of love, as its nut is made of two halves. This is thus a symbolic representation of Schach's indecision about whether a life with Victoire is possible or desirable, and the duality she is bringing into his life.[23] Old Krist amusingly seems to believe that his own suspicions have been confirmed by the unexpected visit of the young master. He heard frogs croaking earlier in the day and interpreted this as a sign (641). This reference to the croaking frogs recalls the similar occurrence at Tempelhof, where the toads' croaking, the ominous *Unkenruf*, increased as Victoire approached the church. It seems that, in this process of discovering value in that which is not aesthetically pleasing, here is an episode whereby insight or knowledge is found too in an unexpected quarter. As Hoppenmarieken observes in *Vor dem Sturm*: 'De Dummen, so as wi ick, de sinn ümmer de Klöksten'.[24]

The description of the manor's interior appears to unite the imagery of the Berlin representations of both Sala Tarone and the Carayons' salon. As at Sala Tarone, entering Schloß Wuthenow is not easy: Schach and Krist walk down a narrow corridor, and open a half-swollen door with difficulty (642). By contrast, the 'Garten*salon*' with the rococo gilded door evokes the salon of Frau von Carayon (642).[25] The purpose of this room is to view the outside; even its name blurs the boundaries between the interior and the exterior. Indeed, moths enter through the windows at night, unifying the park and the *Gartensalon*, and Schach leaves the room through the window and spends the night in the grounds (644). This communion with the outside world resembles the salon's exterior focus in Berlin. Schloß Wuthenow, the place of Schach's past, and a place he has ignored for a long time, symbolizes the layered quality of human beings, Schach in particular.

Inside the *Gartensalon*, Schach tells Krist: 'Störe den Staub nicht in seinem Frieden' (643), and his own words cause him to remember his parents in the ancestral grave. Schach is becoming aware of a more complicated world. The double-meaning of his remark, the double doors leading into the room, and the twin-branched candlestick are all representations of the increasing duality in Schach's previously monolithic mindset (642). Pierre Bange's interpretation of Schach's sleeplessness and night walk are in this light particularly enlightening. The Schach who wakes and leaves the room is, according to Bange, Schach's *Doppelgänger*.[26]

Schach steps out into the garden, which, like the house, appears unchanged since his mother's days and in need of 'eine ordnende Hand' (644): Schach has ignored his own soul for a long time. Like Tempelhof church, decaying yet ancient, time seems to stand still in this garden, which is on the way to becoming a wilderness. The moment and eternity are side by side, as the summer flowers stand inside their evergreen borders. Müller-Seidel has highlighted the fact that the mechanical (i.e. the clock), which has replaced the organic heart of Prussian soldiers, is suspended here.[27] Schach's circling of the sundial certainly underlines the seemingly timeless state of the garden, and in this garden, the organic proves to be more real than the mechanical: the clock is not in fact suspended, and indeed does show that time is passing slowly, but because it is night time, the time feels long, and thus the sundial, which does not register time in the dark, is a truer reflection of time as Schach experiences it.

Müller-Seidel's insight has the potential for a much broader application, however. The garden is a place where Berlin society, its values, and its way of life are negated: Schach attempts 'die Zeit, mit guter Manier hinter sich zu bringen', a phrase reminiscent of the cultivated circles in which Schach moves, of a society built around distractions. What Schach fears about life with Victoire is in part boredom, the *Langeweile* he is also forced to endure in these long night hours in the garden. Schach's crisis is that the social distractions he craves have been turned against him in Berlin. This is reflected in Wuthenow in the moths which drive him out of the *Gartensalon*. Thus Schach flees to the garden as he flees to Wuthenow: it provides a freedom he does not desire, because it entails isolation, but it offers the peace he needs. In this garden free from distraction Schach has space and time to think quite literally forced upon him. As the night cannot be spent 'mit guter Manier', Schach begins a walk, and although he has trodden the garden paths many times before, it is only now that he engages in that deeper interaction with his surroundings explored by Fontane in the *Wanderungen*, and which is of central importance in the later novels: he inhales the perfume of the flowers.

It becomes apparent that Schach is involved in a process of realization when he begins to contemplate motifs of difference and contradiction. He measures the distance between the light and the shadow on the path; he stops to ponder the statues of eternal gods and goddesses, made not of marble, but of more transient sandstone. This is a more contemplative Schach. The walk thus includes conflicting elements, the momentary and the eternal, the organic and the mechanical which are illustrated both in Schach's behaviour and the corresponding descriptions. Schach's garden experiences represent his psychological development, as he becomes aware of the complications and contradictions of the world; they indicate his increasing awareness of human depth.

Schach finds rest on the lake, where he is rocked to sleep by the current, in a moment of communion with his mother.[28] Schach abandons himself to those organic, eternal elements that had been present in various forms during his walk. The mechanical soldier discovers another world, and gives himself to it. Schach's journey ends in an act of resignation, as he falls asleep at dawn with both the stars and the rising sun in the sky (646). Schach's 'retreat' occurs on several levels. He retreats psychologically from adulthood to childhood in the garden and eventually is rocked like a baby on the lake. He retreats temporally from the deadlines and schedule of the wedding that Frau von Carayon had imposed, to a place where time seems suspended. He retreats spatially from Berlin to Wuthenow, and spatially and temporally in terms of civilization: from the house, a civilized space, to the garden which is ordered nature, to the lake which is free from man's influence, where he abandons himself to the natural current.[29] Schach's experience is a period of imposed reflection, contemplation, and exploration of long-neglected truths, a walk along the paths of an untended soul. Schach's eventual rest on the lake, in an organic world, a place of real depth, indicates perhaps that his eventual suicide may in fact be his only way of abandoning himself fully to the eternal nature represented by Victoire.

Summary

Schach von Wuthenow is a finely spun text about complexity, about the puzzle of events and human beings, and, as often in Fontane, the inadequacy of clear-cut world-views. Schach, an apparently simple man, has an affair with a pockmarked girl, which leads to a journey of discovery about the nature of human beings, and above all himself. He finds out that they are not simple, but complex creatures, full of imperfections and contradictions, whose exterior shell can hide a deeper, more meaningful self. The spatial representation in

Schach von Wuthenow functions to trace these developments: the text creates a structural representation of Schach's psychology based on the dichotomy interior/exterior, on the recurrent theme of complexity, and on the character that represents humanity, Victoire.

Graf Petöfy

> In November days,
> When vapours rolling down the valleys, made
> A lonely scene more lonesome.
>
> WORDSWORTH, *The Prelude*[30]

Introduction

Fontane's next novel, *Graf Petöfy*, also explores issues of knowledge, this time the danger of self-delusion. A young actress, Franziska, is invited by an old, theatre-loving Graf to take part in an artificial marriage, based neither on love nor on dynastic considerations, but rather on his desire to be entertained by her stories. She accepts his proposal, and they withdraw to Hungary, a world that she knows only through poetry. Here the relationship between the Graf and Franziska changes, in that the Graf, who had previously maintained that his marriage to Franziska would allow her perfect freedom in amorous matters, loses sight of that original arrangement and reacts emotionally when he finds out Franziska has had an affair with his nephew, Egon. The Graf begins the marriage in a state of awareness, but eventually believes the illusion that their marriage represents. Reflecting on their marriage, shortly before his suicide, he remarks: 'Während ich sie beständig warnte, das Leben nicht als Märchen zu nehmen, hatt' ich mir doch meinerseits ein Märchen ausgedacht, und ihr guter Wille, mir zu Willen zu sein, bestärkte mich in dem Glauben an eine Märchenmöglichkeit' (858). Franziska makes a similar, if less obvious, error in her attachment to Egon. As Fontane explains in a letter to his wife, while Franziska loves Egon, he is indifferent towards her.[31] His falsehood is revealed in the search for the lost child Marischka, which is only a game to him (832), and much like his uncle's marriage based on calculation, Egon's decision to pursue the affair with Franziska is consciously made (843). Franziska falls victim to this conscious acting.

It will be suggested that Adam and Franziska's drift towards delusion is reflected in spatial models in the text. In order to elucidate the argument, the representations of three locations will be examined in turn: Vienna, Öslau, and Arpa. The descriptions of the Petöfy house and Franziska's flat in Vienna will be analysed in terms of characterization and the prefiguration of later conflicts. Here it will be argued that the narrator establishes the Graf's problematic relationship with the theatre. The representation of Öslau explores the theme of theatrical knowledge in greater detail, evincing the difference between being involved in an illusion as an actor or a knowing spectator, and believing an illusion. The text develops this further in the representation of Arpa. Here the description of the arrival, the spatial divisions within the castle, as well as Franziska's views of the landscape will be discussed. The position of her rooms inside the castle points to and sows the seeds of a disastrous marriage, and her view of the landscape from the castle provides a spatial model which may be interpreted in terms of the conflicts she will face in her married life. Finally, it will be argued that the representation of the landscape at Arpa may be analysed in terms of constituting two realms: one which represents knowledge of an illusion, and the other which represents delusion. The movement of the characters into the second realm underlines the increasing self-deception of Franziska and Adam.

Vienna

The novel begins in Vienna with a description of the Petöfy town house, which represents the state of the Austro-Hungarian Empire at the end of the nineteenth century, and Graf Adam Petöfy's old age. The house is a baroque palace, built in the glory days of the Empire, at the time of Prince Eugene of Savoy (1663–1736), the victorious general and patron of the arts. It is, however, in a state of disrepair: the iron gates in front of the house are rusting and to look at it for the first time a passer-by would think it long uninhabited (685).

A visit by the younger Graf Egon provides the motivation for a description of Adam's lodgings (687), which communicates mixed messages about Adam's character. On the one hand, there are numerous images of the theatre and superficial artifice: potted plants in the middle of winter, a gallery of pictures of theatrical greats, as well as the women in the outfitters across the road, who provide a theatrical chorus (693). This seems self-evident, as does the image of the bird in the cage, a seemingly obvious prediction of Franziska's isolated existence at Arpa (687); but all is not as clear as it first appears.

It could be assumed that a semantic field stressing the exterior, openness, and visibility would be appropriate for a spatial representation reflecting theatrical influences. The Graf's lodgings, however, are at the end of a long corridor, and at the furthest extremity from the main *corps de logis*, in the front of the wing of the house. Adam himself is not present in the room where Egon waits for him, but is dressing behind closed doors. These details indicate the Graf's problematic relationship with the theatre: it represents for him distance from reality, an escape and a shelter. In spatial terms, it signifies not a move forward, but a retreat. Correspondingly, the Graf's interest in theatre and the arts begins with his indecision in the 1848 revolution, when he leaves the country (791), and his love of theatre is linked again to fleeing from difficult situations when he departs unexpectedly for Paris because of his growing affection for the actress, Franziska (709). It is arguably the same mental process which motivates the withdrawal to Arpa and Adam's reluctance to return to Vienna (847).

The home of the Prussian actress Franziska is in many ways the antithesis of the Petöfy town house. Its distance from the centre of Vienna suggests a humbler milieu than the baroque mansion (705). The building has a 'Flachdach' (708) rather than a 'Doppeldach' (685), and pots are only planted in the summer months (708). Rather than being set back from the street and protected by iron gates, this actress's flat is in the foremost corner house, and as such occupies a dominant position of relative power and importance (705). It is visibly well lit, unlike the Petöfy house, and is thus a welcoming space. Considering these elements together, it might be suggested that whereas Graf Adam's rooms and his town house in general suggest a state of withdrawal, retreat, and decay, Franziska's more humble home suggests a more external and vibrant character. This might be said to reflect Franziska's youth and Adam's advanced years and, by analogy, the relative vitality of the Prussian state vis-à-vis Austria.

The question of nationality is significant primarily as a means of discussing freedom, a key theme in this novel of marriage and isolation. The Catholic priest, Pater Feßler, considers the virtue of the Prussians to be their intellectual and spiritual freedom tied to their Protestantism, which gives them the unique possibility of choosing to return to the law of the Catholic Church. 'Freiwillige[r] Unterordnung' is his ideal (696). Franziska will eventually fulfil that ideal when she converts to Catholicism at the end of the novel and elects to remain in Arpa after Adam's death (866). The question of Franziska's freedom also finds expression in the description of her flat. Indeed, rather than staying indoors, she and Hanna proceed out onto the roof (708), where she reflects for the first time in the narrative upon her childhood days (708–09). The function of the roof space appears at first to be to highlight Franziska's freedom at this stage of the narrative: beyond the social space of the house, she looks over the city, transformed and silenced by the covering of snow. However, while Franziska lulls herself into almost believing that she can hear the sea near her Prussian home village, the night wind has no respect for her homeward greeting, and destroys the snowball she throws to the north, perhaps signifying change. Whereas elsewhere snowflakes are associated with a yearning for freedom, here the snow has been brought up to the railings, a barrier that extends upwards into the free roof space from the social realm of the house, prefiguring Franziska's caged existence on the veranda and the balcony at Arpa.[32] Her rocking chair (706), like the one in Petöfy's room (687), is a symbol of the indecision and wavering that weaves through the novel, as is her 'ziellos' wandering back and forth on the roof top (708).

Finally, it might be suggested that the distance of Franziska's house from the centre of Vienna is analogous to the distance between Adam's rooms and the centre of his house. As will be demonstrated later, Franziska shares Adam's problematic understanding of the theatre, and this spatial correspondence in Vienna may be an early indicator of their shared psychological trait. In addition, it is Egon who leads Franziska home before the ambivalent signs concerning her freedom are enumerated. Egon is the man with whom Franziska will have an affair and acheive a brief, dangerous, and ultimately false sense of freedom from her marriage. This might indicate that while on the surface Franziska's freedom is threatened by her marriage, in fact it is her delusional affair with Egon which will present her real problem. On balance, then, Franziska's flat may represent her difference from Adam and her current freedom, but the description points also to her fatal similarity to Adam Petöfy and prefigures her troubled future.

In brief, the spatial representations of the Petöfy house and Franziska's flat weave together symbols of characterization and prefiguration in a complex web. The analysis has underlined allusions to Adam's problematic relationship with the theatre and the question of Franziska's freedom. The homes of Adam and Franziska constitute mixed pictures, corresponding to their complex psychologies. The obvious signs are undermined, and subtler shades of prefiguration suggest how their fates may later be intertwined.

Öslau

As in the representation of Vienna, the representation of Öslau prefigures potential problems in the union of Adam and Franziska. Whereas in Vienna the social gap between Franziska and the Petöfys was to a certain extent covered by the distance between their two homes, here the relatively humble 'halbes Parterre' rented by Phemi and Franziska stands diagonally opposite the big hotel (710), the 'König von Ungarn', in which Judith's room is situated upstairs, reflecting her social superiority (718). Furthermore, the presentation of both of these buildings seems to reflect the cooling of relations that has taken place between Franziska and the Petöfys (709). Beyond each of the buildings an additional boundary is noted by the narrator: the hotel is surrounded by oleander trees (711), while the veranda of Franziska's house is described as being protected by windows and canvas screens (710). There are, however, subtle links between the represented places: both the lilies in Franziska's garden (710) and the oleander trees produce red or pink flowers, symbolizing the love of the Graf that will join the two houses. But these symbolic overtones are ambiguous and prefigure later problems: because the lilies described in Franziska's house are not white, but red, this negates lilies' usual connotations of purity; and pink though the flowers of the oleander may be, the tree is poisonous.

More importantly, the presentation of Franziska's lowly veranda and Judith's elevated balcony not only suggests that social hierarchy may cause problems in the marriage, but also indicates the role of the theatre in that union. From their balcony, Judith and Adam look down on the actresses Phemi and Franziska on their veranda, like spectators in a box watching a play on a stage, and Adam even does so with opera glasses (731). The stage-like veranda has a curtain that is half pulled back when Adam approaches the women (729); he visits Franziska and Phemi on the veranda and steps onto it. Franziska for her part later abandons the veranda and joins Judith upstairs in the hotel. These movements between the veranda and the hotel, the stage and the box, indicate that the boundaries between act and reality are becoming increasingly blurred in the relationship between Franziska and Adam.

The theatre theme is developed during a 'Partie' into the mountains, occasioned by a visit from Egon and the young Graf Pejevics (721). More specifically, the *Landpartie* explores the theatrical process, the creation of illusions, knowing what is an act, and what is not. This is an elaboration of those issues seen in the representations of the Vienna and Öslau residences. Previous scholarship has highlighted Adam's lack of understanding in this area, and it is noteworthy that Adam does not take part in this *Landpartie*.[33]

To learn how a spectacle is produced, one must go behind the scenes. This is precisely where the journey takes Phemi, Pejevics, and Franziska, and it is Phemi, the most accomplished actress, who leads them (722).[34] Proceeding behind the hotel, they come to a field where a fair is being set up. Past a motionless carousel, Phemi takes them along a side path that leads behind the stalls, with the remark: 'hier sind wir hinter den Kulissen' (723). Here they meet the characters of the fair: the sword-swallowing Spaniard, the fire-eater, and the strongman among others, but they see the actors as people, not as their acts: 'alle traten einem hier in schöner Menschlichkeit entgegen' (723). The walk through the fair led by the actress is an exposé of the theatrical process, of the difference between the man and the act, that lies at the heart of the conflict in the novel.

This part of the narrative is particularly important; it questions Franziska's relationship with the truth, revealing that she is more like Adam than might be initially expected. Returning from the mountain walk, all of the characters pass through the fair, and the harlequin figure seems to announce that the show, which was earlier seen in preparation, is now being seen in performance (726). When Phemi tries to go and see the fortune-teller, Franziska reacts angrily: 'ich hasse jede Neugier, die den Schleier von dem uns gnädig Verborgenen wegreißen will' (729). In this utterance she predicts Petöfy's downfall, which is arguably the result of his curiosity to know about the affair. At the same time it is delusion and ignorance of the theatrical process that is to blame for Petöfy's decision to marry Franziska, as John Osborne has argued.[35] Simultaneously, through this utterance Franziska gives value to her marriage with Petöfy; she would refuse to know the unhappy outcome, which might have prevented her from marrying him. Her belief in the value of benign illusions places her nearer to Adam in character than might otherwise be assumed.

So far the analysis has focused primarily on the theatre as the key to understanding the construction of illusions, but the text also builds elements of the *Landpartie* around a related theme: visual art and appreciation. After passing the caravans in which the show people live, Franziska, Phemi, and Pejevics come across the baggage train accompanying the travelling fair (723). The rows of wagons present the walking spectators with a series of 'Genrebilder' (723); they walk through a gallery of living pictures. The gallery motif recurs throughout the text, perhaps as a reference to Franziska's desire for a community and a place where she feels she belongs: from the Graf's gallery of actors and actresses and his picture book in Vienna (687), to the corresponding gallery of ancestors at Arpa, which, upon thinking that one day she might have to join it, fills Franziska with feelings of fear and insecurity (782). As in *Schach von Wuthenow*, reflecting on a potential future artwork brings reality into focus (650).[36]

Knowing how to appreciate the landscape, and moreover how to consider it in an artistic way, is an aspect of Fontane's narrative technique that has been the subject of extensive recent research, as was highlighted in the Introduction.[37] In short, Fontane's representations of landscapes, and the way in which his characters react to them, need to be understood within the context of travel literature during the nineteenth century. Moving from an initial position of providing information about a location, texts increasingly emphasized the aesthetic qualities of the countryside, at a time of growing aesthetic appreciation of the landscape in general.[38] Given this context, the 'Genrebilder' and the beautiful landscape at Öslau, which the party sees from the 'Aussichtspunkt' on the hill, take on a new significance. The text constructs a landscape which the characters view and appreciate as a work of art, not simply as an indifferent external reality. The theatrical world of the fair and the artistic world of scenic appreciation are related, in that they are both shown to involve constructed images, one constructed by the actor, the other by the viewer. This is an important consideration when taking into account previous criticism of the novel's portrayal of Hungary as unrealistic and purely artistic or invented. In its representation of Öslau, the text explores the relationship between the viewer and what is seen. It highlights on the one hand the way in which illusions are created, in the theme of the theatre, and on the other the fact that even reality may be seen through a subjective, cultural filter, in the theme of artistic appreciation.

Arpa

Following the honeymoon, the newly-weds Adam and Franziska proceed directly to the Petöfy residence at Arpa (763). The description of the arrival appears idyllic, and Franziska is enchanted by the poetic magic of the Hungarian place names (763). From the steamer's last stop, the couple must take a coach up to the castle, which provides Franziska with a chance to take in the landscape: 'Sieh', the Graf tells her (764). The overwhelming impression is welcoming: the Petöfy colours are flying, the bells are ringing, and the locals are out to wish the couple well. Even the landscape seems on parade, with the corn standing high on both sides of the road, and the idyllic harmony between man and nature appears to be epitomized by the harvest image of the straw-covered ground, and the great beds of watermelons watered by a stream.

Yet on closer examination, the picture is more ambiguous. The poetic place names Franziska found so delightful are revealed by Petöfy to be entirely prosaic (763). Furthermore, Franziska and Adam will not live in the happy and fruitful valley, but begin a difficult ascent to reach the castle, and the description of the corn as 'über mannshoch' (764) has reminiscences of the 'mannshoch' bird cage of Adam's rooms in Vienna, with the consequent implication that Franziska will be a prisoner at Arpa (687). In addition, the harvest image is not only ironic because of the lack of life and vitality in the marriage to the old Graf; it also announces the onset of the autumn months, and with it the rain that will effectively bring about Franziska's captivity (Chapter 22 onwards). Beyond the final station of the steamer the castle seems distant and remote, and rises 'steil und mächtig' over the lake (764). Faced with this awe-inspiring view and the 'tiefe Geläut der Glocken', the diminutive horses and the 'Ton ihrer Glöckchen' suggest Franziska's underlying sense of insecurity and inferiority.

The ambiguity of the arrival is reflected in the distribution of rooms inside the castle. An important aspect of Adam and Franziska's married life is their relative independence and separateness. Karla Müller bases her analysis of the novel on aristocratic marriage as a social model, a dynastic union of two individuals who maintain a large degree of freedom. This relationship is reflected in the creation of private apartments within aristocratic homes.[39] In the case of Adam and his wife however, whom he has clearly not married for dynastic reasons, the already distant relationship of the aristocratic marriage breaks down further, because their rooms at Arpa are not opposite each other, as Müller suggests would be the normal practice.

The Petöfy town house is described as divided into two spheres, inhabited by the siblings Adam and Judith, thus creating the pair of living spaces one might expect for a married couple, following Müller's model. The arrival of Franziska does not change this established pattern. Indeed, when they visit Arpa, while

Judith stays downstairs in rooms next to the Graf's as usual, Egon is put in a room at the top of the tower (817). Franziska thus need not have been given rooms upstairs when she arrived at Arpa; she could have been given rooms next to her husband. The matching pair of rooms appropriate for man and wife has thus been deliberately avoided. This may be partly explained by the Graf's initial desire to give Franziska a degree of freedom in the marriage (74), but also it implies a continuation of the relationship in Vienna between brother and sister, devaluing the marriage. Furthermore, the division between the Graf and his sister downstairs, and Franziska and Egon upstairs also seems to tempt fate, not only because the rooms upstairs are linked, as both Franziska and the reader are made aware of on her tour of the castle (780), thus potentially facilitating the eventual affair, but more importantly because it seems to group the two young characters together, emphasizing what the Graf recognizes in the end as the natural desire of 'junges Blut' in the face of social correctness (751). The fact that Franziska is not accorded what might be called the spatial rights of a Gräfin is further clarified by the limited dimensions of her rooms; just as the carriage was small in a large and daunting landscape, so Franziska's rooms are small in a large house (766), another representation of limitation and containment.

Symbolic spatial dichotomies and the Arpa landscape

On Franziska's first morning at Arpa, she looks out of her window and surveys the countryside (769). She observes the hilly landscape to the left, covered in villages and vineyards; to the right are the mountains, and in the centre is the 'Schloßberg'. The contrast between the farmed hills and valleys, and the uninhabited mountains is on the one hand a typical symbolic dichotomy, opposing society and reality on the one hand, with romantic escape into the unknown on the other. More specifically, however, through accumulated references the text creates an opposition between left and right, and a corresponding structure based on the dichotomy west/east, in which the left and the west symbolize knowledge, safety, and social norms, while the right and the east are associated with danger and delusion.

The west/east dichotomy recurs as a leitmotif throughout the novel, and is woven into the text in a particularly subtle way in the person of Prince Eugene. This figure features in the description of the Petöfy house in Vienna (685) and it is reported that he once sat in the hall at Arpa looking out over the lake (775). Prince Eugene, originally from France, is famed for defeating the Turks. He can thus be seen as a western defender of Christendom against the foreign and heathen invader from the east. His mention recalls each time this battle between west and east, a conflict which has left its scars on the landscape in the shape of ruins visible at Öslau (724). This repeated historic reference establishes in the text a spatial model in which the west signifies safety and the east signifies danger.

This west/east axis also functions to elaborate further the thematic conflict between theatrical knowledge and delusion. References to the west identify that zone with awareness of the difference between reality and illusion, while the east is described as a place in which little or no distinction is made between art and reality. Considering the east first, two references exemplify the characteristically eastern *étroitesse* between life and art: the Hungarian Barscai ballad (794–95) and the figure of Scheherazade (855). Franziska translates the ballad for her Hungarian language tutor, the local curate. In their discussion about the poem, he insists on the parallels between real life and the *Volkslied*, life's mirror image (796). The figure of Scheherazade brings the relationship between art and life a step closer. The narrator of *The Arabian Nights*, she is to be put to death by order of the sultan when she finishes her story. By virtue of the sultan's command, the duration of Scheherazade's existence becomes synonymous with the length of her narrative: she can exist only as a narrator. In the figure of Scheherazade, life and narration are bound to the extent that the end of one will bring about the end of the other.[40] The eastern pole of the west/east axis, which through Prince Eugene signifies danger, is thus elaborated through literary references and assumes new connotations of a synthesis of life and art.

The meaning of the western axis is more obscure. In Öslau a discussion emerges between Adam and Phemi about France and the French. The Graf considers the French to be a 'Theatervolk' (733). By this he means that they do not distinguish between their lives (reality) and theatre (fantasy), thus attributing to the west the qualities this discussion has identified so far with the east. However, the Graf is an unreliable judge. Müller-Seidel argues that his comments are to be read ironically, and Franziska draws attention to Adam's lack of understanding of the theatre and the arts in general: 'der Graf hat mehr Begeisterung als Verständnis' (773).[41] Phemi provides a more credible testimony to the nature of France. She is, according to John Osborne's analysis, the most accomplished and knowledgeable character with regard to the theatre.[42] Furthermore, Phemi reveals knowledge about the theatre elsewhere in the text, by taking Franziska and the others 'hinter d[ie] Kulissen' at Öslau, as has previously been demonstrated, and Phemi's comments confirm that the Graf is in error. Phemi says she would love to go to France to learn about being an actress, 'um [ihrer] Kunst willen' (733). Indeed, Phemi repeats the word 'Kunst' three times in her short utterance, underscoring the difference between her view of France and the Graf's. Rather than France and the west being associated with the synthesis of life and art, as the Graf implies, Phemi sees France as the opposite, as a place where an understanding about the artistry of illusions might be gained. Through Phemi, the western end of the axis is identified with the knowledge about illusions that was outlined in the Öslau chapter. What emerges then is a structural dichotomy between the west and the east in which the west signifies the separation of life and fantasy, which is based upon knowledge and awareness, and the east signifies a fusion of life and art, which is delusion. Within this context, Adam and Franziska's move eastwards from Vienna to Hungary is significant, as it is a symbolic indication of a move away from knowledge and towards self-deception, which will be the fate of Adam and Franziska.

Turning to the left/right dichotomy, it becomes apparent that the text ascribes similar values to these spatial markers as to west and east. Franziska's initial view from her window places the social, hilly landscape to her left, and the mountains to her right, as has been shown. When Franziska and Hanna later look out over the courtyard from the great hall (776), Franziska notices that to her right there is a wilderness. Where the wall has crumbled, the vines are overgrown, and rowan and elder, with their red and black berries, are growing into the courtyard. The vines, recalling the vineyards on the hills Franziska saw to her left from her room, are here overgrown on her right, indicating a lack of order. The uncultivated plants (rowan and elder) invade the courtyard from beyond the wall (i.e. further to the right), and the defensive structure, the wall itself, is crumbling. Even the detail that the berries on the outside of this wall are red and black has meaning within this context. Their colours point to the love, but also the mourning, that lie to the right, beyond the realm of social conformity that the left-hand side represents. The right hand side represented here by mountains, weeds, and crumbling walls thus stands for disorder and passion, while the hills, vines, and courtyards of the left indicate civilization. These symbolic details reflect the movement of the characters in the landscape at Arpa: Egon and Franziska go out into the mountains together (the realm labelled originally as being to the right from Franziska's perspective); and, as the search parties set out to look for Toldy's lost daughter, the old Graf goes off to the left, while Franziska and Egon take their party to the right (830). Franziska's move to the right thus signals a move away from her marriage.

In summary, the relative markers, left and right, are shown to carry specific symbolic value in Franziska's focalized descriptions of the landscape at Arpa, which then correspond to her movement in the landscape. She moves increasingly towards the right with Egon, which is a step away from her marriage and towards the affair and its consequences. This dichotomy complements a wider structural pattern based on the historical conflict between the west and the east, and around which the thematic oppositions knowledge/delusion, safety/danger are constructed.

This structural network of directions informs our reading of the topography at Arpa. The spatial representation of the landscape at Arpa is constructed of two spheres which mirror the two opposing states of mind that have been the focus of the discussion so far: the artificial landscape of the park represents awareness; the wild lake and sheer cliff face that form the more romantic side of the Schloßberg represent delusion. This is a development of the pattern already revealed in the analysis of the representation of Öslau, where the difference between the production of theatre and the illusion that theatre creates was explored in the description of the fair. The spatial construction of the Arpa landscape is also an elaboration of the left/right and west/east dichotomies previously discussed, in which left and west are associated with knowledge, safety, and separation of life and fantasy, while right and east are associated with danger, delusion, and the merging of life and fantasy.

The difference between the two sides of the Schloßberg is made clear by the narrator: while the lake side is 'steil und mächtig' (764), the back of the hill falls gradually away (778). The back of the hill is terraced, with an artificial stream running into ponds, and a serpentine track leading down past the houses and mausoleum at the bottom, out onto a meadow. This park was built in the days of Adam's grandfather, and the text suggests that the Graf has added to it, as his artistic influences can be seen. The text thus makes explicit the fact that the park (the back of the Schloßberg) is a physically constructed space. There are parallels between the representation of the park and Adam and Franziska's marriage, in that the park is purely ornamental, and not a productive garden. Unlike the gardener Toldy's house which is hidden behind vines, emblems of fertility (792), the willows (778), plane trees (779), and cypresses (785) of the park have an aesthetic function only, and do not produce anything. Finally the representation of this manifestly constructed, purely aesthetic park contains clearly symbolic elements, such as the roses and cypresses (785), motifs which Adam used earlier to describe Franziska's youth and his own old age (749).

The other side of the Schloßberg is more romantic. Rather than man-made terraces, it has mountains; in place of artificial pools and streams, it has a lake of unpredictable currents, which even sinks a boat carrying a priest and the communion bread and wine (798). Evil is rumoured to dwell in both the mountains and the lake (798). Furthermore, the island where Egon and Franziska begin their affair is on this side of the Schloßberg. While the park is a manifestly constructed environment, the mists of the lake evoke mystery and a lack of clarity.

Lieselotte Voß has analysed Fontane's representation of Hungary in terms of Lenau's poetry, in particular the poem 'Nach Süden'.[43] This is the poem that Franziska recites at the beginning of the novel (703). Franziska imagines Hungary as a place of poetry, and Voß draws parallels between the details of the Arpa description and the Lenau poem. These observations are only valid for the misty, mountainous, lake side of the Schloßberg, however, not the park landscape. While this does not entirely invalidate Voß's conclusion, namely that the narrator deliberately constructs a landscape based not on reality, but on the poetic preconceptions of Franziska, it does modify it and limits its application. The text makes evident, through references to Lenau's poem, that the landscape to the lake side of the Schloßberg, viewed and explored by the characters (not just Franziska), constitutes a realm in which the division between art (poetry, and also artifice, spectacle, illusion) and reality (physical reality and life) becomes blurred: the landscape is, in part, a subjective construct of the viewer, it is perceived through the filter of the poem.

As with the directional symbolism, movements in the Arpa landscape function as expressions of narrative development. The text constructs two spheres, the park and the lake side of the Schloßberg, between which the castle, the married couple's home, stands. During the early stages of their relationship, Adam and Franziska's *Spazierfahrten* take them into the park landscape (778). The manifestly constructed landscape articulates their awareness of the artifice of their lives. Increasingly, however, Adam drives them into the mountains, in other words the lake side of the Schloßberg, the area to the right seen from Franziska's window. This movement from one sphere to another correlates with Adam's increasing delusion about his marriage: he comes to take Franziska's act for reality. He believes the 'Märchen' he himself created (859). For her part, Franziska is led astray by Egon. She and Egon go out to the mountains together frequently (823); when they look for the lost child Marischka, they travel across onto the lake side of the Schloßberg. This search, which becomes an adventure for Franziska (834), and which ends on the island where she falls for Egon, is but a game to him (832). Like Franziska, he acts a part; when looking for Marischka he merely pretends to be interested. Franziska believes the act, which the movement to the lake side of the Schloßberg represents. Both she and Adam stray here as they become deluded about their lives and relationships.

Conclusion

Fontane saw Realism in broad terms as the representation of truth, 'das Wahre'. A spatial analysis of the two novels *Schach von Wuthenow* and *Graf Petöfy* reveals two texts which explore the related issue of awareness. Ultimately, *Schach von Wuthenow* is a story of dawning self-awareness. Through Victoire, Schach perceives a deeper, more internal sphere; he becomes aware of human complexity, of the distinction between superficiality and true, inner meaning. His progressive development towards this realization and deeper understanding of human nature is charted in three stages, in the representations of Berlin, Tempelhof, and Wuthenow.

In *Graf Petöfy*, the theatre is a vehicle for the discussion of created illusions; knowledge or awareness of theatrical processes prevents the individual from slipping into self-delusion. The marriage of Adam and Franziska begins with them both being aware of the artificiality of their life together. After a short time, however, the Graf allows himself to believe that there is more to the marriage than performance, while Franziska is led astray by Egon's advances. They both fall into the trap of self-deception. The spatial representations of Vienna and Öslau prepare the ground for this fall, exploring and elaborating the themes of delusion and awareness of illusion with recourse to imagery based on the theatre and artistic appreciation. In the analysis of the representation of Arpa, spatial models were proposed by which the text charts the progression of Franziska and Adam's straying from reality.

The theme of awareness and its spatial expression is an early exploration of an issue which, as will be demonstrated, comes to be central in Fontane's later novels. Schach's tentative and short-lived moments of reflection in the garden at Wuthenow also point to the importance of sensitive interaction with the environment, which will be explored in *Irrungen Wirrungen*, while the impact of poor aesthetic understanding in *Graf Petöfy* will become a key concern in *Unwiederbringlich*.

There is no doubt that in both texts spatial representation is manipulated by Fontane in a sophisticated way, that it is a key means of literary expression, and that its investigation has uncovered unexpected layers of subtlety in both texts. Yet there are differences between the two works. The spatial structure of *Schach von Wuthenow* is more integrated. The spatial symbolism in this novel is linked with the other themes of the text to such an extent that unravelling them is challenging, and each description may be charged with a range of complementary meanings on different levels. This is arguably less so in *Graf Petöfy*. The various locations in the text's world (Vienna, Öslau, Arpa) appear more distinct, and while they are all linked by the themes of theatre and illusion, each operates according to its own laws, whereas in *Schach von Wuthenow* each of the places (Berlin, Tempelhof, Wuthenow) used the same basic spatial language or expression: separation or union, the internal or the external, simplicity or complexity were determining in all three zones. What seems to be happening in *Graf Petöfy*, however, is that Fontane is treading new ground, such as investing directional terms like 'left' and 'right' with specific symbolic meaning. What Fontane achieves here on a small scale, the semiotic landscape at Arpa, he will later be able to develop more fully in the mature works *Irrungen Wirrungen* and *Effi Briest*, as Klaus Haberkamm has shown. In addition, Fontane conflates subtle focalization with topographical symbolism, which is later developed in *Unwiederbringlich* and *Der Stechlin*. It may thus be the case that *Schach von Wuthenow*'s textual weft is closer, but *Graf Petöfy* explores new potential structures of meaning.

Notes to Chapter 3

1. HA II, I, 332.
2. Benno von Wiese, 'Theodor Fontane: Schach von Wuthenow', in Benno von Wiese, *Die deutsche Novelle von Goethe bis Kafka*, (Düsseldorf: Bagel, 1962), II, 236–60 (p. 239).
3. See AA, III, 623–29, 627–28.
4. Jolles, *Theodor Fontane*, p. 55.
5. Jean-Jacques Rousseau, *Émile ou de l'éducation*, ed. by François and Pierre Richard (Paris: Garnier, 1964), p. 271.
6. Christian Grawe's treatment of the novel in the *Fontane-Handbuch* is an exception, to some extent, inasmuch as he addresses the question of Schach's character, but even here the emphasis shifts to decadence and false honour, issues which inevitably bring out Schach's quality as a representative, rather than an individual. See Christian Grawe, 'Schach von Wuthenow: Erzählung aus der Zeit des Gensdarmes', in Grawe and Nürnberger, *Fontane-Handbuch*, pp. 533–46, 543–45.
7. Wiese, p. 240.
8. Wandrey, pp. 156–57.
9. Kenneth Hayens, *Theodor Fontane: A Critical Study* (London: Collins, 1920), p. 32.
10. Page numbers in brackets throughout this chapter refer to HA I, 1.
11. 'Doppelte Optik' is von Wiese's phrase. See von Wiese, p. 240.
12. For a specific discussion of this aspect of Victoire, see Walter Müller-Seidel, 'Der Fall des Schach von Wuthenow', in *Theodor Fontanes Werk in unserer Zeit: Symposion zur 30-Jahr-Feier des Fontane-Archivs der Brandenburgischen Landes- und Hochschulbibliothek Potsdam*, ed. by the Theodor-Fontane-Archiv der Brandenburgischen Landes- und Hochschulbibliothek (Potsdam: Brandenburgische Landes- und Hochschulbibliothek, 1966), pp. 53–66.
13. Fontane's emphasis.
14. Manfred Dutschke, 'Geselliger Spießrutenlauf: Die Tragödie des lächerlichen Junkers Schach von Wuthenow', in *Text + Kritik; Sonderband Theodor Fontane*, ed. by Heinz Ludwig Arnold (Munich: edition text + kritik, 1989), pp. 103–16 (p. 105).
15. According to Demetz (p. 116), this is the principal function of location in a social novel.
16. Sylvain Guarda, *'Schach von Wuthenow', 'Die Poggenpuhls' und 'Der Stechlin': Fontanes innere Reisen in die Unterwelt* (Würzburg: Königshausen & Neumann, 1997), p. 30.
17. Aust, *Verklärung*, p. 148.
18. *Erläuterungen und Dokumente: Theodor Fontane 'Irrungen, Wirrungen'*, ed. by Frederick Betz (Stuttgart: Reclam, 1979), p. 8.
19. *Handwörterbuch des deutschen Aberglaubens*, ed. by Hanns Bächtold-Stäubli and others, 10 vols (Berlin and Leipzig: de Gruyter, 1927–42).
20. Guarda, throughout, but especially pp. 28, 33, 34, and 41. In brief, Guarda's argument rests on the fact that the Carayons were crusaders, and that Victoire, but not her bourgeois mother, inherits this tradition. Her illness and consequent scars are the marks of the sins of her forefathers (p. 34). Perhaps more convincingly, Guarda draws attention to the fact that Victoire and Schach are brought together by the ghost story about the Templar knight (p. 28). He sees the reference to the Templars as a prefiguration of Schach's affair with Victoire, or more specifically his guilt, and describes the novel as 'eine parodierte Kreuz- und Bußfahrt zugleich' (p. 28).
21. Demetz, p. 116.
22. For example, Schloß Stechlin, in *Der Stechlin*.
23. Bachtold-Stäubli, entry 'Walnuß'.

24. HA I, 3, 659.
25. My emphasis.
26. Pierre Bange, *Ironie et dialogisme dans les romans de Theodor Fontane* (Grenoble: Presses Universitaires de Grenoble, 1974), p. 112.
27. Müller-Seidel, *Soziale Romankunst*, p. 145.
28. Among others, Bange, *Ironie et dialogisme*, p. 112.
29. This opposition between Berlin and the Mark is an important antecedent of a similar, if more complex, structure in *Der Stechlin*. See Chapter 5 of this book.
30. William Wordsworth, *The Prelude, or Growth of a Poet's Mind*, ed. by Ernest de Selincourt, rev. by Helen Darbyshire (Oxford: Clarendon Press, 1959), p. 26.
31. 15 June 1883, HA IV, 3, 256.
32. See *L'Adultera*, HA I, 2, 11.
33. Müller-Seidel, *Soziale Romankunst*, p. 414.
34. John Osborne argues that Phemi is the only character really to understand the theatre. See John Osborne, 'Graf Petöfy: Eine Separatvorstellung', *FBl*, 80 (2005), 70–90 (p. 74).
35. Osborne, 'Graf Petöfy', throughout, but especially pp. 73–74.
36. Compare also Lene in Hankels Ablage in *Irrungen Wirrungen*, HA I, 2, 386, and problematically, Holk in *Unwiederbringlich*, see Chapter 4 of this book.
37. See Delf von Wolzogen, *Geschichte und Geschichten*.
38. See Fischer.
39. Müller, p. 30.
40. The Graf's reference to this figure as a comparison for Franziska may be thus considered ironic (855): it is the Graf who ends his life when his play has come to its close.
41. Müller-Seidel, *Soziale Romankunst*, p. 414.
42. Osborne, 'Graf Petöfy', p. 71.
43. Voß, pp. 123–27.

CHAPTER 4

~

Spatial Representation and 'die künstlerische Betrachtung des Lebens': *Irrungen Wirrungen* and *Unwiederbringlich*

> Schöne Welt, wo bist du? Kehre wieder,
> O holdes Blütenalter der Natur!
>
> SCHILLER, 'Die Götter Griechenlands'[1]

Introduction

This chapter, like the previous one, will discuss a pair of novels, one of which is set in Berlin, the other abroad. *Irrungen Wirrungen* (1888) and *Unwiederbringlich* (1892) have both been acknowledged as highpoints of Fontane's oeuvre, deal with related subject matter, and share common themes.[2] In *Irrungen Wirrungen* the young Baron Botho von Rienäcker loves his mistress Lene, a lower-class girl who lives outside the city, but is bound to marry his rich, pretty cousin Käthe out of duty to his family and the need to rescue the family finances. The middle-aged Helmuth Holk in *Unwiederbringlich* is unhappy in his marriage to his religious and self-righteous wife Christine, so has an affair in Denmark with a young Swede, Ebba von Rosenberg. After breaking ties with his wife, Holk finds his offer of marriage turned down by Ebba, and is left alone. A reconciliation between the spouses is attempted, but results in Christine's suicide. In many respects the titles of the two novels seem almost interchangeable, and describe shared traits and issues explored by the two works.[3] The second half of *Irrungen Wirrungen* is devoted almost entirely to Botho's reflections on his love which is irretrievably lost; while in *Unwiederbringlich* Holk's moral error is precipitated quite literally by his straying away from home and lack of firm guiding principles.

In both texts, Fontane weaves together spatial structure and insightful accounts of individual spatial experience in an intricate way. In these mature works, Fontane returns to themes treated in the *Wanderungen*; he explores the way individuals look at the world, how real-world objects become carriers of meaning, and in so doing, shows himself to be deeply reflective on the nature of art and poetry. The discussion of *Irrungen Wirrungen* will begin by examining the relationship between imagination and reality in the presentation of the market garden, where the author creates a real world in the text with which an imagining subject interacts. This idea will be developed further in the second section which will focus on the relationship in the text between the presentation of the affair, or Botho's thoughts about it, and the numerous objects associated with it. This will lead into the final section which will examine the abandonment of concrete symbols and the importance of the affair as an alternative fiction. The discussion will conclude by suggesting that the structural relationship between the zoological and the market garden may be interpreted as a comment on the place of art vis-à-vis other cultural products such as popular literature or entertainment.

The analysis of *Unwiederbringlich* will focus more closely on the novel's structure. It will first be argued that the text appears to construct a spatial framework based around two opposite and separate realms, which in turn corresponds to a series of antithetical characters and sets of values. It will be shown however, that on closer examination the text works in a more subtle way, and that a movement corresponding to Holk's mental confusion is a more appropriate model. In the second section the analysis will turn to issues related to those studied in *Irrungen Wirrungen*. It will be demonstrated that while an imaginative interaction with space has a positive impact on the lives of Botho and Lene, for Christine and Holk the effect is negative, as they interpret and respond to the signs and stimuli of reality in a problematic way. This flawed response will be considered within the wider context of education, and the spatial structure as discussed earlier. The study draws the conclusion that the text promotes an anthropocentric understanding of the formal aspects of literature, and thus of art more generally. The novel suggests that art, and the knowledge of it, is a form of education about human beings, and thus essential to life.

Irrungen Wirrungen

'Gib nur wieder her', lachte Lene. 'Du hast kein Auge für diese Dinge, weil du keine Liebe dafür hast, und Auge und Liebe gehören immer zusammen.'

Irrungen Wirrungen[4]

Introduction

As its title suggests, *Irrungen Wirrungen* is a novel of great complexity and apparent contradictions. '[Es] enthält Idyll und Ironie, Illusion und Nüchternheit, Schein und Sein, den Vorbehalt des Anführungszeichens und das rechte Wort'.[5] It combines a late Realism where attention is given to poorer social classes, with attributes more easily reconcilable with the notion of German Poetic Realism, such as the portrayal of an idyllic garden, and a dominantly aristocratic perspective. Since the 1980s, the novel has proved fertile ground for analyses which have emphasized the imagination in Fontane's Realism.[6] This is arguably because the imagination and the poetic appear to be the objects of representation, most clearly in the 'liebevoll gezeichnete Lokalität',[7] the market garden, seen as a *locus* of poetry,[8] but also because Fontane's techniques of representation incorporate subjectivity to a high degree.

Scholars are generally in agreement that Botho's subjective perspective plays a major role in the narrative, particularly in the presentation of the market garden.[9] What remains less clear is whether or not Botho's focalizations are to be read negatively, and form part of the novel's wider social criticism, as Peter James Bowman suggests for example.[10] While most scholars do see Botho as a romantic and Lene as more down to earth,[11] some emphasize a positive development in Botho: Walter Hettche argues that, by the end of the narrative, Botho is 'bewußter geworden',[12] and Rosemary Finlay and Helga Dunn suggest that Botho comes to cultivate an appreciation for the fine arts.[13] Furthermore, Frances Subiotto argues that, while Fontane concentrates on the presentation of Botho's remembrances in the second half of the novel, in the first half both Botho and Lene engage in a shared act of 'remembering the future'.[14] The emphasis on a shared experience is also suggested by Reuter's interpretation of *Irrungen Wirrungen* as a 'Liebesgeschichte', in contrast to the 'Leidenschaftsgeschichte', *Cécile*,[15] and those analyses which highlight the common fate of Botho and Lene further seem to favour a more balanced view.[16]

This discussion of the significance of space in *Irrungen Wirrungen* draws on several strands of previous research: firstly, the overall acceptance that the most important issue with respect to the represented world in the text is the question of subjectivity and imagination; secondly, that the modulating process of imagining and remembering is shared, though primarily shown through

Botho's eyes; thirdly, the concept of development, particularly with regard to awareness and artistic understanding.

As well as a 'Liebesgeschichte' and a story about the possibility of happiness,[17] *Irrungen Wirrungen* is an exploration of how space becomes meaningful through subjectivity: how objects and places acquire symbolic importance to the individual either through direct association with or by analogy to private experience in memory or imagination. Indeed, as Christian Grawe argues, through *Irrungen Wirrungen*, Fontane reflects on his own artistic processes:

> Für Fontane selbst wird *Irrungen, Wirrungen* zum Vehikel klärender literarischer Reflexion, etwa über die fruchtbare Spannung von Intuition und Rationalität beim Schaffensprozeß [...] über die illusionären Elemente auch des lebenstreusten Realismus [...] über die dichte Symbolik seines Erzählens [...] und auch über das sozial Provokante des Themas.[18]

The novel is part of Fontane's profound reflections on the relationship between meanings in artistic texts, the external world, and the individual. Seen within the context of Fontane's *Verklärungsästhetik*, the experience of space as presented in the text is positively valued. Botho and Lene do not idealize; circumstance, their personalities, and their shared life allow them to perceive beauty and meaning which is existent in the world around them.

A representation of looking

The novel's opening paragraph details a complex representation of looking. This is achieved firstly through the observing figure on the street, but also through the spatial representation of the situation (319).[19] The novel begins at a crossroads. Two roads meet, the Kurfürstendamm and the Kurfürstenstraße, one an aristocratic, the other a middle-class place,[20] and at this intersection of two similarly named locations, the narrator describes two gardens in close proximity: a market garden situated 'schräg gegenüber dem "Zoologischen"'.[21] Although it is only mentioned, the zoological garden connotes spectacle and display: a zoo is a social place where living animals, mysterious because of their exotic provenance, are exhibited to a viewing public.

On a certain level, the market garden is not wholly different from its neighbour. Like the two streets, both locations have an implied affinity in their names: they are both gardens. Furthermore, one of the few things that can be deduced from the rather limited view of the 'Gärtnerei' is that there are animals there, albeit rather unexotic ones: pigeons and a dog. What is more, the market garden is in fact being looked at in this first paragraph; it is defined in the initial scene as a place which is observed.

Despite these similarities however, the two spaces are distinct. While a zoo displays openly, the market garden is rather more complex. The house, though small and a hundred yards from the street, can be quite easily seen by a passer-by, as the narrator relates. This small, visible house is not 'die Hauptsache' however, which remains concealed (319). Covering, hiding is more the essence of this place. The description includes a number of details which hint at unseen life and something hidden: the wooden tower, the pigeons and the sound of the dog barking. Tantalizingly, the house door is open, allowing a glimpse of the courtyard. The only appropriate response for the potential viewing subject, or casual observer to use Hardy's phrase, is to hypothesize, 'vermuten', about what might be beyond his or her gaze (319).

The garden is presented here as something not simply viewed by a passer-by. The situation is also more than the simple creation of narrative suspense. Here the consideration of something which is all the more enchanting for being veiled is depicted. This is a spatial representation of the kind of beauty represented by Victoire in *Schach von Wuthenow*, and given poetic expression by Paul Verlaine (1844-96) in his 'Art Poétique': 'C'est des beaux yeux derrière des voiles'.[22] That which is partially uncovered not only entices in a crude way, evoking desire, but also promotes the greater interaction of the imagination. The imagining subject goes beyond the small detail which is exposed and creates in the mind potential solutions to the mystery.

Thus, in the initial paragraph, the emphasis is clearly on viewing, on looking at the world, on the relationship between observer and observed, subject and object. Two differing, if related, methods of presentation and reception are contrasted: the exotic spectacle of the clearly visible animals in cages, albeit only suggested by the name zoo, and what the narrator concentrates his energies on, the contemplation of a hidden mystery. In the first, the role of the imagination is necessarily minimal: the point of a zoo is to see the animals as they really are. In the second, the imagination must play a greater role, projecting ideas about what might lie beneath the surface, and at the same time, through this imaginative process transporting ordinary, everyday, one might go as far as to say *real*, objects (houses and pigeons) beyond the mundane and into the captivating.

The scene which immediately follows is also a representation of viewing, as the lovers Botho and Lene are reported as being seen. The wife of the garden's owner, Frau Dörr, is visiting Lene's stepmother, Frau Nimptsch, and the two of them discuss the young couple (320). According to Frau Nimptsch, Lene 'bildet sich was ein'; she is getting carried away by her thoughts, and for Frau Dörr, this is a dangerous business: 'immer wenn das Einbilden anfängt, fängt auch das schlimme an' (321).

The lovers are seen through the window by Frau Dörr as Botho takes his leave of Lene at the garden gate (322). This action, indicative of Botho's gentlemanly behaviour, confirms a more ideal relationship than the supposed reality expected and described by Frau Dörr. She looks on and comments: 'Ja, das glaub' ich; so was laß ich mir gefallen... Nei, so war meiner nich' (322). The text creates here two spheres, one attributed to the lovers, the other to the old ladies indoors. Outside, on the same street as in the first paragraph, there is shown the rather idealized (beyond expectation) gesture of the respectful lover, that is to say, precisely that kind of relationship that could be imagined or dreamt. Inside, however, the view was articulated that only a matter of fact attitude is healthy. The two spaces are separated by the wall, and yet the wall itself is permeable, it has a window, and Frau Dörr contradicts her own advice by looking out and being pleased by what she sees. The text thus shows reality and imagination to be divided yet linked; they exist side by side here and complement each other. The affair between Botho and Lene attains its special difference, its own significance, partly by being seen and described by a woman who contrasts what she observes with her own memories and expectations. The lovers enter the narrative at this stage by being seen by Frau Dörr. The text thus presents two spaces in mutual dependence, suggesting that neither a world-view dominated by the imagination nor one ruled by a prosaic, crude outlook is sufficient for a meaningful human existence. Both the ideal and the real coexist.

The coexistence of reality and a more poetic alternative is exemplified by the market garden, of which the narrator offers two contrasting views. In the evening, it is 'märchenhaft' (320). Seen in the daylight, however, the garden is a different place altogether, which is most apparent with regard to the 'castle':

> Ja, dies 'Schloß'! In der Dämmerung hätt' es bei seinen großen Umrissen wirklich für etwas Derartiges gelten können, heut' aber, in unerbittlich heller Beleuchtung daliegend, sah man nur zu deutlich, daß der ganze bis hoch hinauf mit gotischen Fenstern bemalte Bau nichts als ein jämmerlicher Holzkasten war. (322)

The narrator's earlier indication that the garden possesses a 'halb märchenhafte Stille' in the evening (320) is significant as it makes clear that the romanticism of the situation is not restricted to Botho's experience, while at the same time acknowledging the influence of circumstance in creating a specific spatial experience, which may not be valid at all times. The fairy-tale experience is partial, but it is not false, and it is not Botho's alone.

As Lene and Botho walk in the garden, the narrator's description indicates just how the favourable circumstances promote a shared, idyllic spatial experience:

> Drinnen im Garten war alles Duft und Frische; denn den ganzen Hauptweg hinauf, zwischen den Johannis- und Stachelbeersträuchern, standen Levkoien und Reseda, deren feiner Duft sich mit dem kräftigeren der Thymianbeete mischte. Nichts regte sich in den Bäumen, und nur Leuchtkäfer schwirrten durch die Luft. (342)

Here again, the narrator links the objects which are perceived with the earlier, daytime description of the garden. Earlier, a scene had been depicted in which the neighbour's dog had caused a stir by chasing Dörr's favourite cockerel, which took refuge in the tree and raised the alarm (325-26). The narrator's indication, that nothing stirred in the trees, confirms the fact that the same space is being inhabited, but that the stillness of evening makes it quite a different place. That only fireflies (rather than cockerels) are flying creates a mood of romantic tranquillity in what was earlier a place of comic disorder — and, as earlier in *Vor dem Sturm*, the narrator makes the reader aware of both potentials.

As the couple stop and look at the moonlight, the narrator once again underlines the link with reality and the influence of a specific moment: 'Wirklich, der Mond stand drüben über dem Elefantenhause, das in dem niederströmenden Silberlichte noch phantastischer aussah als gewöhnlich' (343-44). This is a description of a reality transfigured by circumstance, perspective, light, in other words, *Verklärung*. The image has the effect of promoting a happy, contemplative state in the two onlookers, who awake eventually as if from a dream (344). Recalling the first paragraph again, a similar case of space seen in specific circumstances evokes here an imaginative response, and an engaged response from the viewer. In the first paragraph, it was the projection of *Vermutungen*, here it is a happy quietness, a dream-like state. It is clear that this is a shared experience. It is Lene who suggests that she and Botho look at the crescent moon. Their physical proximity further suggests a common view. The description of what they see in the garden is given from the largely unbiased perspective of the narrator, emphasized by the word 'wirklich'; it is not the product of negative idealization.

It is thus not the case that the market garden is in a fixed sense a realm of the imagination. It is a real world within the text where certain conditions (not least the fact that Botho and Lene are in love) promote a specific experience of space which is different from the ordinary way in which space is experienced by its inhabitants. Thus the real and the poetic have the same source, they abide in the same objects, in the same world; but it is subjectivity which renders that world meaningful, the specificity of lived experience which stimulates the interaction of the mind.

The discussion of symbolism

Irrungen Wirrungen tells the story of a lived experience, the affair, and how that experience, as memory and an imagined alternative, as a quantity of private knowledge, then informs the way the world is perceived. Because of the affair, the characters look at the world in a different way: it has a new meaning for them. This is shown primarily through Botho's eyes. In a small, limited way, the reader is shown in this novel the construction of one level of subjectivity: the text leads the reader through the process by which the affair gives the world a new layer of significance. The novel is a thus literary representation and exploration of the process by which 'lived space' comes into being. Within the text, the represented world and its objects are no longer an environment with a preordered meaning created by the artist; the characters are now seen as active participants in the construction of significance, topographical and otherwise, relevant to themselves. In this literary representation, Fontane may be said to anticipate twentieth-century theorizations of subjective spatial experience.[23]

For Botho, Berlin becomes a series of locations which act as symbolic stimuli. Relating how the affair with Lene began to Gideon Franke in his Berlin home, Botho comments: 'Ich begleitete sie nach Haus und war entzückt von allem was ich da sah [...] [ich frug], ob ich wiederkommen dürfe, welche Frage sie mit einem einfachen "Ja" beantwortete' (442). Botho's initial attraction to Lene is transferred to her surroundings: the continuation of their relationship is expressed in terms of Botho being able to visit the garden again. The situation of their love has become a metaphor for their love itself. Botho's emotional experience informs his entire spatial experience. This then works in reverse. The remembrance of space is part of the path to reliving emotion: 'Rienäcker, als das alles wieder vor seine Seele trat, stand in sichtlicher Erregung auf und öffnete beide Flügel der Balkontür, als ob es ihm in seinem Zimmer zu heiß werde' (442–43). Having just mentioned the garden, the memory of that place stimulates an emotional response. As Bachelard would later observe, spatialization preserves our memories; it is through space that we access these past feelings.[24]

A similar episode occurs earlier in Chapter 16, after Botho and Käthe return from their honeymoon. Their house on the Landgrafenstraße overlooks the zoological garden and a church tower is a landmark on the horizon. Käthe asks Botho what the village to which the church belongs is called, and in his response, '"ich glaube, Wilmersdorf"', his emotional attachment to the place is clear to Käthe:

> 'Nun gut, Wilmersdorf. Aber was heißt das: "ich glaube". Du wirst doch wissen, wie die Dörfer hier herum heißen. Sieh nur Mama, macht er nicht ein Gesicht, als ob er uns ein Staatsgeheimnis verraten hätte? Nichts komischer als diese Männer.' (413)

Not only places, but also objects related to the affair acquire symbolic significance. The presentation of Botho and Lene's emotional attachment, particularly during the period when Botho decides to end the affair and after it has ended, concentrates greatly on artefacts and their meaning to the two of them. Paramount among these are the love letters Botho received from Lene and the posy she gave him in Hankels Ablage. These are physical evidence of Botho's enduring love for her even after his marriage, an outward sign of inner faithfulness. These 'Träger der Erinnerung' 'beleben und auffrischen, was tot ist und totbleiben muß' (454–55), and it is Botho's awareness of their power as relics which causes him to destroy them in an attempt to forget.

The way in which the characters respond to places and objects not directly linked to the affair is also influenced by their love and predicament. Like the narrator in the *Wanderungen*, the reader frequently finds Botho and Lene interpreting signs by analogy, or ascribing a symbolic, almost metaphysical meaning to the world, often in a melancholically playful way. When Botho's canary bothers him for affection, he concludes: 'Alle Lieblinge sind gleich, [...] und fordern Gehorsam und Unterwerfung' (347). Similarly, his inability to swat a fly, which he gives the generalized name 'Unglücksbote', prompts a musing on the inevitability of failure: ' "Wieder fort. Es hilft nichts. Also Resignation. Ergebung ist überhaupt das beste. Die Türken sind die klügsten Leute." ' (400). For Botho this tendency to interpret the world has life-determining repercussions: a turning point in the novel is his ride to the Hinckeldey monument and the sight of the factory workers at lunch (404–06). Botho interprets what he sees, and what his horse led him to by chance, as a sign with relevance to his own life: the senselessness of individual resistance and the need for social order. If the tendency towards generalization is frequently an aspect of Botho's humour, then here it has serious consequences.

Lene too reacts to the world and interprets symbols, and whereas this is often the product of humour with Botho, with Lene it is often linked to her tendency towards superstition. When Lene sees a maid washing dishes at Hankels Ablage, she says to Botho: 'Weißt du, Botho, das ist kein Zufall, daß sie da kniet; sie kniet da für mich, und ich fühle deutlich, daß es mir ein Zeichen ist und eine Fügung' (389). In these episodes, Botho and Lene are shown reading the world with reference to their lives. We see Lene and Botho interpreting the world according to a shared experience of which we as readers have been allowed a glimpse — through the affair the world acquires a new level of meaning for them. An earlier example at Hankels Ablage suggests that rather than this personal, biased view of the world being inaccurate, unobjective, and therefore less real, it can in fact be a way of seeing what normally lies hidden: as in the novel's opening paragraph, the imagination sees a more interesting reality. In a meadow, Botho complains that he would like to pick a posy for Lene, but there are no flowers (377). Lene, by contrast, says: 'Du hast kein Auge für diese Dinge, weil du keine Liebe dafür hast, und Auge und Liebe gehören immer zusammen [...] Es sind aber Blumen und noch dazu sehr gute' (378).

Botho and Lene's behaviour, and in particular her comments cited above, need to be understood in a wider context. Fontane frequently alludes to the inevitable subjectivity of perception and judgement. In *Vor dem Sturm* Berndt von Vitzewitz remarks that 'ein jeder sieht was er zu sehen wünscht; darin sind wir alle gleich',[25] and in *Schach von Wuthenow*, Victoire makes the following statement on literary evaluation: 'das Allerpersönlichste bestimmt immer unser Urteil'.[26]

There is significant textual evidence to suggest that, rather than assessing personal bias negatively, Fontane saw positive value in subjective interpretation.[27] In the second foreword to the *Wanderungen*, for example, Fontane writes that to appreciate the Mark, both 'den guten Willen' and historical knowledge are necessary.[28] The meaning and ultimately beauty of a place or object is not to be sought by considering the object in a distanced, unprejudiced way, but rather by emphasizing its specific relationship with the individual, in this case the fact that it is his local area, and the knowledge he brings to it, in this case historical knowledge. As Lene promotes looking with love, Fontane suggests that the viewer predisposed to find value in an object will be best placed to do so, which will often involve drawing on information extraneous to the object itself.

Fontane also consistently stresses the need to look positively at the world as an artistic imperative. Writing to his wife in 1883, he comments: 'die Schönheit ist *da*, man muß nur ein Auge dafür haben',[29] and in 'Unsere lyrische und epische Poesie seit 1848' (1853) he argues: 'Das Leben ist doch immer nur der Marmorsteinbruch, der den Stoff zu unendlichen Bildwerken in sich trägt; sie schlummern drin, aber nur *dem Auge des Geweihten sichtbar* und nur durch seine Hand zu erwecken'.[30]

The concept of the observing artist is a topos of Realism, but in Fontane's case, it is a highly personal one.[31] The 'künstlerische Betrachtung des Lebens' he advocates and represents in his literary writings is also biographically determined.[32] As a correspondent, war reporter, and *Wandrer*, Fontane himself was an imagining observer, and, as has been shown in the *Wanderungen* discussion, the interpreting narrator is a significant and recurrent feature of this *magnum opus*. Fontane's letters record his tendency to interpret and generalize about what he sees in a similar way to the examples in *Irrungen Wirrungen*.[33] In this context, the imagining figure at the beginning of the text acquires a far more profound meaning: it is a poetical and biographical symbol, an image of a way of life, and of artistic behaviour which draws out the full truth of the world. As will be suggested later, this aspect of Fontane's writing anticipates early twentieth-century critics, such as Georg Lukács or I. A. Richards.[34] In *Irrungen Wirrungen*, the imagining figure is a prelude to the way in which the reader sees Botho and Lene engaging with their surroundings, an announcement of their symbolic understanding or their lives.

From artefact to art

The love affair between Botho and Lene is, as has been argued, often presented via concrete artefacts in the text, and is linked to specific locations, such as the market garden and the Wilmersdorf church tower, which Botho can see from his balcony (445–46). There is, however, a period of transition, during which these concrete signs are abandoned, and the physical, worldly reality of the affair's existence disappears.

Both Botho and Lene are confronted after the affair abruptly with the reality of life, and in each case journeys involving symbols of change mark the decisive shift in their lives. Lene sees Botho and Käthe out together; trying to get home, she faints and dies, as Christian Grawe argues, a symbolic death (415–16).[35] After these events, Lene decides that she and Frau Nimptsch have to move away from the market garden (420–21). Botho is told by Gideon Franke of the latter's intention to marry Lene, that she now lives on the Luisenufer and that Frau Nimptsch is dead (440–45). Botho's experience is especially interesting from a spatial perspective, because of the symbolic role that the representation of Berlin plays. Hearing the news about Frau Nimptsch, Botho remembers his promise to the old woman that he would place a wreath of everlasting flowers on her grave, and sets off to the new Jakobikirchhof (446).

Botho's journey is significant because it indicates a shift in his mental and spiritual state: Franke's revelations have broken the physical reality of the market garden world for Botho. It no longer exists as it once did, and perhaps more importantly for this investigation, the physical markers which previously reminded Botho of his days in the garden no longer point to a real-life alternative, but rather to a memory. As the narrator comments: 'Nun war alles anders, und er hatte sich in einer ganz neuen Welt zurechtzufinden' (445).

Berlin is that world in a concrete sense, in that it is where Botho lives, but Fontane also manipulates the historical reality of Berlin's rapid expansion to express the evolution in Botho's emotional world. Botho's revelation about his changed circumstances is revealed in the journey to the cemetery, during which a vision of the modern, expanding Berlin of the *Gründerzeit* is focalized through him: Botho sees his new reality. In particular, the *Schaubuden* present a view of the varied and international life of modern Berlin. The world is perceived in motion and presented in succession (449), indicating the increasing 'Tempo des Daseins'.[36] As Reuter comments:

> Bothos einsame Wagenfahrt [...] bleibt der deutschen Literatur als erster gelungener Versuch einer epischen Nutzung der Kontraste der modernen Großstadt. Der Modernität des Stoffes entspricht die Modernität der Erzählweise. Raffiniert macht sie die Möglichkeiten raschen Wechsels disparatester äußerer Eindrücke auf dem Wege über die Optik des Helden der Vergegenwärtigung innerer Vorgänge dienstbar.[37]

This movement creates a sense of contrast with the market garden, where the still observer contemplated the world. Here, in modern Berlin, that contemplation is no longer possible; Botho's thoughts are explicitly interrupted by the scenery outside (449). This is an early example of Fontane's portrayal of the haste of Berlin life, later explored in greater depth in *Der Stechlin*.[38] The circus and traders' stalls recall furthermore the zoo of the first scenes, through their direct, visual appeal to a spectator: Botho's final visit to Frau Nimptsch is thus a symbolic return to his past. He journeys to the city's outskirts once again, yet now, in this new topography of his present, the green spaces are graveyards, and a symbol of urbanization, modernity, and social problems rises high: the *Mietskaserne*.[39] Botho's journey to the threshold of Berlin and his decision to lay down both a modern and an old-fashioned wreath symbolize transition in his life. The song 'Denkst du daran', which he hears sung by a poor couple and a flirtatious woman, underlines the sense that the affair is confined to a time of memory, and through the distorted repetition of the past, emphasizes the impossibility of the affair's existence in the present. Botho has his coachman wait, not by the churchyard, but back in the city, the new world where he knows he now belongs.

Having made the journey, Botho also burns Lene's letters and posy (455), the latter being the physical remains of a place they enjoyed together, Hankels Ablage. The laying down and destruction of concrete symbols mean that now the world of Lene can only be experienced as a memory or as an imagined might-have-been. Losing its physicality however, the affair is sublimated. Though a real-life past experience, it now becomes unreal. In the second half of the novel, which is dominated by memory and reflection, the affair, its world, and its values are an alternative fiction which Botho can experience through the mind.[40] Patricia Howe makes the point succinctly: 'the real event becomes a picture, and the picture lives on in the mind to inform attitudes and actions'.[41] Again, Fontane anticipates the phenomenologist Bachelard, whose study of space is based on the detachment of the imagination from its remembered, real sources.[42]

Botho's consciousness crosses over into his heterocosm frequently. In Chapter 22, the narrator describes how, while thinking about Käthe, Botho's mind wanders to earlier days and places: 'Er hing dem [Gedanken, M.W.] noch eine Weile nach, dann aber wechselten die Bilder und längst Zurückliegendes trat statt Käthes wieder vor seine Seele: der Dörrsche Garten, der Gang nach Wilmersdorf, die Partie nach Hankels Ablage' (454). Often thoughts of Lene are provoked by circumstances which recall specifically his affair, such as the dance with Käthe to the music drifting over from the zoo (419), or the newspaper announcement of Lene's marriage at the end of the novel (475). These are, however, short-lived moments. The narrator stresses in Chapter 17, as Botho increasingly reflects on the superficial nature of his wife, that he often thinks of Lene, but that her image disappears just as quickly as it came (419). Whether a conscious act of remembrance or a painful surprise, memory and imagination provide only temporary disengagement from reality; Botho can only cross over into the imaginary world of his for a short interlude.

These fleeting moments of reflection are in part the result of a longing for values which Lene and her world represent, which are absent in Botho's life and in his wife in particular. When Botho thinks of Lene and their hours together in the market garden, or Hankels Ablage, or on the path to Wilmersdorf, he considers Lene's personal qualities, 'Einfachheit, Wahrheit, Unredensartlichkeit' (419), or the notions of happiness and beauty: 'Das war der letzte schöne Tag gewesen, die letzte glückliche Stunde' (454). Even taking into consideration the relative weakness of the German 'schön' compared with the rarer English 'beautiful', it is not difficult to see that Botho's imaginative experience, his forays into the world in his mind, allows him to access qualities which are commonly attributed to art: a classical simplicity, truth, sincerity, and beauty.[43] Botho thinks of his affair with Lene — something which as we have seen has been disengaged from reality — in aesthetic terms.

This is especially clear if we compare Käthe. Just before thinking of 'den letzten schönen Tag', Botho calls his wife 'hübsch': the qualitative difference is clear. And whereas Lene embodies truth and sincerity, Käthe is 'unterhaltlich', 'oberflächlich'. She constantly repeats stock phrases, above all 'zu komisch', in contrast to Lene's 'Unredensartlichkeit': Lene is original, whereas Käthe is not. When it is also considered that the places associated with Botho's friends and family are often places of entertainment (the club, the restaurant) it becomes apparent that the text is elaborating a structure of oppositions which functions by analogy as a comparison of real art on the one hand, and popular entertainment and kitsch on the other.[44] Dresden is not loved by Käthe for its works of art, but for its cakes. What does Botho call her but his doll?

The Lene/Käthe, art/entertainment structure leads back to the beginning of the text and this discussion. The novel begins by describing a garden opposite a zoological garden: both are gardens and both engage a spectator but in different ways. One, the zoo, while only mentioned, connotes accessibility and a tendency to display, superficiality, and openness. The other, the market garden, commands and rewards imaginative interest; it engages through objects which are real, but which attain a new significance through this imaginative interaction. Seen in the context of the antipodal structure outlined above, and the argument that the imaginative, subjective, and symbolic interpretation of the world is associated with the market garden and Lene, the opening paragraph may be said to create a representation of entertainment and popular literature in the zoo, and art in the market garden.

In life and then in remembrance, Botho is able to visit this garden for brief periods, breaks from his everyday existence. This of course does not stop him from living in the everyday world; it is where he belongs and there can be no prolonged retreat into the imagination. However, those fleeting moments grant him access to values beyond those he encounters in his own life, and enable him to look at the world in a new, critical way. His market garden experience allows him to see through the sham of his modern existence. This is not to make Botho a poet, nor to deny the reality of the affair; and certainly, the text is ambivalent in that Botho's sensitivity and aesthetic understanding do not make him able to change his life in a concrete way. The novel's ending, in which Botho remarks 'Gideon ist besser als Botho', makes clear that Fontane does not see imaginative art as a path to happiness in an immediate sense (475). Yet it is not necessarily negative that at this final stage of analysis the text is not clear cut: Fontane's symbolism is often deliberately nebulous, and *Irrungen Wirrungen* is not a parable. Rather, at a level beyond the literal meaning of the text, Fontane shows us that symbolic worlds where we can access truth and beauty enrich our lives.

Unwiederbringlich

> Zeit, sagt man, ist Lethe; aber auch Fernluft ist so ein Trank, und sollte sie weniger gründlich wirken, so tut sie es dafür desto rascher.
>
> THOMAS MANN, *Der Zauberberg*[45]

The antipodal structure and its problems

Fontane's novel of 1892, *Unwiederbringlich*, lends itself to analysis in terms of two opposing worlds, sets of values, and groups of characters.[46] Helmuth Holk, an affable Junker from Schleswig-Holstein, is dissatisfied with his life at home and the frequent arguments with his wife, Christine. Her religiosity and self-righteousness do not combine well with his own apparent indifference to what she considers important issues, such as the education of their children and the reconstruction of the family vault, which is in a dangerous state of disrepair. Holk is thus pleased to receive news that he is expected earlier than usual across the water in Copenhagen, where he is a gentleman-in-waiting to Princess Maria Eleonore of Denmark, although Christine, who views Copenhagen, and Denmark in general, as degenerate, is less than happy at the prospect of her dissatisfied husband spending months alone in a den of iniquity. In Copenhagen, Holk is at first attracted to his landlady's daughter, Brigitte, and then to the young Swede Ebba von Rosenberg, a lady-in-waiting with a questionable history. During a prolonged trip to Frederiksborg castle, Holk finally succumbs to Ebba's charms, but that very evening, a fire breaks out in the castle and the lovers only manage to escape via the roof. The escape from the fire appears to Holk as a sign that a new life with Ebba is preordained, but his thoughts are a clever piece of dramatic irony. The state of shock into which Ebba and the princess have fallen prevents him discussing his plans and hopes with them before he returns to Holkenäs and tells Christine. Returning to Copenhagen, Holk finds himself rejected by Ebba. After some years apart, Holk living in London, and Christine living in Gnadenfrei, the Herrnhut establishment where she was educated as a child, they are brought back together through the efforts of family members and a local priest. The church blesses their reunion, and they take up their old lives again in Holkenäs. Christine is, however, deeply unhappy; she is unable and unwilling to forget Holk's infidelity, and eventually commits suicide.

From this brief recapitulation of events, it is clear that the novel may be said to operate around two opposing poles. Firstly, there are the two contrasting characters Christine and Ebba: the one is Holk's wife of seventeen years and her name indicates her strong Christian beliefs. The other is briefly Holk's mistress, and she herself indicates that 'Ebba ist Eva' (659), the biblical Adam–Christ oppositional pair being here transferred onto this pair of females. Around these two incompatible alternatives, two antithetical realms are constructed. The two worlds, Holkenäs and Denmark, are divided by the sea; they are completely separated. Holk's world at home is one based on agriculture and farming (576), whereas Denmark is characterized rather by its island nature (587), thus creating the opposition land/water. The classical building Holk has erected as his family home in Holkenäs (567) may be contrasted with the romanticism of Frederiksborg with its towers (723) and ghosts (702), and similarly the park landscape around Holkenäs, and the veranda where the family sit together (567) appear to be the antithesis of the wilder landscape and activities in Denmark: the forests and the ice of Frederiksborg for example,[47] or the deer-herding spectacle Holk is privy to at the Eremitage (665).

A strong argument in favour of this model of analysis is Fontane's choice of location and the historical setting. The novel is set in Schleswig-Holstein shortly before the war between Denmark and Prussia and Austria, fought to decide whether Schleswig-Holstein should be integrated into the Danish kingdom, or form part of the German Federation. The historical situation, well known to the author from his work as a war correspondent, provides a pre-existing adversarial spatial and ideological structure. As regards the characters's politics, Holk's position is ambivalent. He is largely for maintaining the status-quo,[48] while the women in his life represent differing views: Christine's political sympathies lie with a unified federal Germany, whereas Ebba's Swedish heritage has been suggested as representative of the political movement towards a pan-Scandinavian federation.[49]

These two worlds may further be perceived as representing two different sets of values in the text. The gulf between *ancien-régime* court-life and provincial married life are summarized in the two *Weltanschauungen* of Ebba and Christine: one advocates a policy of 'alles leicht nehmen',[50] the other cannot help taking all matters too seriously (618). Yet this is not simply a matter of personalities. The entire experience of Denmark, especially Copenhagen, is one of distraction and entertainment, such as Vincent's restaurant (629), or the stories Holk has told to him every morning by his landlady (640–46). Similarly, Christine's sombre personality ('Christine war eigentlich nie heiter' (585)) seems to extend over the whole way of life in Holkenäs: Holk and his brother-in-law Arne have to go outside to smoke their cigars for fear of upsetting her, for example (576).

It is clear, then, that in the first analysis the text does indeed construct a spatial world which may be viewed with advantage in terms of oppositional pairs, and that this corresponds to similarly divided groups of characters and sets of values. This initial analysis has only scratched the surface; other scholars, such as Karla Müller, have developed more elaborate models based on this pattern.[51] It might appear that the text itself encourages this spatial reading: Holk engages in frequent comparisons between Denmark and Holkenäs (667), and the letters from home serve as a constant reminder of the alternative world Holk has left behind;[52] yet, this also creates a situation in which both places, sets of values, and women coexist in the text. A more detailed investigation of how the text constructs the two spatial worlds Holkenäs and Denmark will show that the view of two separate spheres is difficult to sustain.

Let us consider firstly the representation of Holkenäs (567). The new castle built by Holk (though in fact there had been plans for a new building since his grandfather's days (568)) is classical, in the style of Palladio, as the narrating observer at the beginning of the novel notes (567). Nevertheless, the inspiration for the 'Schloß am Meer' is romantic in tone; it is in part the result of Holk's incomplete knowledge of Uhland's ballad of the same name (569). The opposition between the Danish romantic north and classical allusions in Holkenäs is further undermined by the continued existence of the former seat of the Holk family. The old castle dates from the Middle Ages, and is haunted (568). There is, in addition, Arne's irony about Holk's new building, evoked at the beginning of the novel:

> Es war ein nach italienischen Mustern aufgeführter Bau, mit gerade so viel Anklängen ans Griechisch-Klassische, daß der Schwager des gräflichen Hauses, der Baron Arne auf Arnewiek, von einem nachgeborenen 'Tempel zum Pästum' sprechen durfte. Natürlich alles ironisch. (567)

Even if Fontane, with typical ambivalence, then continues: 'Aber doch mit einer gewissen Berechtigung', the reference to Holk's brother-in-law's well-intentioned humour is significant. The family humour woven into the description signals a level of acceptance of Holk's weaknesses: Holk has had the freedom to indulge his 'Baupassion', regardless of its inconsistent inspiration or anything else. Furthermore, Holk does succeed in creating a home in which his family are, for a time at least, happy. Holkenäs appears on this level, then, to represent the tolerance and acceptance of eccentricity and imperfection that are only to be found at home, among family and friends. This is implied in the initial description and gains importance as the novel progresses.

To turn to the depiction of Frederiksborg, the place where Holk and Ebba become lovers, this site epitomizes northern romanticism, and thus might be construed as logically opposed to classical Holkenäs. On closer inspection they are not as different as they seem. The castle is indeed first described as 'märchenhaft' (705), tall and with many towers. The second description, however, indicates that the castle is constructed of two towers, and from these towers extend forward two wings, which in turn are joined by a colonnade (707). This recalls obliquely the characteristic 'Säuleneinfassung' of Holkenäs (567).

This on its own would be insufficient to justify abandoning the pattern previously established, were it not for the fact that Holk himself compares the area with his own Holkenäs. Looking over the village Hilleröd near Frederiksborg, Holk considers the peace of the place and is reminded of home: 'In solcher Stille zu leben', sprach er vor sich hin, 'welch Glück!' und als er sich dann vergegenwärtigte, daß Holkenäs dieselbe Stille habe, setzte er hinzu: 'Ja, dieselbe Stille, aber nicht denselben Frieden' (732). This episode is significant for several reasons. Firstly, the reader becomes aware that the differences between Denmark and Holkenäs may not be as great as is first imagined. The reader is alerted to the fact that many of the judgements upon which the oppositional model is based come from characters not in a position to make an objective statement: Holk is having to convince himself here, he is determined that Hilleröd and Hölkenäs should be different. Similarly, Christine's condemnation of Denmark's decadence (590) is just as questionable as Holk's claims that Holkenäs is dull (667). Perhaps more importantly, the text hints here that what Holk is seeking is not only waiting for him at home, but also that his ideal (here 'peace') is at odds with what he appears to be striving for in his relationship with Ebba. The 'Glück' observed by Holk here is also much closer to his wife's concept of happiness than might be expected, given that Holk and his wife believe themselves to be so different. The idea of peace and rest announced in the Waiblinger poem 'Die Ruh ist wohl das Beste', sung in an early scene at Holkenäs (592), and the Gräfin's rather extreme and sentimental reaction to it introduces the theme of peace at an early stage, although it is primarily Christine who is identified with it (609). In the above quotation, Holk shows himself also to be desirous of a peaceful life. Holkenäs, the classical building may thus be said to symbolize a harmony which both Holk and Christine enjoyed in their early marriage and yearn for in their present lives. It might further be suggested that, because Holk eventually begins the affair in earnest in Frederiksborg, with its subtle allusions to Holkenäs, that in his heart of hearts, Holk does not want to be unfaithful, although this is not to deny the fact that thoughts of home are not enough to prevent his adultery, and indeed encourage it. Rather, spatial indicators point to thoughts and emotions lying deeper than Holk's conscious reasoning, which, as has been shown, is flawed.

Even the apparently clear and exclusive way in which the groups of characters are assigned to the two regions in the text cannot, on closer examination, be maintained. In his letter to Holk informing him that he is required in Copenhagen (604–05), Pentz also indicates that the Danish king is in Glücksburg (604), one German mile from Holkenäs (567). The king later arrives in Fredericksborg as well (738). Furthermore, the captain of the ship Holk takes to Copenhagen is the subject of some innocent romantic remarks from Asta, Holk's daughter (622). The verbal presence of the sea-captain in Holkenäs, as well as the arguably negative moral effect he has, mirrors, if to a lesser degree, the connotations surrounding Captain Hansen and his wife in Copenhagen, creating yet another link between these apparently divided and opposed worlds.

The presence of numerous locations which do not properly fit into an analysis based on two antithetical sites further complicates matters. It has already been noted that the new and the old castles at Holkenäs are to be distinguished; so too are Copenhagen, the Eremitage, and Fredericksborg in Denmark, to say nothing of the frequently named Gnadenfrei of Christine's youth, and Holk's travels to Italy, France, and finally London, where he settles in Tavistock Square. Even the broader Germany/Denmark opposition is hard to maintain, given that Ebba is Swedish, of Jewish extraction, and ultimately marries a Scot who owns a large portion of London.

Closer scrutiny thus suggests that Denmark and Holkenäs are not opposed, and this raises the question about other, non-spatial differences. The opposition between Christine and Ebba has been seen by many as essential to the plot, and on the first level of analysis it is. Yet, they both display similarities. They are, according to their own philosophies, women of principle in the sense that they stick rigorously to the ways of life they have chosen. For Christine this means living according to her religious beliefs; for Ebba, this means observing the spirit of play typical of the court. A further similarity is signalled by the narrator when Holk attempts to ask Ebba to marry him: he is exasperated at her distance, yet finds her 'überheblicher Ton' enchanting (789). This mirrors the narrator's comment early in the novel revealing that it was Christine's piety which Holk had actually found attractive when they were young (595). Holk is attracted to the women's shared sense of superiority in both cases.

The question of values and the difference between *leicht* and *schwer nehmen*, Christine's religiosity, and Danish decadence is a key area of divergence. Yet here again, the idea that these might be assigned to two zones is an oversimplification. In this instance it is the secondary characters who play an important role. The character Pentz, in many ways the personification of

Copenhagen, has a counterpart in Arne who lives near Holkenäs. Arne, like Pentz, believes that taking one's own principles too far can be dangerous (619), and it is Arne who advises Holk to allude to an affair in Copenhagen to make Christine jealous (736). The description of his and Schwarzkoppen's scheming (592–99), and the engagement of others generally in the private affairs of Holk and Christine, is not far removed from the gossiping of the Danish court. Finally, not everything appears to be morally above board even in Holkenäs: Elisabeth Petersen is, according to Asta, really called Elisabeth Kruse, and the absence of her parents remains curiously unexplained (620).

It is thus clear that on closer examination the novel does not present two entirely distinct spaces. Making this observation has led us to question and re-examine the other apparently evident oppositions in the text and now raises the question of what form the spatial structure may more appositely be said to take. The representation of space in the novel clearly functions as a means of illustrating Holk's psychology. He leaves for Denmark eagerly because of a failing marriage. It seems that marital difficulties also shape his experiences there, in that he is attracted to two (younger) women. Yet as has been shown, Holk is himself at pains firstly to create an artificial level of distinction between two places and women who share common traits and that he is also attracted to qualities (spatial and feminine) which might be said to characterize his world at home. Holk is running away from a troubled home ostensibly on a search for a new life but invariably seeks out that which is unrealizable (a life with Ebba) and which in fact resembles the home he has left behind (Hilleröd). What Holk is seeking is what he has left: Christine and Holkenäs. The question is whether Holk can return and the answer appears to be no.

Holk's psychological and emotional state thus cannot be described as oscillating between two alternatives, and the text makes this clear. Holk's thoughts are on two occasions described as moving in a circle: 'In einem Kreise drehten sich all seine Vorstellungen, und das Ziel blieb dasselbe' (766). The novel does not work on a model of binary oppositions, but rather on a series of journeys around a central point, a circular movement in pursuit of a home and origin which lies back in space and time. When, on the occasion of the above quotation, Holk is mentally disoriented, the narrator indicates that he is in need of an outsider to help him (766). This, it could be argued, is Christine, or being in Holkenäs: Holk's search for otherness is a mistaken search for an earlier time, for a sense of self which has been lost but is ultimately at home with his wife.

A key theme in the novel is education. It is a source of considerable strife between the couple: Holk thinks little of formal education, whereas Christine is strongly in favour of sending the children away to school (600). In the case of the daughter, the education will be religious and will serve to give her faith as an anchor in a storm, in other words a strong sense of moral orientation, exactly what Holk lacks, or rather lacks without Christine and Holkenäs. It is not entirely clear whether Holk's journeys can be seen as a journey of education, or self-development: while at first thinking that he would achieve freedom away from home, as he sits alone in London, he realizes that he is only free at home (792). He has learnt something, at least. This appears to make *Unwiederbringlich* into a *Bildungsroman* characteristic of the Realist model, as the journey into the world is typically completed in Realist narratives with a return home.[53] But in fact the problematical structure of the novel, the erosion of the difference between home and abroad, as well as the failed attempt at a reconciliation calls into question any 'return' to a former state, spatial, temporal, or moral. That Christine is buried in the still crumbling mausoleum further illustrates Holk's lack of real progress in understanding his wife, while Christine's explicit statement that she does not want to return to former days, 'ich wünsche sie [verschwundene Tage, M.W.] *nicht* zurück' (807), questions the desirability and possibility of any return.[54] In the final analysis, Christine and Holk are both tragically similar, not different as they believe: they are both searching for peace, and because they are not prepared to make do or accommodate the ordinary inconveniences of life, they pay a heavy price.[55]

The subject–space relationship

So far the argument has focused on the spatial structure of the novel. It has been argued that while an initial overview of the novel might support an analysis based on two opposing realms, this is hard to maintain when specific details are analysed more closely. This ambivalence reflects the mental state of Helmuth and to a lesser extent Christine: he is searching abroad for what he can best find at home, and ultimately for a past which is lost to him altogether, no matter how far he roams.

The analysis will now turn to focus less on the structural aspects of the novel, and more on the relationship between the individual, or subject, and the world, or space. Christine and Holk both attach great importance to the world around them. Christine is initially unwilling to move from the original family home because the site on which it is built is close to the church and the family mausoleum, where their child who died early is buried (568). Here it is the emotional attachment to the site itself which is important, not the building; as the narrator reports, she would have preferred to rebuild the old home rather than move to a new one. Holk too shows a deep-rooted attachment for his home. It is 'der Fleck Erde, daran er mit ganzer Seele hing' (792), and it is eventual homesickness which leads him to return to Christine, rather than love for her (792).

Despite this profound sense of belonging to a specific location, however, both Christine and Holk can be distracted by their immediate surroundings. This is most evident with respect to Holk. When he is in Denmark, his wife writes: 'Ich weiß, daß Du Dich allemal von dem einnehmen läßt, was Dich unmittelbar umgibt' (690). This statement is confirmed by Holk's general lack of concern for events at home while away, and the infrequency of his letters, but Holk's impressionability is also seen when he returns home to break the news to Christine about his plans for a life with Ebba. He enters the house decorated for Christmas, sees the piano and the park outside, and begins reminiscing, half forgetting what he came to do in the first place (775). This is, it would appear, part of Holk's character as an 'Augenblicksmensch', 'schwankend und wandelbar' (608). Christine, however, is also shown to be affected in similar ways. Christine is at first firmly against the new Holkenäs manor. Seeing the 'Schloß am Meer' in its completed state, however, especially the panoramic views from its roof, makes her forget her misgivings about moving there (571). This should be seen within her general tendency towards strong emotional reactions, most frequently observed with regard to songs and poems.

Thus, as in *Irrungen Wirrungen*, the relationship between subject and space is pivotal. Ultimately, however, the relationship that Holk and his wife have with their surroundings may be described as problematic. Both Holk and Christine turn out to be more attached to remembered and imagined places of happiness than to their real situation. Holk's desire to return to Holkenäs when he is in London is essentially a wish to undo his mistake and return spatially and temporally to a past family home, whereas memories of Gnadenfrei and the old Holkenäs dominate Christine's outlook. The building projects of both spouses should also be understood within this context: they focus their energies on plans and ideas, rather than realities.

Like Botho and Lene, Holk and Christine are shown to read or interpret space. As Holk is the character who goes beyond the confines of home, it is through his eyes (in a similar way to Botho) that the world is seen for most of the novel, and in two specific examples the text makes explicit that Holk interprets reality as if it were giving him a sign. When the princess's court has returned to Copenhagen from Frederiksborg, Holk goes to meet the princess with the intention of asking her blessing on his proposed union with Ebba. The sight however (not the words) of the princess and her surroundings make him change his mind, and ask simply for a leave of absence. The princess assures him verbally that Ebba will forever be in his debt, which is just what he wanted to hear. The sight, however, of the grey, elderly woman under the portrait of a man who neglected, betrayed, and divorced his wife[56] leads Holk to the conclusion that the real message of the audience is in fact: 'daß bei Lebenskühnheiten und Extravaganzen in der Regel nicht viel herauskomme [...], vor allem aber eine richtige Ehe (nicht eine gewaltsame) der einzig sichere Hafen sei' (771).

The narrator comments: 'Holk hätte die Schrift gern anders entziffert'; Holk is reading the world. The spatial experience of the audience presents Holk with a message at odds with and more powerful than the words the princess speaks. On this occasion Holk decodes the signs correctly; he reads his experience accurately, even if he chooses to ignore the message. At a key turning point in the novel, however, Holk reads reality badly.

By the time of the audience, Holk has decided that his marriage has no future, but that a new life with Ebba is assured. Holk's confidence is in part based on the fact that he sees his salvation from the fire as a sign that his affair with Ebba has a higher sanction (765). Like many of Holk's actions and desires, his interpretation of the fire is highly ironic: what he might have taken as a warning, a lucky escape, and a chance to reform, he sees as sanctification of his current behaviour. This is tellingly expressed by him in spatial terms which betray his lack of judgement: the narrator relates in reported speech Holk's thoughts about 'wie dieses Hinaustreten [aus dem Turm] ihnen doch die Rettung bedeutet hatte' (765). In fact Holk's escape onto the roof was in no way his and Ebba's rescue, it provided only momentary relief. It is only when the king's men make a hole in the roof of the main part of the castle, permitting a re-entry, rather than an exit, that Holk and Ebba are brought to safety (760). The metaphorical use here of entry and exit takes on greater significance when considered within the broader context of the home/abroad dialectic discussed above. Here again Holk believes that what he needs is outside, beyond Holkenäs, when in fact his thoughts are leading him in the wrong direction. He steps out on to the roof 'ins Freie', but is trapped by the fire. In the same way, Holk eventually realizes that the freedom he gains through his divorce and his European travels is illusory, if he is not free to return to his home (792).

Much of the narrative focuses on Holk; the narrator rarely gives insight into Christine's thought processes directly, as he does for Holk, and for this reason, examples of Christine's spatial readings are harder to find than her reactions to poetry and songs reported as seen by members of the family. Yet, when Holk leaves for Denmark, Christine and her friend Julie watch the ship as it goes into the distance. The sight of the disappearing ship causes Christine to reflect, and after a time her friend notices that she is crying (623). Christine admits that she had been thinking of a prophetic dream about a burial, and also about the potential for Holk's infidelity (623–24). The image of the disappearing ship instigates a chain of thoughts, whereby Christine is all but convinced that her marriage is doomed. It might be suggested that this fatalism then translates into her inability (like Holk's) to create an intimate tone in their letters and Holk's increasing distance. Thus while for Botho and Lene the interaction of imagination and memory with spatial experience added value to their lives, for Christine and Holk similar processes occur, but their readings often have negative effects on their later conduct.

Christine and Holk's spatial misreadings reflect their misunderstandings of people, notably of themselves and of each other. Holk believes he can be a cavalier, but Ebba shows him he is in fact cut out to be a good husband (787). Christine believes Holk to be without principles (626), yet Holk attempts to legitimize his affair with Ebba through marriage (759). Holk believes that Christine is cold and unfeeling towards him (772), yet he is unaware of her admissions of love and real tenderness to Julie Dobschütz (626). Christine and Holk embody Fontane's view of human beings as full of 'jener halb rätselhaften Widersprüche, [die] sich in jeder Menschennatur vorfinden', and, by failing to recognize and accommodate these in each other, Holk and Christine demonstrate their ignorance of human nature, and of each other.

Christine and Holk's unsuccessful readings of signs in the world, and their inability to see their own similarities, also correspond to their inappropriate responses to art. Poems and songs play a frequently pivotal role in this novel, and both Holk and Christine are shown to deal with literature in a problematic way. This is again most obvious with Holk: he is inspired to build a 'Schloß am Meer' by the Uhland poem, of which he knows only the first stanza, as his wife is quick to tell him. Holk gets carried away with a romantic idea, a foretaste of his susceptibility to the romantic allure of Denmark, and Frederiksborg in particular. For all their differences, Christine's reactions to poetry are essentially similar to her husband's: she is overly sensitive, and in the same way as Holk is led astray by romantic ideas in Denmark, so she is prompted to despair and eventual suicide by the poems 'Der Kirchhof' and 'Denkst du'.

There is no doubt that Christine is more artistically aware than her husband, but both are shown as having limited aesthetic understanding. Christine assures Holk 'ich bin nicht blind für all das Schöne, was da drüben [in Kopenhagen, M.W.] zu finden ist', but she focuses her attention on the negative aspects of Copenhagen in her damning assessment of moral life there, and ultimately refuses to accompany her husband (606).[57] Her plans for a family mausoleum are grandiose and in poor taste: she plans a *Totentanz* in imitation of the one in Lübeck, even if it has to be painted by third-rate artists (575–76).

There is, however, evidence that for Fontane, knowledge of art and beauty fosters moderation, law, and insight, those qualities Christine and Holk are lacking:

> Das Predigen von Himmel und Hölle versagt den Dienst. Man pflege (wie es unsere größten Geister geraten) den Sinn für das Schöne, statt diesen Sinn immer mehr zu verwirren, und mit dem Maß und Gesetz und dem klaren Erkennen in der Kunst wird der erste Schritt geschehen sein zur Wiederaufrichtung eines Banners, das berufen ist, die zersplitterten Geister um sich zu scharen.[58]

Indeed, the topography of this novel, with its disparate elements and apparent contradictions, can be read as an image of Christine and Holk's marriage, but also as an image of each of them, and arguably of human beings in the modern world in general. In their journeys through the novel's artistic world, Holk and Christine are shown to misunderstand, misread the signs in front of them, as they fail to comprehend each other and themselves. In this novel, Fontane shows that art is *menschlich*. It is as 'rätselvoll' and multifaceted as human beings themselves.[59] Topography appears in *Unwiederbringlich* to function as an authorial canvas, a map with designated locations of fixed meanings and clear antipodes. In fact, it is an environment which is constantly misread by those who inhabit it, characters lacking insight and adequate human understanding. Through this 'rätselvolle Modelung' *Unwiederbringlich* becomes testimony to and symbol of the need for aesthetic education.[60]

Conclusion

Essentially this study has focused on how *Irrungen Wirrungen* and *Unwiederbringlich* explore the individual experience of space and the relevance of this experience to spatial structures. The texts have been shown in the final analysis to have a high degree of reflexivity; they give the reader insights not only into complex matters of psychology and social interaction, but have important messages about art itself. *Irrungen Wirrungen*, it was found, exposes the process by which space and the objects in it achieve special and additional significance for individuals by means of the memories, emotions, and imaginative potential they attach to them. Here Fontane conveys insights into the complex matter of how and why human beings adopt and use symbols, what they are and how they come into being. The fact that Fontane shows how this occurs with everyday objects in a modern setting makes this text a reflexive discussion of Realist poetics too, something which will have greater significance in *Der Stechlin*. The fact that Botho is shown in imaginative interaction with real-life objects indicates an author who views the processes of artistic production and reading as inherently linked to ways in which concrete reality may be apprehended; yet Fontane demonstrates how Botho's memory of the affair becomes increasingly detached from the physical objects associated with it, and in so doing argues at the same time for a knowledge of the boundary between art and real life, a theme already seen in *Graf Petöfy*.

This detailed and subtle discussion of the imaginative responses to space which the text constructs was considered within the context of the initial description of the zoo and the market garden. Here it was argued that Fontane examines the scope and nature of human cultural production. Two areas are described, related but different in essential ways: the market garden, Lene, and thus with it the world of memories and associations linked to the affair are representative of art of a higher and profound nature. The qualities of Lene which Botho accesses and reflects on through his memory and imagination are the essential qualities of meaningful art. The text thus elaborates a view on the function of art in society: it is a temporary means of accessing a set of values higher than can be achieved in reality. The zoo was equated with Käthe, Botho's world, the club and restaurants and his life after Lene. This is everyday reality, and its equivalence in terms of cultural production is popular art and entertainment. Fontane does not disregard these: he draws attention to the similarities between the zoo and the garden, and to Käthe's charms. He acknowledges the existence of popular art in the same way as Botho must accept his marriage, but the imaginative realm of real literature offers to its initiate a new and deeper world of significance.

In *Unwiederbringlich* similar themes are explored and space functions in interaction with characterization and historical aspects to create a dense web of associations and impressions. This interpretation was based firstly on a critical assessment of the novel's spatial structure. It was found that this reflected Holk's psychology and rather than an antithetical structure, this study advocated seeing the novel in terms of a futile, circular search for something which has been left behind, spatially and temporally: a happy marriage. The intricate structure which creates and then undermines a series of oppositional pairs reveals the extent to which the main character Holk is seeking his home and his wife. Holk and Christine have a problematic relationship with space; unlike Botho and Lene, their interaction with and interpretation of space, as well as their knowledge of themselves and each other, their human knowledge, are flawed. The paradoxical nature of the structure functions additionally to lift the novel beyond that of a troubled marriage. The structure reflects the similarity between the spouses, and the belief in their difference which drives them apart; it is a symbol of man's divided and contradictory nature, his inability to be straightforward and constant. Artistic form and the human soul are placed on a level platform here: artistic form emanates from human paradox. This gives the artistic qualities harmony, unity, multiplicity, and paradox a timeless power. In *Irrungen Wirrungen* the text explores how it is human experience which first gives the world symbolic significance; in *Unwiederbringlich* aesthetic understanding is suggested as the Royal Road to understanding mankind.

Notes to Chapter 4

1. *Schillers Sämtliche Werke*, ed. by Eduard von der Hellen and others, 16 vols (Stuttgart and Berlin: Cotta, 1904–05), I, 159.
2. Throughout this study, *Irrungen Wirrungen* is written without a comma, consistent with the spelling in the 1962 Hanser edition to which references are given, though as Frederick Betz has shown, this variant appears in 1910 for the first time. See Betz, *Erläuterungen*, p. 5.
3. Max Rychner has alluded to this. He calls Holk's love for Ebba an 'Irrung, Wirrung'.

Max Rychner, 'Fontanes *Unwiederbringlich* (1952)', in Max Rychner, *Aufsätze zur Literatur* (Zurich: Manesse, 1966), pp. 237–50 (p. 247).
4. HA I, 2, 378.
5. Ingrid Mittenzwei, *Die Sprache als Thema: Untersuchungen zu Fontanes Gesellschaftsromanen* (Bad Homburg: Gehlen, 1970), p. 97.
6. For example, Howe, 'Reality and Imagination'.
7. Rost, p. 129.
8. For example, Karl-Gert Kribben, 'Großstadt- und Vorstadtschauplätze in Theodor Fontanes Roman *Irrungen, Wirrungen*', in *Studien zur deutschen Literatur: Festschrift für Adolf Beck zum siebzigsten Geburtstag*, ed. by Ulrich Fülleborn and Johannes Krogoll (Heidelberg: Winter, 1972), pp. 225–45 (p. 238).
9. For example, Cordula Kahrmann, *Idyll im Roman: Theodor Fontane* (Munich: Fink, 1973), p. 160.
10. Peter James Bowman, 'The Lover's Discourse in Theodor Fontane's *Irrungen, Wirrungen*', *Orbis Litterarum*, 62 (2007), 139–58 (pp. 150–52).
11. See Bance, *The Major Novels*, p. 95. Bance argues that Botho idealizes the lower class; Lene can keep dream and reality separate.
12. Walter Hettche, '*Irrungen, Wirrungen*: Sprachbewußtsein und Menschlichkeit', in Grawe, *Interpretationen*, pp. 136–56 (p. 149).
13. Rosemary Finlay and Helga Dunn, 'The Pictures in Fontane's *Irrungen, Wirrungen*', *Seminar*, 24 (1988), 221–36 (p. 226).
14. Frances M. Subiotto, 'The Use of Memory in Fontane's *Irrungen, Wirrungen*', in Thunecke and Sagarra, pp. 478–89.
15. Reuter, *Fontane*, II, 667.
16. For example, Peter Wruck, 'Viel Freud, viel Leid. Irrungen, Wirrungen. Das alte Lied', *FBl*, 39 (1985), 79–97 (p. 95).
17. Reuter, *Fontane*, II, 667.
18. Christian Grawe, '*Irrungen, Wirrungen*', in Grawe and Nürnberger, *Fontane-Handbuch*, pp. 575–84, at p. 576.
19. Page numbers in brackets throughout this chapter refer to HA I, 2.
20. Hertling, pp. 28–29.
21. Hertling (pp. 28–29) draws attention to the fact that the two gardens are similar, seeing the zoo as 'künstlicher' and the market garden as 'naturhafter'.
22. *Verlaine et les poètes symbolistes*, ed. by Alexandre Micha (Paris: Larousse, 1943), pp. 36–37, 36.
23. See Introduction.
24. Bachelard, *Poétique*, p. 28.
25. HA I, 3, 176.
26. HA I, 1, 616.
27. This should be understood within the wider context of nineteenth-century subjective criticism. See William K. Wimsatt and Cleanth Brooks, *Literary Criticism: A Short History* (New York: Vintage, 1957), pp. 491–96.
28. HA II, 1, 12.
29. Letter to Emilie 14 June 1883, Erler, *Briefe*, II, 103.
30. My emphasis, M.W. HA III, 1, 241
31. Martini, *Deutsche Literatur im bürgerlichen Realismus*, p. 97.
32. HA IV, 4, 472.
33. See letter to Martha Fontane of 9 August 1891, HA IV, 4, 143. After a moth he had allowed to shelter in his room is eaten by a bird, Fontane comments 'Es ist mit den Rettungsversuchen oft so'.
34. See Conclusion.

35. Grawe and Nürnberger, *Fontane-Handbuch*, p. 580.
36. Reinhard Rurüp, 'Vergangenheit und Gegenwart der Geschichte: 750 Jahre Berlin', in *750 Jahre Berlin. Stadt der Gegenwart. Lese- und Programmbuch zum Stadtjubiläum*, ed. by Ulrich Eckhart (Berlin: Ullstein, 1986), p. 80, cited in Charlotte Jolles, '"Berlin wird Weltstadt": Theodor Fontane und der Berliner Roman seiner Zeit', in *Berlin: Eine Großstadt im Spiegel der Literatur*, ed. by Derek Glass and others, Publications of the Institute of Germanic Studies, XLII (London: University of London; Berlin: Schmidt, 1989), pp. 50–69 (p. 53).
37. Reuter, *Fontane*, I, 495.
38. See Chapter 5 of this book.
39. Charlotte Jolles describes the *Mietskaserne* as 'ein hervorstechendes Charakteristikum der städtebaulichen Entwicklung Berlins'. See Jolles, '"Berlin wird Weltstadt"', p. 58.
40. At this stage of the text, Botho's perspective dominates. German Realism concentrates on middle- or upper-class perspectives, and as such Botho is here the appropriate agent of Realism. Yet there are reminders that Botho and Lene's fate is shared. The visit by Gideon Franke has its equivalent when Lene sees Botho and Käthe out together (415), and the newspaper announcement of Lene's marriage is another example (475).
41. Howe, 'Reality and Imagination', p. 354.
42. Bachelard, *Poétique*, p. 10.
43. It is possible to see these attributes in terms of post-Classical heritage. Martini, *Deutsche Literatur im bürgerlichen Realismus*, p. 2, argues that post-1848 poetics continues the Classical tradition. Reuter also argues that in Fontane's critical writings there is a 'bewußte Anknüpfung an die Ästhetik der Klassik' (H.-H. Reuter, 'Entwicklung und Grundzüge der Literatur Kritik Fontanes', in Preisendanz, *Theodor Fontane*, pp. 111–68 (p. 112)).
44. Jochen Schulte-Sasse gives a structured summary of the typical evaluative opposition between art and kitsch, in Jochen Schulte-Sasse, *Literarische Wertung* (Stuttgart: Metzler, 1971), pp. 9–19.
45. Thomas Mann, *Der Zauberberg* (Frankfurt a. M.: Fischer, 1960), p. 6.
46. H. C. Sasse, *Theodor Fontane: An Introduction to the Man and his Works* (Oxford: Blackwell, 1968), p. 104: 'Closely related to the antithesis of character (Ebba/Christine) is the antithesis of milieu (Kopenhagen/Holkenäs)'.
47. Compare Ebba's reaction on the journey there (703).
48. Holk favours Denmark over Prussia, but is anti-Danish in supporting Schleswig-Holstein's special status.
49. For detailed historical analysis, see Stefan Blessin, '"Unwiederbringlich" — ein historisch-politischer Roman? Bermerkungen zu Fontanes Symbolkunst', *Deutsche Vierteljahrsschrift für Literaturwissenschaft und Geistesgeschichte*, 48 (1974), 672–703.
50. Compare Ebba's rejection of Holk's proposal (788).
51. Müller, pp. 62–93.
52. Frances M. Subiotto, 'The Function of Letters in Fontanes *Unwiederbringlich*', *MLR*, 65 (1970), 306–18 (p. 318).
53. Becker, pp. 165–66.
54. The question of returning to lost states is raised later in *Der Stechlin* in an anecdote about restoring virginity: HA I, 5, 198–200.
55. Jost Schillemeit has argued persuasively that Holk and Christine are similar: Jost Schillemeit, *Theodor Fontane: Geist und Kunst seines Alterswerks* (Zurich: Atlantis, 1961), p. 72. His argument is similar to that proposed here, suggesting that what is at fault in the marriage (and what the novel criticizes) is that Holk and Christine take their own dreams too seriously (ibid., p. 77).

56. For a commentary on the references to art, see Helen Chambers, 'Afterword', in Theodor Fontane, *No Way Back*, trans. by Hugh Rorrison and Helen Chambers (London: Angel, 2010), pp. 233–48 (p. 242). The first mention of the painting refers to Christian VII, the second to Christian VIII, although the indicator 'noch' suggests Fontane meant to refer to the same portrait. Chambers bases her analysis on the painting of Christian VII.
57. Christine's comment is of course an ironic reference to beauty of a specific kind.
58. 'Kristallpalast-Bedenken' (1856), HA III, 1, 128.
59. HA III, 2, 847.
60. Ibid.

CHAPTER 5

~

The Spatial Representation of a *poetische Weltanschauung*: *Der Stechlin*

> Wer das tiefste gedacht, liebt das Lebendigste.
> Hohe Tugend versteht, wer in die Welt geblikt,
> Und es neigen die Weisen
> Oft am Ende zu Schönem sich.
>
> HÖLDERLIN, 'Socrates und Alkibiades'[1]

Introduction

Any treatment of space in Fontane's works needs to give consideration to his final novel, *Der Stechlin* (1898). Unlike many of Fontane's other novels, the title of this work is not taken from a character, such as *Effi Briest* or a state of affairs, such as *Unwiederbringlich*, but from a place, the Stechlin lake. Fontane had already written about this lake many years earlier in his *Grafschaft Ruppin*,[2] and the imaginative return to a familiar location seems to bring with it some of the traces of those early years: there are similarities in breadth and length between this *Zeitroman* and Fontane's first historical novel, while action is replaced by conversation, *Genrebilder*, and anecdotal interludes. There is furthermore a closeness between reader and author in this final, undeniably personal novel: Fontane's familiar penchant for memorable aphorism and *zugespitzter Satz* is developed to an extent unparalleled in the earlier novels, and it is above all in the figure of Dubslav, 'der Typus eines Märkischen von Adel, aber von der milderen Observanz, eines jener erquicklichen Originale' (9), that the author seems to find the mouthpiece and living example of a particular philosophy.[3]

The idea that a novel by Fontane may have a message does not seem to fit with the ironic, distanced narrator, who in novels treating difficult moral issues otherwise doggedly refuses to take sides in the various entanglements in his characters' lives. In this last novel, there are no real moral mazes, no affairs, no suicides, no acts of defiance against king and country, but there are two things that single this work out from all others in Fontane's writings: the issue of choice and example. The inevitability of events and resignation are defining characteristics of Fontane's other novels. In terms of narrative technique, the fate of the individual is signalled in advance to the reader through prefiguration, and there is no escape from its unalterable course. *Der Stechlin*, however, is primarily a novel about decisions. Of only a handful of significant events in the novel, two involve a choice made by the younger Stechlin, Woldemar: which of the two Barby daughters should he marry, and where should he live, in Berlin or Stechlin? In this novel, there is no longer a preordained order of things; the individual has free will.

Woldemar is representative of the generation who will shape the future and it is that future and its values that this novel is concerned with above all else. Indeed, the novel ends: 'es ist nicht nötig, das die Stechline weiterleben, aber es lebe *der Stechlin*' (388). This imperative reveals that there is something beyond the individual at work in this novel, an idea which Woldemar and the reader are not left alone to figure out for themselves, but are given examples to follow: Dubslav, Lorenzen, old Graf Barby. The message these exemplary figures communicate is one of tolerance, 'tiefe [...] Humanität' (9). Richard Brinkmann has called Fontane 'der strenge Zeitgenosse, der versöhnende Dichter', and it is as if Fontane's aesthetic reconciliation becomes transformed in this novel into a model way of life.[4] Fontane, the old artist, recommends through Pastor Lorenzen that rather than abandoning tradition in favour of all things new, Woldemar and the new generation continue 'mit dem Alten, soweit es irgend geht' (31). The novel's ethos is built around the capacity of individuals to tolerate and promote differing opinions through conversation, and to accept that 'paradoxes are the only truths'[5]: 'Unanfechtbare Wahrheiten gibt es überhaupt nicht, und wenn es welche gibt, so sind sie langweilig' (10). This is a *Weltanschauung* in which language, in particular the unifying, playful language of poetry, occupies a central position.

The discussion will begin by considering the representation of interior spaces in the text, and how these function to distinguish Dubslav and the Barbys from other characters. We will then address the topographical relationship between Berlin and Stechlin; it will be demonstrated that Stechlin represents a place where *Verklärung* is possible and practised, while Berlin is not. On the basis of these insights, we will consider the specific symbolic import of the Stechlin lake as a symbol of poetic language, and the parallels between Stechlin and Fontane's late poetry.

Interior Spaces

In a cultural historical study, Sabina Becker makes the general observation that in the novel of Poetic Realism, people are essentially portrayed as belonging indoors.[6] Fontane's writing reflects this general tendency, in that individual characters are frequently allotted interior spaces, and the description of these spaces serves the purposes of characterization. This has been seen in *Vor dem Sturm*, *Graf Petöfy*, and *Schach von Wuthenow*, for example. *Der Stechlin* marks a move away from these earlier procedures. This might at first seem like the logical consequence of Fontane's characterization through dialogue; however, not only is dialogue essential for characterization in the early novels too, but *Der Stechlin* does have recourse to characterization through description of personal interior space. The difference is that in *Vor dem Sturm*, for example, practically all of the characters are assigned rooms which are described in detail, and this applies to both main and secondary characters, from Berndt von Vitzewitz to Frau Hulen; in *Der Stechlin* this technique of characterization is restricted to secondary characters, such as Frau Schickedanz and Adelheid von Stechlin. The principal characters are indeed assigned personal spaces, but this occurs relatively loosely; long descriptions in which the character's personality is presented through material evidence accumulated in a particular location, or the description of a place they have created and from which their desires, qualities, and flaws may be deduced, are absent.

Considering firstly the description of Frau Schickedanz's parlour (122), this is an excursion in the narrative of almost no significance to the plot, given the relative irrelevance of this character. The inconsequential Frau Schickedanz and her story are detailed as part of a more thorough description of the Barbys' Berlin home (117–25), how they came to live there, and they serve to give the reader information about the Barby family. Frau Schickedanz is the widowed owner of the house, and upon his death bed, her husband had made her vow only to take in respectable people as tenants, not the *nouveau riche* (120). Fontane thus expands the reader's knowledge of the house and, through this spatial expansion, augments the reader's knowledge about the family from which Woldemar will choose his bride. It is a spatial variant of his technique of conversation: in talking about each other, his characters relate information about one another. Here the same operation occurs: the relationship between the house's various inhabitants is explained, which then leads to a deeper understanding of the principal characters, in this case the Barbys.

Frau Schickedanz is overwhelmingly characterized through her relationship to her belongings, and in particular those related to the cult of her dead husband. A rosewood cabinet contains anniversary gifts, neatly arranged: a silver goblet depicting St George, an album containing photographs of all the sights of Caputh, a laudatio with watercolour arabesques, among other items, described in detail by the narrator (122). These objects are linked to the past married life of Frau Schickedanz and her husband, and the Realist narrator illustrates here, through the rather simple woman's devotion to her collection, the power that such objects can have, a power and significance Fontane explores in *Irrungen Wirrungen*.

It is not only the items within the cabinet which attract the narrator's attention, however. A bust, floral covered sofas and chairs, a chandelier in a gauze dust-cover are also listed. Finally, the objects around Riekchen, or Frau Schickedanz, even extend to her person: not only does she have lily of the valley on the windowsill, but she also always wears them in her caps (122). Frau Schickedanz is a figure wholly integrated into her surroundings; her life and character are objectified, rendered concrete through the cult-like dedication to her husband and the objects he left behind (not least the house). This is alarming, as until the Barbys' arrival, something was broken on a monthly basis during cleaning, suggesting that fixation on concrete objects is dangerous, because of their transience.

The above description may be compared with advantage to other passages in Fontane's oeuvre. The cabinet is reminiscent of a similar one to be found in *Vor dem Sturm*, and the image of a humble parlour may also be found in *Schach von Wuthenow*.[7] In neither of these instances however, is the comic element so apparent as here. Not only are Frau Schickedanz's belongings, which the narrator lists, a curious mix, but also his mention of 'großblumige[n] Überzügen' seems to indicate that they are in rather poor taste (122).

If the description of Frau Schickedanz and her possessions is almost entirely dominated by humour, then a similar representation of personal interior space earlier in the text is not as straightforward: the representation of Adelheid von Stechlin's *Salon* in Kloster Wutz (81–82). The room is low ceilinged, old fashioned, and blackened with smoke. The furniture is large, recalling that from Schloß Stechlin, the pieces are described as 'lauter Erbschaftsstücke', and even the tablecloth is heavy. Within the small room, the furniture appears, according to the narrator 'beinahe grotesk'. The place is a 'stilloses Durcheinander', a phrase which might well be equally applied to Frau Schickedanz's parlour. In a similar way to Riekchen, Adelheid is linked to the room through objects attached to her person. The connotations of the heavy décor, the age, and large scale of the furnishings are carried over onto Adelheid herself, not simply because she is old too, but because of the 'Karlsbader Granatbrosche' she is wearing, humorously called the 'Sieben-Kurfürsten-Brosche' by Dubslav (82). Nevertheless, her room has a homely feel, not least because of the fire in the hearth and the open windows, recurrent elements in Fontane's descriptions of cosy and ideal living room conditions, although the fact that the heavy curtains are all but drawn adds yet another contradiction to this mixed picture (82).[8]

The image is thus part of a characterization: Adelheid is linked here to ideas of tradition, but in a limited and provincial setting. Her delusions of grandeur are entirely at odds with her reality, signalled by the large furniture in the small room. The importance she attaches to family is represented by the inherited furnishings, but in this 'Kloster', these ironically underline Adelheid's own childlessness and indicate the end of a line, rather than continuity. Thus the narrator's reference to a 'Durcheinander' (81) refers not only to an incoherence of décor, but also of person. The narrator reveals here that the proud, vitriolic, and prejudiced petty aristocrat has points of weakness and human foibles, producing a balanced picture of this character. Human paradox or contradiction is an important thematic aspect of the novel, of which this description may be considered a part.

It is not only that the description reveals inconsistency, however, it is precisely irony which permits the positive, or at least qualified, image of Adelheid to shine through. Wanting to appear grand, Adelheid puts herself 'in Staat' (82), in keeping with her sense of pride, yet her room is, as has been shown, homely and welcoming, and it is precisely the provincial and limited nature of her person and her salon which allow the reader to forgive the faults shared by them both. The text thus presents the reader here with an image which is based upon contradiction, in terms of what it represents and the manner in which this is achieved, and which gives a human face to an otherwise unsympathetic character.

The analysis of these spaces has been brief, because they operate with essentially the same narrative techniques which have been seen many times before. However, if we now consider the main characters and their spaces, it will be seen that these characterizations through the description of a room specifically identified with an individual character, and in particular the objects within it, are absent. This may most clearly be seen by considering the description of the Barbys' home.

Chapter 11 begins with a relatively detailed description of the Barbys' house, and its location on the Kronprinzenufer. The Barby family occupies the first floor, and the narrator indicates that their apartment is divided into two loggias, with a reception room in between (109), one loggia is the Graf's room, the other belongs to Melusine and Armgard. The Graf's loggia is described at this point as being painted Pompeian red, but no further details are given, while nothing is said of Melusine and Armgard's room. Nevertheless, at this stage, the representation of the house is in part focalized through an observer outside, and a limited view restricted to the exterior is therefore not unusual.

In the next stage of this introductory paragraph, the narrator discusses briefly the family's attachment to their apartment, and mentions Baronin Berchtesgaden's suggestion that the family might consider moving, followed by Melusine's reply. Melusine cites the life and movement visible outside as the particular advantage of their situation, and her detailed response (fifteen lines) provides more information about what can be seen from the balcony. The narrator then leads the reader inside Melusine and Armgard's loggia, providing an opportunity for its description:

> Ein solcher Abend war auch heute; die Balkontür stand auf, und ein kleines Feuer im Kamin warf seine Lichter auf den schweren Teppich, der durch das ganze Zimmer hin lag. Es mochte die sechste Stunde sein und die Fenster drüben an den Häusern der andern Seite standen wie in roter Glut. Ganz in der nähe des Kamins saß Armgard, die jüngere Tochter, in ihren Stuhl zurückgelehnt, die linke Fußspitze leicht auf den Ständer gestemmt. (110)

The readers are given some details: they are told that the balcony door is open, that the lights could be seen from the houses opposite, and that a small fire in the hearth illuminated the whole room. The latter indication of a light source, and the mention of the rest of the room could have, according to Hamon's narratological theory of motivation, led to a focalized description of that which is illuminated, but it does not.[9] The presence of a chair is indicated because Armgard is described as sitting in one, and the text goes on to mention a cup and ball with which Armgard is playing, and some needlework that she had recently put down. The only other object listed in the room not being used by a character is the carpet.

The room and the objects within it are passed over, their existence noted only if they are being used by the characters. Armgard and Melusine exist thus in something of a textual vacuum here. For a Realist, this is a marked avoidance of a principal method of characterization and, for Fontane, an unused opportunity for his frequent prefiguration of later events. The setting ceases to be expressive in the conventional Realist sense, and is reduced to a minimum.[10]

The old Graf's room is treated in much the same way. By contrast to the entry into Adelheid's room, which was followed by description (81), Woldemar's entrance into the Graf's room is accompanied purely by the ensuing dialogue, and again, objects are only mentioned as they are used; they are integrated into the narrative:

> Und nun trat Woldemar in das Zimmer des wieder mal von Neuralgie Geplagten ein, der ihm, auf einen dicken Stock gestützt, unter freundlichem Gruß entgegenkam.
> 'Aber Herr Graf', sagte Woldemar und nahm des alten Herrn linken Arm, um ihn bis an seinem Lehnstuhl und eine für den kranken Fuß zurechtgemachte Stellage zurückzuführen. 'Ich fürchte, daß ich störe.' (126)

It is not essential that the dialogue begin immediately. In *Frau Jenny Treibel*, for example, there are thirteen lines of description between Frau Treibel's entry into Professor Schmidt's living room, and her greeting to Corinna.[11] The avoidance of *Detailrealismus* here is perhaps all the more surprising in the case of the old Graf than his two daughters, as his age would provide ample opportunity for the description of objects associated with his past life, as is the case with Frau Schickedanz. The narrator instead, as for Dubslav (9–14), gives a brief narrative account of the Graf's life (123–25). He deliberately avoids placing the Graf in a room filled with collected evidence of his various experiences. In so doing, the author creates a positive distinction between the principal and secondary characters in terms of the relationship they have with the world around them.

The descriptions of Frau Schickedanz's and Adelheid von Stechlin's rooms, with their somewhat comic collections of objects which sum up their lives and personalities, indicate the mentality of characters who are tied to their material surroundings. Such a character is objectified, rendered concrete and, as a result, incapable of change. Frau Schickedanz's possessions are in danger of being broken through time, while Adelheid's inherited furniture and enormous brooch are ill-adapted to the modern age and her own situation, indicated by her small room in a home for elderly gentlewomen. Furthermore, Adelheid's closed curtains prevent a view of the outside world, while Schickedanz's prized objects are housed in a display cabinet, equally drawing the eye to the inside, rather than the outside.

This may be contrasted with both absent descriptions in the Barby apartment. An absence of personal objects which crystallize personality and experiences in the past signifies the Barbys' freedom and flexibility, something that Adelheid and Frau Schickedanz do not have. Furthermore, the emphasis is squarely placed on conversation: what Melusine, Armgard, and their father say is of relatively greater significance than the objects around them. They are divorced from the fossilized artefact and move instead in the free space of the word.[12] This freedom is represented not by an inwardly oriented perspective, but by looking outside. The Barbys' rooms are loggias, or open-sided rooms. The Graf sits by his window (and is disturbed by periodic carpet beatings) (125); Melusine and Armgard's balcony window stands open, and Melusine looks out at the sunrise (110). Indeed, it is the exterior and its interest which Melusine cites as the reason for the family's choice of address and their somewhat 'beschränkt' living quarters (109). While the typical figure in Poetic Realist writing, and the lesser character in this novel, is a creature of the indoors and their possessions, the main characters in *Der Stechlin* look outward and are not bound by the objects around them.

This informs the way in which the description of Schloß Stechlin might be read. It is true that the text creates a fuller, more complete image of the *Schloß*, than of the Barbys' apartment. Details of the building emerge through the relating of its history:

> Dieser Neubau war das Haus, das jetzt noch stand. Es hatte denselben

> nüchternen Charakter wie fast alles, was unter dem Soldatenkönig entstand, und war nichts weiter als ein einfaches Corps de logis, dessen zwei vorspringende, bis dicht an den Graben reichende Seitenflügel ein Hufeisen und innerhalb desselben einen kahlen Vorhof bildeten, auf dem, als einziges Schmuckstück, eine große blanke Glaskugel sich präsentierte. (8-9)

This description of a typical manor house of the Mark seems to characterize Dubslav according to his heritage, leading the reader to anticipate a personality similar to Briest or any number of figures from the *Wanderungen*. This appears to be *Milieuschilderung* as evocation of a typical representative of a social group, based on the idea that a person is, in large measure, the product of environmental factors, which Dubslav's own comments on locality and identity ostensibly confirm: 'Wer aus Friesack is, darf nicht Raoul heißen' (11). The narrator relates, moreover, that Dubslav is 'der Typus eines Märkischen von Adel' (9), supporting this view. At the same time, it is Dubslav's individuality which is important. He is an aristocrat 'von der milderen Observanz, eines jener erquicklichen Originale' (9). Significantly the typical image of a Mark manor house is given an individual edge in the initial description, and the narrator links Dubslav's own person explicitly to an object described:

> Gleichzeitig war aber doch ein Bestreben unverkennbar, gerade diese Rampe zu etwas Besonderem zu machen, und zwar mit Hilfe mehrerer Kübel mit exotischen Blattpflanzen, darunter zwei Aloes, von denen die eine noch gut im Stande, die andere dagegen krank war. Aber gerade diese kranke war der Liebling des Schloßherrn. (9)

Furthermore, unlike in the representation of the Barbys' apartment, details of the interior of Schloß Stechlin are given in extended descriptive passages, the occasion for which is provided when Rex and Czako are led upstairs to their room in Chapter 2. Walking up the stairs they pass a rococo clock 'mit einem Zeitgott darüber, der eine Hippe führte' and arrive 'auf den mit ungeheurer Raumverschwendung angelegten Oberflur' (19), where the narrator reports what they see:

> Über einer nach hinten zu gelegenen Saaltür hing eine Holztafel mit der Inschrift: 'Museum', während hüben und drüben, an den Flurwänden links und rechts, mächtige Birkenmaser- und Ebenholzschränke standen, wahre Prachtstücke, mit zwei großen Bildern dazwischen, eines eine Burg mit dicken Backsteintürmen, das andere ein überlebensgroßer Ritter, augenscheinlich aus der Frundsbergzeit, wo das bunt Landsknechtliche schon die Rüstung zu drapieren begann. (19)

The room in which Czako and Rex stay is also given relatively detailed treatment. The reader learns about its size, furnishings, and even the objects on the bookcase: a Meißen rococo figurine, and a copy of the New Testament with a chalice, cross, and palm branch on the cover (20). Other items within the house are mentioned in an *ad hoc* fashion and within the context of action, such as the *causeuse* that Dubslav and Czako sit on drinking liqueurs (41).

These details create an impression of age and continuity through the old furniture; a sense of isolation is imparted through this house, seemingly uninfluenced by changing fashion. The presence and significance of family (temporal) and local ties are brought into focus, as Rex and Czako are told that the figure in the painting on the landing is an ancestor buried in the church. Thus the representation of Schloß Stechlin appears at first to be much closer to that of Adelheid's and Frau Schickedanz's spaces than the Barbys'. Schloß Stechlin even contains a museum, a collection of old objects brought together by Dubslav, seemingly recalling the notions of ossification seen earlier.

The question must be asked, however: what do these descriptive passages tell the reader about Dubslav von Stechlin? The answer is very little. The spaces about which detailed information is given are not specific to Dubslav: the guest room might be described as a semi-public space, while the image created by the castle as a whole lacks Dubslav's personal stamp. The many references to inherited furniture, and especially to the rococo, are in fact testimony to the fact that Dubslav inhabits this space; he has not created it. Schloß Stechlin is a place where he fits and belongs, and thus an appropriate setting for Czako's doubts about Woldemar's situation: 'er paßt doch nicht recht an seine Stelle' (21). The significance of this belonging that the house represents is that it is beyond the individual: this is not personal characterization. The house represents a larger totality into which the individual fits — a family — like Hohen Vietz in *Vor dem Sturm*. The house thus mirrors the distinction Melusine makes at the end between values and their proponents in a family and its members (388).

Unlike Berndt von Vitzewitz or Adam Petöfy in their houses, or even Graf Barby in his Berlin apartment, Dubslav is not assigned an interior personal space, a room attributed specifically to him, in this house. He has no study, for example, a recurrent private room in Fontane's fictional homes. As for the museum, it contains weather vanes, symbols of change. These are really in the care of the schoolmaster Krippenstapel (275) and in fact Dubslav's half-hearted approach to his collection confirms rather than challenges the distinction between him and the other main characters. It is furthermore significant that the reader is not admitted to the room in which he dies, but rather remains outside with Agnes.

There is a counterargument to be made that in fact the text does create a space with which Dubslav is specifically identified: the veranda. It is here that the reader first encounters him, and indeed meets him on many occasions. At the beginning of the novel, the narrator paints a detailed picture of the old man, 'ein Bild des Behagens', on his veranda:

> Dubslav, sonst empfindlich gegen Zug, hatte die Türen aufmachen lassen,

> und von dem großen Portal her zog ein erquicklicher Luftstrom bis auf die mit weiß und schwarzen Fliesen gedeckte Veranda hinaus. Eine große, etwas schadhafte Markise war hier herabgelassen und gab Schutz gegen die Sonne, deren Lichter durch die schadhaften Stellen hindurchschienen und auf den Fliesen ein Schattenspiel aufführten. Gartenstühle standen umher, vor einer Bank aber, die sich an die Hauswand lehnte, waren doppelte Strohmatten gelegt. Auf eben dieser Bank, ein Bild des Behagens, saß der alte Stechlin in Joppe und breitkrempigem Filzhut und sah, während er aus seinem Meerschaum allerlei Ringe blies, auf ein Rondell, in dessen Mitte, von Blumen eingefaßt, eine kleine Fontäne plätscherte. Rechts daneben lief ein sogenannter Poetensteig, an dessen Ausgang ein ziemlich hoher, aus allerlei Gebälk zusammengezimmerter Aussichtsturm aufragte. Ganz oben eine Plattform mit Fahnenstange, daran die preußische Flagge wehte, schwarz und weiß, alles schon ziemlich verschlissen. (14)

Dubslav the person is integrated into a descriptive passage, which lists a number of concrete objects, and signals their inevitable decay. It could subsequently be argued that no additional internal space is described because it would interfere with the characterization that the veranda description has achieved. This is true: the image *par excellence* of Dubslav, of him when he is well, is of him sitting outside watching the fountain. However, it is the fact that this is an exterior space which is crucial here: Fontane places Dubslav outside, in direct contrast to his sister Adelheid sitting by the fire with the curtain drawn. He is no longer here a typical Bourgeois Realist figure, identified with a room, and even goes beyond the image of the Barbys looking outside from within a loggia.[13] He does not look, but rather *is* outside, with his back to the building (14), aware of the changing, living world of nature around him. Indeed, when Woldemar and his friends visit the old man, he is found waiting for them 'auf der Rampe' (18). This indicates in a straightforward sense Dubslav's desire for punctuality, the fact that in his lonely existence he has little else to do or think about, and, above all, his love for his son. It is also, however, a sign of Dubslav's willingness almost literally to meet someone half way, of *Entgegenkommen*. Being outside and unbound is a sign of mental freedom and preparedness to have a relationship with the outside, changing, living world.

It is clear, then, that Fontane uses spatial representation, in particular the representation of personal interior space, as a medium for elucidating two tendencies in the novel. Adelheid, Frau Schickedanz, and the descriptions of spaces attributed to them form the first type: inward-looking, dominated by the physical, and in the case of Frau Schickedanz that which is breakable. Their characters are identified with the unchanging nature of what Botho calls 'diese toten Dinge'.[14] Othegraven's observation in *Vor dem Sturm*, 'Was starr ist, ist tod', applies equally here: what Adelheid and Frau Schickedanz lack is the capacity for spiritual movement, evolution, and an awareness of a world beyond their own.[15] These qualities form the basis of the second way space is represented with the characters who inhabit it. Dubslav and the Barbys' private spaces are not described in detail. These individuals are not seen as inherently linked to stable and static objects around them. Their gaze is not directed inward, but outward. Their relationship to space indicates an intellectual freedom and flexibility. This should be considered in relation to the wider moral, social, and political thrust of the text: the need for a union of old and new, home and world.

Dubslav and the Barbys are not associated personally with objects, but with their particular *Weltanschauung*, with reflection and with words. The Realist Fontane moves the emphasis in this 'Roman der Sprache' from the material, to the immaterial, from the fixed, dead world of the object, to the living fluctuating realm of language.[16] The novel is thus in this sense what Mittenzwei describes as a 'Wortgefecht' against the 'Feststehende'.[17]

Bance's observation that prefiguration through symbolically motivated description is absent in *Der Stechlin* may be considered in this context. Indeed, Woldemar's decision to marry Armgard and their choice to retire to Stechlin are not prefigured as in earlier novels. Yet the concept of destiny is a major theme. Dubslav remarks when dying: 'Ein ewig Gesetzliches vollzieht sich, weiter nichts, und dieser Vollzug, auch wenn er 'Tod' heißt, darf uns nicht schrecken. In das Gesetzliche sich ruhig schicken, das macht den sittlichen Menschen und hebt ihn' (372). Similarly, it is with the concept of continuing values that the novel ends: 'es ist nicht nötig, daß die Stechline weiterleben, aber es lebe *der Stechlin*' (388); and, after Armgard has suggested moving back to Stechlin, the narrator indicates that Woldemar had long been fighting the inevitable (or so he feels):

> Das alte märkische Junkertum, von dem frei zu sein er sich eingebildet hatte, [begann] sich allmählich in ihm zu regen [...]. Jeder neue Tag rief ihm zu: 'Die Scholle daheim, die dir Freiheit gibt, ist doch das Beste.' (387)

The novel may well distinguish between being tied and being free by means of the spatial representation of the Barbys', Adelheid von Stechlin's, and Frau Schickedanz's spaces, but with Schloß Stechlin, Dubslav's exteriority, and the context of Woldemar's return, this concept of freedom is nuanced: individual freedom is found in balance with limitation; individual identity exists alongside group identity (the Stechlin family). In a spatial variant of the Goethean 'das Gesetz nur kann uns Freiheit geben', the Stechlin house and the assumption of an identity which is in part socially created and exists beyond the individual create in fact an arena for true individual freedom.[18]

Fontane's shift from the concrete, breakable, and fixed realm of things to the fluid, paradoxical, playful realm of words cannot thus be interpreted as a foretaste of twentieth-century linguistic scepticism,[19] but as a vote of confidence in poetic literature, in language as the only solution to the potential *Starrheit* of society and the human soul.[20] Unlike the lives and cosmos governed by prophecy and destiny in *Vor dem Sturm*, *Der Stechlin*'s world and the events in it are no longer presented as a preordained order of things. The objects which would otherwise prefigure later events and shape the destinies of characters are lacking: the individual is here left to choose.

The Topographical Structure

Now the discussion will proceed to address the question of topography in the novel: the represented locations in the textual world and their meanings as constructed through their relation to each other. From rooms and houses, our interest passes to villages, towns, and countries. In fact, *Der Stechlin* has global scope: Russia, Italy, England, China, and Java are all mentioned. Within this international context, however, only two places are of real interest to the reader and are represented in detail, Berlin and Stechlin. The two places are linked through Woldemar, who lives in Berlin but whose family home is in Stechlin; there is communication between the two by way of letter and characters from each zone visit the other. Furthermore, the novel ends significantly with a decision made by Armgard and Woldemar to leave Berlin to live in Stechlin, indicating that the relationship between rural Stechlin and urban Berlin is antithetical, rather than complementary. Moreover, this antipodal topographical structure in the text functions as an appropriate framework for the organization and expression of the various thematic oppositions, such as old and new, *Heimat* and *Welt*, solitude and society. Many of these conclusions can be reached even from a superficial reading of the text. As will be shown in this section however, the relationship between the represented world and apparently simple thematic oppositions is finely nuanced. As was shown in the discussion of *Unwiederbringlich*, Fontane is capable of constructing and simultaneously undermining an antithetical structure, creating an 'im Helldunkel sich bewegenden Schwankezustand' between clarity and obscurity.[21] More significantly, a specific study of spatial representation reveals that topography in the text is not simply a canvas onto which wider thematic concerns may be painted, space is more than 'an organizing element around which its [the text's] non-spatial features are also constructed'; rather it creates layers of meaning itself, the investigation of which contributes to a fuller understanding of the text.[22]

At the most basic level, the distinction between Stechlin and Berlin is constructed around an 'old' versus 'new' opposition. In Berlin, signs of modernity are dominant, whereas in Stechlin they are hard to find. This is not to say that there is no industry in Stechlin, nor that Berlin lacks old buildings or nature; rather, on balance, the signs of the old dominate in Stechlin, while in Berlin modernity is everywhere. A more detailed analysis reveals that the opposition between Stechlin and Berlin has less to do simply with temporal issues; it is the nature or quality of what modernity and tradition represent which is significant. The distinction here is between movement and stillness. Berlin's signs of modernity are signs of change, perceived on the move and at speed; in Stechlin, history dominates in representations which are constructed around fixed images. Fontane's letter to Georg Friedlaender of 21 December 1884 sheds light on this opposition between movement and stillness:

> Bismarck, der so oft Recht hat, hat auch Recht in seiner Abneigung gegen die Millionen-Städte. Sie schreiben selbst 'bei weniger "Carrière" hätten wir mehr Wahrheit in der Welt'. Gewiß. Und nicht blos mehr Wahrheit, auch mehr Einfachheit und Natürlichkeit, mehr Ehre, mehr Menschenliebe, ja auch mehr Wissen, Gründlichkeit Tüchtigkeit überhaupt. Und was heißt Carrière machen anders, als in Berlin leben und was heißt in Berlin leben anders, als Carrière machen. Einige wenige Personen brauchen ihrem Berufe nach die große Stadt, das ist zuzugeben, aber sie sind *doch* verloren, speziell für ihren Beruf verloren, wenn sie nicht die schwere Kunst verstehn, in der großen Stadt zu leben, und wiederum auch *nicht* zu leben. [...] Aber das alles ist Ausnahmefall. Als Regel steht es mir fest, die große Stadt macht quick, flink, gewandt, aber sie verflacht und nimmt jedem der nicht in Zurückgezogenheit in ihr lebt, jede höhere Produktionsfähigkeit. [...] Die große Stadt hat nicht Zeit zum Denken, und was noch schlimmer ist, sie hat auch nicht Zeit zum Glück. Was sie hunderttausendfältig schafft, ist nur die 'Jagd nach dem Glück', die gleichbedeudend ist mit dem Unglück. [...] Wenn ich dann zugleich an *Ihr* Haus denke, an Ihre Frau und Kinder, an gesunde Luft und Natur, so finde ich, Sie leben im Paradiese. Dies ist meine aufrichtigste Meinung.[23]

In this letter, Fontane states that life in Berlin is dominated by careerism and social advancement, and that this life robs individuals of their capacity to think, reduces the existence of core values in society ('Einfachheit', 'Natürlichkeit'), and specifically makes the production of higher things, intellectual endeavours and specifically art, impossible. Although no regressive romantic, there is no doubt Fontane has contemporary urban life in mind: he criticizes life in 'Millionen-Städte', which should be understood within the context of Berlin urbanization in the *Gründerzeit*.[24] Fontane sees the antidote to the disadvantages of this modern life in distance: intellectual distance within the city, or physical distance from it in the case of the Friedlaenders' house.[25]

Similarly in the novel, Berlin and Stechlin are distinguished by the capacity of characters to make aesthetic judgements: in the haste of Berlin this is generally not possible, whereas it is in Stechlin. The representations of Berlin and Stechlin are furthermore at variance in that they obey different poetics: the moving images are not subject to the same kind of *Verklärung* as seen in the still images. In Berlin and Stechlin, then, Fontane creates places which do represent old and new, but age itself is not the measure of value. Rather, Berlin and

Stechlin become representative of two alternative ways of living in the modern world: one involved in hectic modern life, the other distant, yet because of this intellectual distance capable of critical engagement and artistic perception. There is a dual topography at work here: within the story, Woldemar chooses between Berlin and Stechlin, a place which is physically distant. At a level beyond the story, Berlin represents the world and Stechlin the intellectually remote, observing individual.

Considering the representation of Berlin first, Chapter 13 opens with a strikingly modern description of Woldemar's journey to visit the Barbys and what he sees on the way there:

> Und so ging er denn [...] auf die Hallische Brücke zu, wartete hier die Ringbahn ab und fuhr, am Potsdamer und Brandenburger Tor vorüber, bis an jene sonderbare Reichstagsuferstelle, wo, von mächtiger Giebelwand herab, ein wohl zwanzig Fuß hohes, riesiges Kaffeemädchen mit einem ganz kleinen Häubchen auf dem Kopf freundlich auf die Welt der Vorübereilenden herniederblickt, um ihnen ein Paket Kneippschen Malzkaffee zu präsentieren. An dieser echt berlinisch-pittoresken Ecke stieg Woldemar ab, um die von hier aus nur kurze Strecke bis an das Kronprinzenufer zu Fuß zurückzulegen. (125)

What is being described here is a journey, not a fixed image: Berlin is seen by the passer-by. Indeed, the elements which are listed here by the narrator, and which thus stand for the space 'Berlin' in the reader's mind, are in fact points on a journey; most are simply names, such the Potsdam Gate, or the Brandenburg Gate, while the modern image of the Kneipp advertisement is described by the text in detail partly as a means of signalling where Woldemar is. He is at 'jene [...] Reichstagsuferstelle'. Berlin is here identified with motion, with a journey which serves as a metaphor for change and progress. The 'Ringbahn' is named as the mode of transportation, indicating a new way of making that journey and suggesting speed. Berlin itself is composed of 'Vorübereilende[n]', people who literally pass by, people on individual journeys, people in a hurry. Woldemar is seen as an individual making a journey among a mass of others, each with different destinations, and his use of public transport places him literally with other travellers.

The large malted drink advertisement is unusual in a German Realist text, because of its modernity and urban provenance. The girl is 'wohl zwanzig Fuß hoch', 'riesig', looking down from a 'mächtiger Giebelwand'. This symbol of modernity thus dominates the view, but also the description as a piece of text: older, more familiar elements (the Potsdam Gate) are simply named. There are other comparable descriptions of contemporary urban Berlin in Fontane's oeuvre, such as the sign for 'Schulzes Bonbonfabrik' in *Die Poggenpuhls*.[26] That sign of modernity is part of a humorous presentation; here by contrast the presence of the 'Kaffeemädchen' renders the spot 'sonderbar' and 'echt berlinisch-pittoresk'. What could otherwise be seen as the intrusion of a modern, oversized symbol of industrial society and mass production is given positive value by the narrator. This occurs partly as a result of its inclusion in a passage alongside more conventional and, to a traditional Poetic Realist aesthetic, acceptable elements (Potsdam Gate), but also partly through the narrator's positive aesthetic judgment, 'picturesque'.

An analysis of this brief passage thus illustrates that the new dominates in terms of what is being represented. This is evident firstly through the coffee advertisement which dominates both the skyline and the text itself, and secondly through the fact that a journey by modern transport is represented. This accords with the manner of presentation: not only is a journey the represented object, but also that journey becomes a vehicle for the representation of Berlin, in that only those places Woldemar passes are mentioned by the narrator.[27]

Similar tendencies may be observed at greater length in the narration of Woldemar's, the Barbys', and the Berchtesgadens' outing 'Nach dem Eierhäuschen' (109). The party meet at the Jannowitzbrücke to take the boat journey up the Spree (137). Once the boat has set off it increases speed and runs parallel to the 'Stadtbahnbögen' or arched railway bridge (139–40). The narrator describes the effect of this on what is perceived by the gathered spectators on the boat: 'Jeder Bogen schuf den Rahmen für ein dahinter gelegenes Bild, das natürlich die Form einer Lunette hatte' (140). Once again, movement and change are the themes of this description: signs of urbanization and modern transport are represented via a series of changing pictures perceived on a journey, the metaphor of change. Through each 'Lunette' an urban landscape can be glimpsed:

> Mauerwerk jeglicher Art, Schuppen, Zäune zogen in buntem Wechsel vorüber, aber in Front aller dieser der Alltäglichkeit und der Arbeit dienenden Dinge zeigte sich immer wieder ein Stück Gartenland, darin ein paar verspätete Malven oder Sonnenblumen blühten. (140)

However, while these images are indeed dominated by evidence of work, industry, and building, this is interspersed with small areas of garden and elements of nature: sunflowers and mallow.

On one level, this description of railways and work buildings with intermittent greenery is an accurate representation of the urban suburbs, and particularly of growing Berlin. Within the context of those images analysed earlier, however, what is significant about this description is the mixture of industrialization and nature, of new and old, a mixture in which the signs of industry dominate. What the text presents is not an entirely bleak cityscape; Fontane does not create a 'Coketown' here.[28] Nevertheless, work and 'Alltäglichkeit' set the tone, gardens are mere pieces of greenery, the fruit and flowers they provide are few in number and late survivors; they are anomalies.

The gardens, sunflowers, and mallow represent on the one hand 'the old', in a Romantic sense, as evidence of nature and a more harmonious relationship with it, and in a more concrete sense, as remnants of once pre-industrial rural landscapes and lives now dramatically altered, a theme explored by contemporaneous texts, such as Wilhelm Raabe's *Akten des Vogelsangs* (1895). Fontane draws on these discourses. At the same time, however, these references to the old, to 'verspätete' natural beauty in the face of ('in Front') industrialization, and perhaps above all these symbols of beauty found among it are reflexive representations of Fontane's art as a Realist writing late in 1898: he defines art by its beauty in an age of Naturalism, and seeks to find that beauty in a world in which it is becoming increasingly rare. Fontane thus creates in these images a reflection on his own writing. The question of how poetry is possible in the modern age continues to be relevant for the Realist Fontane in 1898, and has arguably gained in significance.

As the boat travels further into the countryside, the railway recedes and poplar-lined avenues and meadows become visible. The gardens evolve into meadows bringing a physical increase in the amount of countryside. Yet still there is evidence of industry, of man, and the narrator explicitly states that it dominates the landscape here:

> Und wo das Ufer kaiartig abfiel, lagen mit Sand beladene Kähne, große Zillen, aus deren Innerem eine baggerartige Vorrichtung die Kies- und Sandmassen in die dicht am Ufer hin etablierten Kalkgruben schüttete. Es waren dies die Berliner Mörtelwerke, die hier die Herrschaft behaupteten und das Uferbild bestimmten. (140)

Again, it could argued that what is being described here are nothing more than the less than picturesque areas that the party must travel through in order to get to the desired destination. It is, however, significant that so far, although the images have been dominated by prosaic, everyday things, they have not necessarily been valued negatively. They are not explicitly associated with bourgeois characters, as in the description of the factories in *Frau Jenny Treibel*,[29] nor are they transposed into an idealized image, such as Botho's view of the factory in *Irrungen Wirrungen*.[30] This may suggest that in itself modernity and change are not perceived negatively; indeed Charlotte Jolles sees the journey up the Spree as a poetic rendering of the 'Triumph der Technik sowie die neue Industrielandschaft Berlins'.[31]

However, the lack of evaluative comment is also a result of the rapidity with which the images are moving past the focalizing characters: 'Unsre Reisenden sprachen wenig, weil unter dem raschen Wechsel der Bilder eine Frage die andre zurückdrängte' (140). It is the pace of change, and thus life in general in Berlin, which allows no time for reflection and comment. If this is the case for the characters on the boat, the internal focalizers, then it is perhaps equally true for the narrator, the external focalizer. Are these images less selective, less *verklärt*, because the haste of modern life makes this impossible?

This argument may be strengthened by focusing on the beginning of the journey. The *Landpartie* narrative begins when the characters meet and take their seats on the boat to look at the scenery (137). In the initial view of Berlin, a light fog creates a 'verschleiertes Stadtbild'. In response to the veiled image, Melusine comments:

> 'Da heißt es nun immer [...] Berlin sei so kirchenarm; aber wir werden bald Köln und Mainz aus dem Felde geschlagen haben. Ich sehe die Nikolaikirche, die Petrikirche, die Waisenkirche, die Schloßkuppel, und das Dach da, mit einer Art von chinesischer Deckelmütze, das ist, glaub' ich, der Ratshausturm.' (138)

Seen at a particular moment, Berlin can rival the beautiful cities on the Rhine. This is significant, because, in this discussion of a *verklärtes* image, Melusine's comments reveal firstly that modern Berlin is not incompatible with universal or conventional standards of beauty (Cologne and Mainz), nor is a representation of Berlin incompatible with the Poetic Realist aesthetic of *Verklärung*. At this point of the journey, however, the boat is still. The text thus differentiates between an image seen at speed and one seen at a standstill: in the latter there is both *Verklärung* and aesthetic judgement on the part of the characters. Fontane links the external conditions of life represented in his text to both potential levels of focalization, internal and external. What is valid for the characters in the story is valid for the narrator and the novel as a whole.

The link between modern life (in Berlin), aesthetic judgement, and even creation may further be observed when the party finally arrives at their destination. By this time they are further out in the country, 'in halber Einsamkeit' as Melusine remarks (141), yet even out here, a sign of industry, the chimney stacks of Spindler's factory can be seen on the horizon, in the twilight (143).[32] This is not perceived as any kind of intrusion onto the landscape, indeed it is not Spindler's factory that the narrator and Woldemar name, but rather 'Spindlersfeld'. The chimneys thus emerge from a field, not a factory: industry and landscape are here integrated in a name current among the population of a modern city. This mixture and integration where in a traditional Realist text a distinction and process of selection would have been expected, namely between industry and the country, mirrors the Baronin's comments that class boundaries are increasingly broken down through conveniences and developments in modern society:

> Es ist mein' ich nicht passend, auf einem Pferdebahnperron zu stehen, zwischen einem Schaffner und einer Kniepenfrau, und es ist noch weniger passend, in einem Fünfzigpfennigbasar allerhand Einkäufe zu machen und an der sich dabei aufdrängenden Frage: 'Wodurch ermöglichen sich diese

> Preise?' still vorbeizugehen. Unser Freund in Spindlersfelde da drüben degradiert uns vielleicht auch durch das, was er so hilfreich für uns tut. (143)

What the aristocracy is losing through progress in the modern age is difference and distinctiveness, and with it their function in society. Here the paternalistic role of the aristocracy is undermined by their willingness to buy consumer goods at prices which they suspect to be disadvantaging the producer. A way of life, a right to moral authority, and a landscape scene are brought together here, as the text raises the common social and aesthetic question of what belongs together, of what is 'passend'. With Spindlersfeld, Fontane goes against traditional Realist approaches and creates an image which reflects a modern society where boundaries are increasingly blurred.

It is thus clear that the textual representations of Berlin consist of descriptions which present evidence of modernity, urbanization, and industry, as well as those elements more traditionally associated with a Poetic Realist aesthetic: gardens, countryside and respectable, historic areas of the city (the Potsdam Gate). Contrary to traditional Realist poetics and Fontane's own practice, these are shown together in an undifferentiated way, and modernity dominates, both in terms of what is seen and also in the method of presentation in these views of a new, changing world. It is above all movement which is the metaphor for this change. This movement inhibits aesthetic judgement and silences criticism, however. The question of aesthetic judgement is linked to the binding of old and new in the descriptions, but also in society: Fontane creates through the *Landpartie* a discourse on the relationship between poetics and life.

The representation of Stechlin, the lake, village, and manor house, is from the outset the antithesis of the Berlin world. The first paragraph begins by locating the Stechlin lake:

> Im Norden der Grafschaft Ruppin, hart an der mecklenburgischen Grenze, zieht sich von dem Städtchen Gransee bis nach Rheinsberg hin (und noch darüber hinaus) eine mehrere Meilen lange Seenkette durch eine menschenarme, nur hie und da mit ein paar alten Dörfern, sonst aber ausschließlich mit Förstereien, Glas- und Teeröfen besetzte Waldung. Einer der Seen, die diese Seenkette bilden heißt 'der *Stechlin*'. (7)

In this first descriptive passage the narrator gives an overview of the area in which the Stechlin lake, and by extension Stechlin itself, is formed. Various points of reference are named — this description serves the purpose of orientation. Specifically, the lake is described as belonging to a chain whose beginning and progression can be charted. Details about the area as a whole are given: it is a sparsely populated, wooded place with a few old villages, glass and tar works. The text creates an image of a place of isolation, at a distance from civilization and mankind, yet this lonely place represents integration and a stability which comes from knowing the surroundings. Rather than a series of partial snapshots, as in Berlin, a landscape seen in motion, Stechlin is presented as a totality.

In fact, stopping and looking at the world from a fixed point of view is what characterizes the interaction of viewer and environment in Stechlin, and thus plays an important role in how Stechlin is represented. This occurs in the narrator's description of the village and the manor house. Having located the lake, the narrator situates the village with reference to the lake. He lists the village's various component buildings, including its layout, the church and the roads; these eventually lead to the manor house (8). The terrain is mapped out as an organic whole, as if from a bird's eye perspective. This way of looking at Stechlin is not restricted to the narrator, however. The 'Poetensteig', a tower from which Stechlin can be surveyed from a single spot, seems to exemplify this form of perception, but there are other examples too. Dubslav's favourite place is a bench by the lake where he stops on his regular walk, the idea of constancy or custom giving this 'fixed' view an additional metaphorical edge. When the reader follows Dubslav on his walk, it is from this specific point that the area is described, not the journey leading up to it:

> Unmittelbar am Südufer, da wo die Wand steil abfiel, befand sich eine von Buchenzweigen überdachte Steinbank. Das war sein Lieblingsplatz. Die Sonne stand schon unterm Horizont, und nur das Abendrot glühte noch durch die Bäume. Da saß er nun und überdachte sein Leben, Altes und Neues. (225)

Another example occurs near the beginning of the novel, when Woldemar, Rex, and Czako are on their way to Stechlin. Coming to the end of an avenue of chestnut trees, Rex and Czako are so struck by the image of Schloß Stechlin, that the narrator reports that they stop and admire the view:

> Unter diesem sich noch eine Weile fortsetzenden Gespräche waren sie bis an einen Punkt gekommen, von dem aus man das am Ende der Avenue sich aufbauende Bild in aller Klarheit überblicken konnte. Dabei war das Bild nicht bloß klar, sondern auch so frappierend, daß Rex und Czako unwilkürlich anhielten.
> 'Allerwetter, Stechlin, das ist ja reizend', wandte sich Czako zu dem am andern Flügel reitenden Woldemar. (17)

In these last two examples, it is of particular interest to this discussion to note that it is actually what is being seen which causes the viewer to pause and stay still. With Dubslav, it is the beauty of the bench's location which implicitly is the reason why he tarries there; in the case of Rex and Czako, the text is explicit. These views are for the most part aesthetically pleasing, and as with the view of Berlin when the boat was still, the stillness of the character and the image provides an opportunity for reflection, both on life, and on the beauty of what is seen. Czako gives an instant assessment of the view in front of him. Dubslav's engagement with the surrounding countryside on his bench is not the hurried reception of new stimuli on a moving vessel; he consistently seeks out a beautiful spot and there contemplates his life. Stechlin is a place of *verweilen*. On his bench by the lake, Dubslav draws figures in the sand, linking this stillness not only to contemplation, but potentially to creative activity, to writing, to signs (226).

Instead of the constant indicators of activity, movement, and industry which dominate in Berlin, in Stechlin man's impact is minimal: 'kein Kahn zieht seine Furchen' (7). This is a world still dominated by nature. In Berlin, the coffee advert filled the skyline, and looked down on those below, and the Spindler's factory chimney was a landmark in the surrounding countryside. Here the primary element in terms of size, and that which gives everything its name, is natural: the lake. That is not to deny that there is some industry. When Woldemar visits his father with his two friends Czako and Rex, Dubslav, unable to show them the lake's crowing cockerel, points out instead the glass blowers' colony, albeit with no great affection:

> 'Das ist die Kolonie Globsow. Da wohnen die Glasbläser. Und dahinter liegt die Glashütte. Sie ist noch unter dem Alten Fritzen entstanden und heißt die "grüne Glashütte."'
>
> 'Die grüne? Das klingt ja beinahe wie aus 'nem Märchen.'
>
> 'Ist aber eher das Gegenteil davon. Sie heißt nämlich so, weil man da grünes Glas macht, allergewöhnlichstes Flaschenglas. An Rubinglas mit Goldrand dürfen Sie hier nicht denken. Das ist nichts für unsre Gegend.'
> (57)

Dubslav's lack of warmth for the industrial aspect of his estate is clear here and although the place is mentioned, the reader is presented with no representation of it. Nevertheless, Dubslav includes it in his tour, and it can be seen by the characters in the tower, thus implying that it does form a part of the Stechlin whole. The situation is thus similar to that of Berlin, in that the reader is aware that both industrial and natural elements make up this landscape, and the life of the area. The difference lies in the 'Mischungsverhältnis'.[33] What matters is what dominates, and how the world is seen and represented. Here, though the existence of Globsow is not denied, it enters the narrative only in a refracted form, it is not represented directly, and in the above example, Dubslav raises the issue of what is 'passend': 'das ist nichts für unsere Gegend'. Thus it can be argued that Stechlin is not only a place of natural beauty, but that at a more abstract level it exists as a poetological antithesis to Berlin. It represents a state where *Verklärung* is possible and practised.

The movement and evidence of modern, rapid transport in the representation of Berlin signify change and the hurried state of modern life. In Stechlin, however, journeys, such as Dubslav's walk and Rex and Czako's horse ride, are interrupted during focalized views of the landscape. This accords with the presentation of Stechlin as an historic place which represents continuity and gradual evolution. The description of Schloß Stechlin begins with an introduction which details the history of the spot on which the castle stands, revealing at once a long history, a stability, and yet the potential for change:

> Etliche hundert Jahre zurück stand hier ein wirkliches Schloß, ein Backsteinbau mit dicken Rundtürmen, aus welcher Zeit her auch noch der Graben stammt, der die von ihm durchschnittene, sich in den See hinein erstreckende Landzunge zu einer kleinen Insel machte. Das ging so bis in die Tage der Reformation. Während der Schwedenzeit aber wurde das alte Schloß niedergelegt, und man schien es seinem gänzlichen Verfall überlassen, auch nichts an seine Stelle setzen zu wollen, bis kurz nach dem Regierungsantritt Friedrich Wilhelms I. die ganze Trümmermasse beiseitegeschafft und ein Neubau beliebt wurde. Dieser Neubau war das Haus, das jetzt noch stand. (8)

The story of Schloß Stechlin reveals that a different building stood there once, of different character and which went through a period of decay, being eventually replaced by a new building. This sets an historical precedent for potential change in the present. Nevertheless, not all elements of the old building vanished: the very ground the current building stands on, the small island, is a product of that time. Moreover, building the new house was less replacement than renewal: the house Stechlin survived as a concept, even if its outward appearance changed. The kind of change Stechlin represents thus involves preservation too. The long history of the site shows stability and evolution at the same time, the delicate balance between the old and the new which Fontane had already explored in his 'Erstling' and which forms the main theme of this final novel.

Associated with history and age is the sense of familiarity that this location evokes. Fontane creates a landscape immediately recognizable to his readers. If Dubslav is 'der Typus eines Märkischen von Adel' (8), then the same might be said for the village and his house, which recall those from the *Wanderungen* and *Vor dem Sturm*. The yellow painted, plain house is in Wolfgang Rost's words 'eine Musterkarte märkischer Schloßreminiszenzen',[34] while the village has the same key elements that the village in *Vor dem Sturm* has, and indeed any small country village might be expected to have: a medieval church, presbytery, schoolroom, public house and 'Eck- und Kramladen' (8).[35] The recognizability of Stechlin is demonstrated when Rex and Czako see it for the first time: Czako identifies castle, church, and schoolmaster's house from a distance (17). It is furthermore noteworthy that in the description of the village, the narrator simply names the various buildings, whereas in the first novel these were given detailed descriptions.[36] By avoiding this practice here, Fontane creates a sense of familiarity, of *Vertrautheit*. Phillippe Hamon has shown that a narrator only describes what is new, of interest to the viewing eye.[37] Here these objects are indeed new to the reader, but by simply naming them, by alluding to them as known, Fontane creates the illusion of a place already present in the collective imagination of his readership. He creates a literary home in Stechlin.

There is a temporal stillness in Stechlin, as well as a lack of motion. Yet it is possible to identify a final aspect of Stechlin's stillness which gives it a specific quality, its quietness: 'Kein Kahn zieht seine Furchen, kein Vogel singt, und nur selten, daß ein Habicht drüber hinfliegt und seinen Schatten auf die Spiegelfläche wirft. Alles still hier' (7). This complete silence recalls the *Wanderungen* chapter 'Radensleben':

> Aber was unser Interesse weckt, das ist ein andres, ist die poetische, beinah absolute Stille, die ihren Zauberkreis um dies Stück Erde zieht. Das Ruppiner Land ist überhaupt eins von den stillen in unsrer Provinz [...] aber die stillste Stelle dieses stillen Landes ist doch das *Ostufer* des schönen Sees, der den Mittelpunkt unserer Graftschaft bildet und von ihr den Namen trägt, *Durchreisende gibt es hier nicht* [...]. Noch einmal also, keine 'Passanten'. Es legt hier nur an, wer landen will.[38]

Speaking more directly to the reader here than in the novel, Fontane identifies lonely silence with poetry and magic. This recalls Czako's words to Woldemar upon seeing Schloß Stechlin for the first time: 'ist das wohl Ihr Zauberschloß?' (17). Fontane creates in his representation of Stechlin a silence and absence of 'Passanten' which had in the *Wanderungen* been associated with a magical and poetic experience of Radensleben, an estate filled with *'italische[r]* Kunst', foreign art in the middle of the Mark Brandenburg.[39] The local legend about Stechlin lake provides a similar link to the outside world:

> 'Wenn's aber draußen was Großes gibt, wie vor hundert Jahren in Lissabon, dann brodelt's hier nicht bloß und sprudelt und strudelt, dann steigt statt des Wasserstrahls ein roter Hahn auf und kräht laut in die Lande hinein.' (7)

The narrator does not explicitly link the Stechlin lake with art, poetry, with actively awakening the imagination as he does in 'Radensleben'; the language is itself poetic. The novel's long first sentence, with enumerated adverbial phrases, recreates the stillness and remoteness of the Stechlin lake, while in the context of these meandering, slow sentences the short phrase lacking a finite verb, 'alles still hier', acquires an enigmatic pregnancy. Moreover, the paragraph ends in a local legend, that is in oral literature, recreated by the narrator and full of alliterated 'b', 's', and 'l' sounds. The description of this still lake thus leads the narrator into a type of literature, in the form of a legend or saga relating to the lake's past. Stechlin is a place of poetry.

The representations of Berlin and Stechlin thus reveal two worlds, one dominated by the new, and one by the old. This opposition is based in part on what is found in the two places: in Berlin, evidence of modernity dominates, in Stechlin nature is the dominant feature, while the history of the manor house is also stressed. Considering this aspect of the opposition leads, however, to the realization that Stechlin and Berlin are not absolute opposites: both contain industry and nature. The antithesis between Berlin and Stechlin is, however, also present in the way the two places are represented. In Berlin moving images dominate, representing change and haste in life, while Stechlin is depicted via still images and in a way which emphasizes its place within a wider totality, indicating stability.

In contrast to Fontane's previous works, the representation of Berlin in *Der Stechlin* often deviates from Poetic Realist aesthetics, which are based on the perception and representation of beauty in reality through *Verklärung* — an evaluative, critical process. The Berlin/Stechlin antipode thus represents perhaps a choice between alternative poetics, between the old and the new, to be interpreted as a critical engagement with unrefining Naturalism. However, this reflexive structure is not primarily related to the opposition of two aesthetic codes of practice. It is a discussion about how human beings see their world, how environmental factors shape their capacity for an aesthetic appreciation of it, and thus the role of and potential for perceiving beauty in the modern world. The dialectic movement/stillness is shown to affect the relationship between viewer and viewed, between human beings and their world. In Berlin, moving images create a disassociation; in Stechlin fixed views promote interaction and reflection. This is a more elaborate variant of models seen previously in *Schach von Wuthenow* and *Irrungen Wirrungen*. The stillness of Stechlin is both consistent with more traditional Realist poetics, but it is also a requirement for the perception of beauty in the world and for the selective reproduction of reality, *Verklärung*. This view seems confirmed by the quotation from *Faust* which functions as the title to the last book in the novel: 'Verweile doch' (354).[40]

This does not of course mean that beauty can only be found in the country. There is an important, *verklärtes* image of Berlin in the fog, which proves otherwise, and in general the distinctions drawn between Stechlin and Berlin are not absolute. Berlin and Stechlin are, however, Woldemar's two alternatives, and as such are the novel's specific expression of the text's more general aesthetic ideas. Through this opposition, the text differentiates two ways of looking at the world, two ways of living. In choosing to live in Stechlin, Woldemar and Armgard take the step towards the critical and evaluative distance it represents. The topographical model at the level of the story allows the moment of stepping back to be expressed, and value to be attached to that decision.

At the same time, however, Berlin and Stechlin function as a single unit: they are a representation of the type of critical reflection advocated by the text. Berlin, the 'Weltstadt' is not simply 'das Neue' that can be ignored or kept at bay. It is quite literally the modern world in which all human beings live, and which is always experienced as new, and changing. What Fontane does in *Der*

Stechlin is create a topography which allows him to use physical remoteness as a metaphor for critical distance. If within Stechlin and Berlin two relationships between viewer and viewed are presented, on a larger scale, Stechlin is the implicit viewer, Berlin the implicit viewed. Woldemar's retirement to Stechlin entails quite literally his stepping outside the Berlin world; he gives up his career and becomes *außer Dienst* (387). However, it is as an outsider that he finds his own sense of identity: he returns home. The distance of Stechlin is a means of securing the individual's distinctiveness at a spiritual and intellectual level.

This reading of *Der Stechlin*'s topography complements the first part of this discussion, where it was argued that the protagonists are free from their surroundings and from the material world in a way which the secondary characters are not. Rather than focusing their attention on the interior of a house on or the *Requisiten*, on that which is superficial, their gaze was fixed on the world outside their own homes.[41] They are examples of the distanced life advocated through the text's topography and of the paradoxical way in which removal from the world leads ultimately to engagement with it. Looking beyond their own lives and contemplating the space outside, their images in the novel are those of thinkers: through their exterior interest they gain insight into the inner human soul.

The idea of freedom, if only mental, spiritual freedom, is important because this novel is about choices and decision-making. Although in many respects a novel without action, the two most significant events in the novel are Woldemar's two decisions, choosing his bride and choosing his home. Thus, despite any overtones of resignation in the novel about the inevitable encroachment of 'das Neue', this work essentially paints a picture of free individuals faced with choices which will shape their lives and the lives of those around them. The life choices of the individual are political and social choices, in which in spite of everything, he is, and must remain, a free agent. In electing to live in Stechlin, Woldemar chooses a world dominated by the old, rather than the new; he turns his back on modern, commercial Wilhelminian society in favour of a humble 'Kate' built in the days before Prussia's greatness. Woldemar's choice is not, however, *fin-de-siècle* love of the moribund. His youth and the money of his young wife promise to breathe life into Stechlin. Despite Melusine's assurance 'es ist nicht nötig, daß die Stechline weiterleben, aber es lebe *der Stechlin*' (388), it is important that someone live on to carry the values signified by 'der Stechlin', lake, novel, and man, into the future. Melusine's remark in the letter to Lorenzen suggests that it is the lake which signifies these values, and it is the lake which will be the focus of the final section of this discussion.

The Stechlin Lake

In the previous section, the spatial representation of Stechlin was examined, with a view to elucidating its function within an antipodal structure, in which alternatives of place specific to the novel's world and characters reflect alternative universal values. In that part of the discussion, 'Stechlin' referred to the place, the location comprising village, manor house, and lake. It is, however, this latter element of Stechlin which is perhaps the most significant for the novel as a whole. The lake is a symbol which has invited varied and contradictory interpretations in scholarship.[42] Fontane was aware of the lake's symbolic pregnancy: it is the 'gedankliche[r] Kern des Ganzen',[43] the theme around which the whole novel revolves.[44] Such is the range of potential meaning attributable to the lake that incorporating it into the previous part of this discussion would have made the argument unwieldy, and so it is assessed here, as a development of the interpretation proposed so far.

The most straightforward interpretation of the lake is as a 'Symbol für ein revolutionäre Veränderung'.[45] As the narrator relates, the lake is in touch with the wider world, and when truly great events occur, 'dann steigt [...] ein roter Hahn auf und kräht laut in die Lande hinein' (7). This ascendant, raucous red cockerel has been seen as a symbol of the world-wide proletarian revolution.[46] No doubt Fontane would have been aware that the symbol could have been interpreted in this way, and there are other references to 'red' in the text which are clearly associated with the recurrent theme of social democracy, such as Dubslav's refusal to have a red strip sewn onto his Prussian flag (15), or the young doctor's red tie (332). Nevertheless, the idea that the lake is a seismograph for a coming revolution seems to be at odds with the overwhelming weight of textual evidence which identifies Stechlin, the lake included, with the old into which the new must be incorporated only when absolutely necessary. It is the social democratic Stechlin pastor, Lorenzen, who crystallizes this thought in his advice to Woldemar: 'Lieber mit dem Alten, soweit es irgend geht, und mit dem Neuen nur, soweit es muß' (31), and it is Lorenzen with whom Melusine makes her pact: 'es ist nicht nötig, das die Stechline weiterleben, aber es lebe *der Stechlin*' (388). Clearly this is a reference to an unarticulated set of values, for which the lake is a symbol, and which Lorenzen shares. It is thus difficult to see the lake as revolutionary, given that Lorenzen is anti-revolutionary, and that Melusine actively makes the lake a symbol of continuity. A revolutionary lake also contradicts our topographical analysis, which identifies Stechlin as a whole with stillness. It might be possible to consider the lake and the red cockerel independently, but this too seems unsatisfactory. The saga of the red cockerel is integral to the depiction of the lake in the first paragraph, and given that the cockerel appears instead of a more common 'Wasserstrahl', the lake and cockerel can be said to behave in similar ways.

The argument that the lake is a revolutionary symbol also disregards the relationship between Dubslav and his lake. The lake constitutes a significant part of Dubslav's sense of identity. Not only do they share the same name, but Dubslav is proud of his lake; owning it gives him a feeling of distinction, even compared with Bismarck. There are more profound links between Dubslav and his lake, however, and Melusine's imperative almost certainly refers to Dubslav's values and way of life, his *Gesinnung*. Dubslav is a humanitarian conservative by nature. The fact that after an election defeat he advocates political ideas which Lorenzen declares to be left-wing does not make Dubslav a revolutionary, but rather serves to indicate that within old, non-revolutionary approaches, there are means of tackling modern problems such as poverty caused by industrialization. Dubslav is flexible, willing to adapt, and concerned about fellow human beings. The text establishes a number of similarities between this character and the lake in the first chapter, when Dubslav is characterized by the narrator:

> Er hatte noch ganz das eigentümlich sympathisch berührende Selbstgefühl all derer, die 'schon vor den Hohenzollern da waren', aber er hegte dieses Selbstgefühl nur ganz im stillen, und wenn es dennoch zum Ausdruck kam, so kleidete sich's in Humor, auch wohl in Selbstironie, weil er seinem ganzen Wesen nach überhaupt hinter alles ein Fragezeichen machte. Sein schönster Zug war eine tiefe, so recht aus dem Herzen kommende Humanität, und Dünkel und Überheblichkeit [...] waren so ziemlich die einzigen Dinge, die ihn empörten. (9–10)

Dubslav is explicitly given the attributes of the lake. Through his ancestry at least, he has the feeling of having been in Brandenburg since before the Hohenzollerns; he is an old man identified with age and heritage. His self-assurance is kept 'im stillen' and yet it can be expressed in a humorous, ironic way. The lake is also silent, and given that the spout of water and crowing cock fable is related in the first paragraph as a local legend, it is not unreasonable to consider that the red cock story is also told in an ironic way. The fact that it is attributed to the locals and presented with considerable alliteration and onomatopoeia also appears to support this reading. Dubslav can, like the lake, however, be enraged, and the word employed to describe his emotion, 'empörten', recalls the upward movement of the water and cock ('empor'). This happens, however, only if Dubslav's 'tiefe [...] Humanität' is provoked by falsehood. The lake, its depth, and its occasional angry reactions are here associated with a humanity which, though usually quiet, can react and make its voice heard.

The lake resembles Dubslav in another, more abstract way, through paradox:

> Paradoxen waren seine Passion. 'Ich bin nicht klug genug, selber welche zu machen, aber ich freue mich, wenn's andre tun; es ist doch immer was drin.

Unanfechtbare Wahrheiten gibt es überhaupt nicht, und wenn es welche gibt, so sind sie langweilig.' (10)

Paradox and antithesis are at the core of Dubslav's speech and way of thinking, and may be seen as the linguistic expression of the essential problematics of this novel about the necessity of coexistence, primarily of old and new. Enumerating some of the lake's key characteristics reveals that it too is paradoxical. The lake is deep, yet its spout of water makes it also ascendant. It is, on the one hand, associated with the old, with continuity and with legend, while, on the other, the implication is that it will rise again when 'was Großes gibt', linking the lake to the future. The lake is silent, but the cockerel 'kräht in die Lande hinein'. Through its frequent mention in the novel and its associations of home for Dubslav and Woldemar, it acquires the connotations of familiarity discussed earlier, but never loses its mystery and danger because of its size, and, according to Melusine, its elemental quality (267). It is distant, on the border, a far-away place, and yet Stechlin is Woldemar's home and entirely provincial. Through the lake, this parochial place is nevertheless in touch with the world, whether Iceland or Java (7). As a natural, poetic milieu it appears to stand against the industry and commercialism of Berlin, but it is viewed as a commodity by Dubslav, as 'seinen See' (11), and as a potential source of wealth by his creditor Baruch Hirschfeld (13). Given the close relationship between Dubslav and the lake, the general importance of paradox in the novel, and the lake's own characteristics, the lake can be said not only to appear paradoxical, but to represent paradox, as Charlotte Jolles argues.[47]

Considering the lake as a symbol of paradox remains unsatisfactory, however, unless we ask what the function of paradox is. Paradox, antithetical contructions, and dialogue are ways of criticizing apparent 'unanfechtbare Wahrheiten' by admitting the possibility of alternative truths (10). Paradoxical structures in *Der Stechlin*, even when not specific examples of social critique, become identified with the potential for the kind of intellectual distance from accepted norms which has been explored above. Yet contradiction as an idea permeates the novel to a much deeper degree, in that being receptive to antithesis is associated with understanding human beings and life in general, primarily through Dubslav. As Fontane states elsewhere, 'Das Leben macht doch die besten Witze und steht obenan in der Kunst der Antithese'.[48] An inclination towards paradox thus characterizes a specific approach or mentality, a *Gesinnung* which permits the apprehension of profound truths, in this case about mankind. Paradox is a means of perceiving and expressing these truths: 'es is doch immer was drin' (10). Once again, as in the topographical discussion, we find the novel representing a way of looking at the world. It is also clear by now that the word 'paradox' or near alternatives such as 'antithesis' are too limited in their scope. What is in fact being represented is symbolic understanding and expression, in that a symbol is the bringing together of two disparate entities, of two separate, different elements, which are to be understood reciprocally within a dialectic relationship of meaning.[49] By representing a 'Vereinigung des Entgegengesetzten',[50] the lake represents more than paradox; it is a symbol of the symbolic itself. Symbolic art is an exploration of humanity's irresolvable, paradoxical mysteries which cannot be summed up in a single truth, but can only be accessed through the ability to reconcile the irreconcilable. In this 'poetologischer Roman', Fontane creates a symbol which stands for the very processes by which artists perceive and communicate ideas.[51]

Der Stechlin is undeniably a *sprachliches Kunstwerk* at the centre of which are dialogue and conversation: it is a novel about language, as many commentators have noted. Not only does conversation play an important role, but speech and the meaning of words become the focus of this last, highly reflective novel in a way unparalleled in Fontane's earliers works; and this focus on language is essential to the meaning of the Stechlin lake. Some aspects of the relationship between the lake and language have already been explored, and need only be summarized here. The lake is the subject of many discussions, and inasmuch as it is constructed of irreconcilable opposites (above, below, near, and far) it represents the conversational to and fro of the novel. The lake is, as we have seen, a *Gegenbild* to Dubslav, the *causeur* who lives consciously 'en philosophe' (9), and whose love of paradox is part of his wider appreciation of *Plauderei* (10). Hence the lake may be seen as an image representative of language and indeed conversation in the novel in a general sense. The lake is not only associated with language in general however, but with poetic language in particular. As was demonstrated earlier, the initial description ends in folklore reported in alliterated, stylized language[52]:

> 'Wenn's aber draußen was Großes gibt, wie vor hundert Jahren in Lissabon, dann brodelt's hier nicht bloß und sprudelt und strudelt, dann steigt statt des Wasserstrahls ein roter Hahn auf und kräht laut in die Lande hinein'. (7)

The lake thus represents symbolic understanding in general (as linked to aesthetic perception described earlier) and poetic expression (of that understanding) in particular. In its paradox and ambiguity, its representation of unity in variety, the lake symbolizes 'in jedem Fall das Wesen der Dichtung', as Müller-Seidel argues.[53]

Seeing the lake as representative of the capacity of poetic language to express symbolic insights is significant, because the prominent position afforded to paradoxical constructions in *Der Stechlin*, the denial of unchallengeable truths, and the conversational, dialectic structure of the text have led certain commentators to see the novel as an expression of linguistic scepticism, a forerunner of *fin de siècle* doubt in language.[54] The relationship between the representation of the lake and language is not one of scepticism, however, but confidence. The Stechlin lake perhaps above all exists as a word itself, and it is this word which gives the novel, family, and village its name. What is more, Melusine's imperative, 'es lebe der Stechlin', assigns this symbol of language an importance beyond any individual and announces it as the way of the future. As we have seen, paradoxical constructions are positively valued. Woldemar's decision to go and live in Stechlin, a place dominated by the existence of the lake, is a topographical indicator of faith in the power of poetic — that is, symbolic — language.

Stechlin and Fontane's Poetry

It could be countered that seeing the lake as symbolic of poetry is all too easy an answer to a difficult, and as some have argued, unanswerable question.[55] It might also be argued that seeing paradox and tension as inherently part of 'the poetic' is a catch-all for any interpretative difficulties. In this case, however, it is possible to read the lake not only as representing language and the symbolic *per se*, but also to consider Stechlin, place and lake, within the context of Fontane's own later poetry.

The link between Fontane's later poetry and his final novel is established, but little heeded. Reuter, in his *Fontane* monograph, sees in Fontane's later poetry a blending of subjective *Bekenntnis* and objective realism, something that, in his assessment, Fontane as a novelist seeks only in his final work, preferring more usually to separate himself from his artistic prose production.[56] Reuter also draws a parallel between what the Stechlin lake stands for (in his view, a 'neue, bessere Welt') and Fontane's later poetry, where, he argues, similar issues are explored.[57] Karl Richter also sees a thematic link between Fontane's late poetry and *Der Stechlin* in the poem 'Die Alten und die Jungen',[58] and in general argues that Fontane's poetic output is to be understood as undergoing similar development processes as the novels, as Reuter arguably does too.[59] Richter also provides insight into the formal aspects of Fontane's poetry and, as will be argued here, there is a profound correspondence between these formal attributes, as well as the aim of the poems, and what this spatial investigation of *Der Stechlin* has brought to the fore.

Throughout this study of space in Fontane's works, it has been shown that Fontane depicts in his texts a way of looking at the world which is aesthetically informed, a 'poetische Betrachtung des Lebens'.[60] In *Der Stechlin* this is expressed spatially primarily through Woldemar's decision to live in Stechlin — a place which represents this way of life and where it is possible. It is thus significant that Richter makes allusion to the similarity between the later poems and the novel in that he identifies Fontane's search for the 'Zusammenhang der Dinge' both in the poems (which pre-date the novel) and *Der Stechlin*.[61] They are both testimony to what Reuter, in another context, calls Fontane's 'poetisch bestimmtes Suchen und Fragen'.⁶²

Richter identifies traits in Fontane's late poems, which arguably are represented in *Der Stechlin*'s topography, particularly in Stechlin and its lake. According to Richter, Fontane combines in his late poems biographical elements, with reflections on society, the personal and the universal, 'Nahblick und distanzierende Überschau'.⁶³ The same might be said of Stechlin, in that this place, which is Woldemar's home, represents closeness, and yet is physically remote from the unspoken centre, Berlin. The author of the late poems has become a foreigner, alien within and critical of the world around him. According to Richter, it is the poetry of a 'skeptisches Beiseitestehens'.⁶⁴ The Stechlin lake seems to symbolize this critical distance which marks out Fontane's poems. It is distant from the 'Weltstadt' Berlin and, through its red cock, critical of modern society, be it via allusion to Dubslav's feeling for humanity, or revolutionary fervour. Nor is this reference to 'Beiseitestehen' simply a *façon de parler* of Richter's. The lyrical *Ich* in Fontane's poems may be seen to be standing by, indeed gazing from a window, like the figures identified at the beginning of this chapter with freedom from the world and intellectual credibility:

> Ich trat ans Fenster, ich sah hinunter,
> Es trabte wieder, es klingelte munter,
> Eine Schürze (beim Schlächter) hing über dem Stuhle,
> Kleine Mädchen gingen nach der Schule, —
> Alles war freundlich, alles war nett,
> Aber wenn ich weiter geschlafen hätt'
> Und tät' von alledem nichts wissen,
> Würd' es mir fehlen, würd' ich's vermissen?⁶⁵

As was seen at the beginning of this discussion, Fontane draws objects of everyday reality into his art, only to question their relevance for human existence. Reading 'Fritz Katzfuß' in the context of this spatial discussion reveals similar thematic correspondences.⁶⁶ The dawdling shop apprentice Katzfuß reads Goethe whenever he is sent from the shop front to the cellar and silently rejects the materialism of the shop's owner and customers:

> '*Eure* Welt ist Kram,
> Und wenn ihr Waschblau fordert oder Stärke,
> Blaut zu, soviel ihr wollt. *Mein* Blau der Himmel.'⁶⁷

Fontane's lyric poetry and last novel both thematize distance: intellectual distance, and the distance which the otherness of poetry provides.

It is not simply critical distance that links *Der Stechlin* and Fontane's *Alterslyrik*. Fontane's poems are frequently constructed around antitheses, the rhetorical figure that the lake represents. This may be seen in 'Ja, das möcht ich noch erleben', for example:

> Eigentlich ist mir alles gleich,
> Der eine wird arm, der andre wird reich,
> Aber mit Bismarck — was wird das noch geben?
> Das mit Bismarck, das möcht ich noch erleben.
> Eigentlich ist alles soso,
> Heute traurig, morgen froh,
> Frühling, Sommer, Herbst und Winter
> Ach, es ist nicht viel dahinter.[68]

In his analysis of the poem, Richter underlines another quality which he has elsewhere singled out in the later poems and is related to antithesis: dialogue. 'Die antithetische Komposition erweist sich als eines der typischen, für die dialektische Beweglichkeit zugeich besonders charakteristischen Verfahrensmuster der späten Gedichte Fontanes'.[69] Richter argues that dialogue in the poems has a new function here: dialogue 'zeigt, daß der Autor aus dem scheinbar Abseits heraus die Auseinandersetzung mit Zeit und Gesellschaft aufnimmt [...] macht Sprache und Sprechen mittelbar zu ihrem Thema'.[70] There are similarities here between what Richter rightly identifies as a core element of Fontane's late lyric poetry and *Der Stechlin*, the novel as a whole and the lake in particular. Despite remoteness, poetry and literature provide a means of engaging with the world, indeed remoteness provides the necessary context for that poetic engagement. Thus in both the poems and the novel, literature (the linguistic expression of symbolic perception) is reflexively discussed, as are the conditions in which it becomes possible.

Richter's conclusions differ from those of this discussion, however, in that, as other commentators have done for *Der Stechlin*, he sees in Fontane's late poetry an expression of scepticism. It is above all the poems' closeness to ordinary speech which leads Richter to this conclusion.[71] As we have seen in *Der Stechlin*, however, Fontane demonstrates faith in symbolic ways of looking at the world and poetry as a means of communicating these insights. As Reuter writes of 'Fritz Katzfuß': 'Es ist ein Credo *zum* Realismus, zugleich ist es ein Credo *im* Realismus: in der blitzartig wiedererkannten und poetisch wiedergegebenen "bedeutenden" Begebenheit "nach dem Leben"'.[72] Fontane, in his last novel, depicts an attitude through which poetry can continue, despite a changing world. Woldemar's move to Stechlin to begin his married life, to bring money and youth to Stechlin, represents Fontane's belief in the power of language, of poetic, symbolic language. If we consider the lake as representative not simply of poetry, but in fact of Fontane's own poetry, then Woldemar's move and Melusine's imperative indicate confidence in the poetic discourse Fontane himself creates both in his novel and his later poetry.

In 'Mein Leben' it cannot plausibly be maintained that Fontane shows lyrical scepticism. The poem uses rather the very essence of poetry, sound, to create an artwork out of the simplest of diction:

> Mein Leben, ein Leben ist es kaum,
> Ich geh' durch die Straßen als wie im Traum.[73]

The description of the lake similarly ends with a play with sounds: 'es sprudelt und strudelt [...]'. Fontane may well abandon traditional motifs in his later poetry and adopt more original images from everyday life. Alan Bance has made a similar observation with regard to *Der Stechlin*, but instead of seeing a crisis, has seen a new stage in Fontane's work.[74] In her analysis of the novel, Charlotte Jolles sees autobiographical symbols in topography, and there is an argument to be made that the lake could be one of them.[75] An analysis of Fontane's later poetry suggests that perhaps rather than signifying its creator, the lake signifies the attitude and poetics of his own lyric poetry.

Conclusion

> Ich betrachte das Leben, und ganz besonders das Gesellschaftliche darin, wie ein Theaterstück und folge jeder Szene mit einem künstlerischen Interesse wie von meinem Parquetplatz No. 23 aus.[76]

Theodor Fontane was, and saw himself as, an observer of life. In his final, most personal novel, the detached consideration of life becomes a key theme which is communicated in various ways through spatial representation. In the description of personal spaces, certain characters are shown to be unbound and spiritually free, compared with others who are tied to their concrete and closed environments. Topographically, the novel explores the potential for thought and reflection in a hectic world, and creates in Stechlin a remote space of stillness, where aesthetic perception, judgement, and artistic creation are possible. Here Fontane places a symbol of symbolic understanding and poetic expression, a sign of confidence in the potential of literature. This spatial reading uncovers parallels between the last novel and the late poetry. The distant space Fontane creates in Stechlin, the paradoxical symbol of the lake, and the allusions to poetic language suggest that the author represents his own poetry here. The lake is thus a poetical symbol of the symbolic, which crows, if not sings, a message of confidence in literature, of its role and capacity to criticize, and through its paradoxical, dialogical process, to engage in an examination of 'tiefe [...] Humanität' (9).

Notes to Chapter 5

1. Friedrich Hölderlin, *Sämtliche Werke*, ed. by Norbert von Hellingrath, Friedrich Seebass, and Ludwig von Pigenot, 6 vols (Berlin: Propyläen, 1922–23), III, 16.
2. HA II, 1, 338–44.
3. Page numbers in brackets throughout this chapter refer to HA I, 5.
4. Brinkmann, *Theodor Fontane*, p. 27.
5. Helen Chambers, quoting Bernard Shaw's *Misalliance* (1910), in Helen Chambers, 'Großstädte in der Provinz: Topographie bei Theodor Fontane und Joseph Roth', in Delf von Wolzogen and Nürnberger, *Theodor Fontane am Ende des Jahrhunderts*, III, 215–25 (p. 223).
6. Becker, p. 166.
7. In *Vor dem Sturm*, it is the pastor's cabinet (HA I, 3, 104); in *Schach von Wuthenow*, it is the 'gute Stube' in the servants' house (HA, I, 2, 648).
8. For fire and open window, see *Unwiederbringlich*, HA I, 2, 628.
9. Hamon, pp. 264–73, for light, p. 266.
10. Karla Müller makes a similar argument, but with reference to the Stechlin castle: 'Das Schloß ist nun weniger semantisierter Schauplatz von Handlungen und Geschehnissen denn Schauplatz von Gesprächen' (Müller, p. 94).
11. HA I, 4, 299.
12. Martin Beckmann arrives at similar conclusions about the relationship between Frau Schickedanz and the Barbys. Martin Beckmann, 'Theodor Fontanes Roman *Der Stechlin* als ästhetisches Formgefüge', *Wirkendes Wort*, 39 (1989), 218–39 (p. 230).
13. There are a number of veranda or similar scenes in Fontane's oeuvre: at Hankels Ablage in *Irrungen Wirrungen*, on the terrace at Holkenäs in *Unwiederbringlich*, on the roof in Vienna in *Graf Petöfy*. It could be suggested that the inhabitation of these liminal spaces is indicative of a search for personal freedom from social norms on the part of the protagonist, but given that most of Fontane's works deal with these types of issues to a degree, such a generalization is perhaps less helpful than it appears. Here for example, as will be shown, exteriority is identified not with a yearning for freedom, but as representing a spiritual freedom which has already been achieved and which can be maintained within society's norms.
14. HA I, 2, 454.
15. HA I, 3, 276.
16. Mittenzwei, p. 171.
17. Ibid., p. 169.
18. *Goethes Werke*, I, 245.
19. Eckhard Czucka, 'Faktizität und Sprachskepsis: Fontanes Stechlin und die Sprachskepsis der Jahrhundertwende', in Delf von Wolzogen and Nürnberger, *Theodor Fontane am Ende des Jahrhunderts*, II, 27–39.
20. Not all critics see awareness of language as linguistic scepticism. See Peter James Bowman, 'Fontane's *Der Stechlin*: A Fragile Utopia', *MLR*, 97 (2002), 877–91 (p. 888).
21. HA I, 3, 486.
22. Lotman, 'Artistic Space', p. 229.
23. HA IV, 3, 368–70. Fontane's emphasis.
24. For a more detailed analysis of Fontane's ambivalent stance towards Berlin and life in cities, see Peter Wruck, 'Fontanes Berlin: Durchlebte, erfahrene und dargestellte Wirklichkeit', in *Literarisches Leben in Berlin 1871–1933*, ed. by Peter Wruck, 2 vols (Berlin: Akademie Verlag, 1987), I, 22–87, specifically pp. 54–79.
25. The Friedlaenders lived in Schmiedeberg, and Fontane met Georg Friedlaender during

one of his 'Sommerfrischen' in the area, his escapes from the Berlin heat of summer. Their house which he mentions here is thus distant from Berlin, but also a symbolic anti-Berlin. See Schreinert, *Briefe*, p. xi.
26. HA I, 4, 479.
27. Phillip Frank argues that the late works are sceptical of technology. See Phillip Frank, *Theodor Fontane und die Technik* (Würzburg: Königshausen & Neumann, 2005), p. 206.
28. The imaginary industrial town Coketown is the setting for Charles Dickens's novel *Hard Times* (1854).
29. HA I, 4, 306–07.
30. HA I, 2, 405.
31. Charlotte Jolles, 'Weltstadt — verlorene Nachbarschaft: Berlin-Bilder Raabes und Fontanes', *Jahrbuch der Raabe-Gesellschaft* (1988), 52–75 (p. 74).
32. Spindler was a well-known producer of cleaning products. See HA I, 5, 943.
33. 'Friedrich Spielhagen, Problematische Naturen' (1860), HA III, 1, 491.
34. Rost, p. 139.
35. See HA I, 3, 53–54.
36. Compare the description of the church in *Vor dem Sturm*, HA I, 3, 36–41.
37. Hamon, p. 264.
38. HA II, 1, 44–45. Fontane's emphasis.
39. HA II, 1, 45. Fontane's emphasis.
40. 'Verweile doch, du bist so schön!' *Goethes Werke*, III, 57 and 348.
41. Richard Brinkmann, 'Der angehaltene Moment: Requisiten — Genre — Tableau bei Fontane', *Deutsche Vierteljahresschrift für Literaturwissenschaft und Geistesgeschichte*, 58 (1979), 429–62.
42. Scholarship is divided on the relative importance of the lake. Some, such as Günther, see the lake as the 'Mittelpunkt', see Günther, p. 95. Others such as Hillebrand see Dubslav as the centre, see Hillebrand, p. 271. In general, however, most scholars see the lake as a defining aspect of the novel in some way.
43. From Fontane's notes, cited in Reuter, *Fontane*, II, 807.
44. Draft letter to Adolf Hoffmann, [May/June? 1897], HA IV, 4, 650.
45. AA, VIII, 426.
46. Jolles, *Theodor Fontane*, p. 95.
47. Charlotte Jolles, '*Der Stechlin*: Fontanes Zaubersee', in Aust, *Fontane aus heutiger Sicht*, pp. 239–57 (p. 249).
48. Letter of 24 September 1895 to Georg Friedlaender, in Schreinert, *Briefe*, p. 21.
49. See P. J. Bowman, who argues that the lake stands for the 'connectedness' of the various dichotomies associated with it, rather than their difference, in Bowman, 'Fontane's *Der Stechlin*', p. 879.
50. Müller-Seidel, *Soziale Romankunst*, p. 451. Müller-Seidel, however, argues that the lake is an allegory, not a symbol. For a discussion of the differing views on whether the lake is a symbol, chiffre, or sign, see Eda Sagarra, *Theodor Fontane: 'Der Stechlin'*, (Munich: Fink, 1986), pp. 92–101. It is argued there that an excessively detailed focus on the type of symbol the lake represents can become inconsequential. It is true that the label given to the lake is of relatively little importance, but it should be acknowledged that describing its — perhaps many — symbolic functions is necessary.
51. Mittenzwei, p. 171.
52. Contrast Derek Barlow's (p. 283) interpretation of the description of the lake as 'matter-of-fact'.
53. Walter Müller-Seidel, 'Theodor Fontane: *Der Stechlin*', in *Der deutsche Roman*, ed. by Benno von Wiese, 4 vols (Düsseldorf: Bagel, 1963), IIb, 146–89 (p. 186).

54. See Czucka, and Sean Ireton, 'The Problem of Language in Nietzsche's *Ueber Wahrheit und Lüge im aussermoralischem Sinne* and Fontane's *Stechlin*', *Colloquia Germania*, 35 (2002), 239–61.
55. Garland, p. 242. Garland argues that it is Fontane's practice to leave symbols vague and ambiguous. He sees the narrative as held together by Dubslav more than the lake (ibid., p. 260).
56. Reuter, *Fontane*, II, 781.
57. Ibid., p. 790.
58. Karl Richter, 'Das späte Gedichtwerk', in Grawe and Nürnberger, *Fontane-Handbuch*, pp. 726–47 (p. 734).
59. Ibid., p. 732.
60. To Martha, 22 August 1895, HA IV, 4, 472.
61. Karl Richter, 'Die späte Lyrik Theodor Fontanes', in Aust, *Fontane aus heutiger Sicht*, pp. 118–42 (p. 122).
62. Reuter, *Fontane*, II, 795.
63. Richter, 'Die späte Lyrik', pp. 121–22.
64. Ibid., p. 126.
65. HA I, 6, 340.
66. HA I, 6, 364–66.
67. HA I, 6, 365. Fontane's emphasis.
68. HA I, 6, 349.
69. Richter, 'Die späte Lyrik', p. 131.
70. Ibid.
71. The situation is complicated by the fact that Richter is using the term 'lyrisch', which has the potential for a narrow meaning.
72. Reuter, *Fontane*, II, 783. Reuter's italics.
73. NyA, XX, 416. This is the version cited by Richter. The text reproduced in the Hanser edition deviates in line 2, reading 'dahin' in place of 'durch die Straßen' (HA I, 6, 346 and notes 981).
74. Bance, *The Major Novels*, pp. 187 and 190.
75. Jolles sees the Grafschaft Ruppin and England as autobiographical symbols. Charlotte Jolles, '"Und an der Themse wächst man sich anders aus als am Stechlin": Zum England Motiv in Fontanes Erzählwerk', *FBl*, 5 (1967), 173–91 (p. 181).
76. Letter of 5 July 1886 to Georg Friedlaender, in Erler, *Briefe*, II, 143.

CONCLUSION

~

> An understanding appreciation of literature means an understanding appreciation of the world, and it means nothing else.
> ARNOLD BENNET, *Literary Taste*[1]

General Findings

A stated methodological aim of this investigation of space in Fontane's works has been to treat each text individually in the first instance, which has produced varied readings. Nevertheless, the study of space has uncovered recurrent themes, and it is the purpose of this final chapter to draw together the general tendencies and developments that have emerged in the preceding chapters. For the purposes of the present discussion, the texts analysed may be assigned to one of three groups, according to the function of space in them and to the types of issues that an investigation of space raises. The first group comprises the *Wanderungen durch die Mark Brandenburg* (*Die Grafschaft Ruppin*); the second, *Vor dem Sturm*, *Schach von Wuthenow*, and *Graf Petöfy*; and the third *Irrungen Wirrungen*, *Unwiederbringlich*, and *Der Stechlin*.

In the chapter treating *Die Grafschaft Ruppin*, the main focus of the investigation was the relationship between the textual and the empirical world. The discussion assessed the extent to which spatial representation functions as a means of creating symbolic meaning within the text, and came to the conclusion that this does occur, and can be highly sophisticated, but is rare. It was demonstrated that such spatial symbolism can be achieved either structurally or through a pregnant description. Significantly, in what was called interpretative representation, the narrator in *Die Grafschaft Ruppin* can often be observed to interpret reality as being symbolic, to read the world, which is of relevance for the later texts, where observing figures act in similar ways within their fictional environments.

In the case of the three novels *Vor dem Sturm*, *Schach von Wuthenow*, and *Graf Petöfy*, the question whether or not the represented world functions in a symbolic manner proved irrelevant and instead the discussions focused on the role of spatial representation as a constructor of meaning. The analysis of *Vor dem Sturm* revealed a variety of strategies whereby the representation of space serves to relativize and place in relief events, individual experiences, and opinions. Spatial references function to create a dissenting voice and through spatial representation the text constantly contextualizes and nuances apparently simple facts. In *Schach von Wuthenow* and *Graf Petöfy*, spatial representation also functions to provide the reader with information beyond the knowledge of individual characters and sheds light on their conduct. In *Schach von Wuthenow*, a complex topography reveals a psychological development in Schach, while in *Graf Petöfy*, the representation of Vienna and Öslau reveals the flawed psychological states of Adam and Franziska, whose straying into delusion is charted in the represented landscape, of Arpa.

Spatial representation continues to play a significant role in the mature novels *Irrungen Wirrungen*, *Unwiederbringlich*, and *Der Stechlin*, and in these works the question about the relationship between human beings and their world resurfaces. The discussion of *Irrungen Wirrungen* concentrated in particular on seeing and viewing, and on how, in this novel, Fontane explores a particular kind of perception: the ability to look at the world and see meaning, specifically with reference to oneself and to individual, private experience. This discussion of symbolism was shown to be part of a wider reflection on art and literature in the text. In this novel, imaginative interaction with the environment is presented positively: it adds value to Botho's life; in *Unwiederbringlich*, the other side of the coin is shown. A complex antithetical topography was here exposed as the creation of Holk's and Christine's minds. The characters misapprehend themselves and their environment, misreading signs in the world. Holk's and Christine's failures are related to their lack of artistic sensitivity. As in *Irrungen Wirrungen*, Fontane makes a case for art and literature as a means of improving how we grasp the significance of our surroundings, that is, their meaning for us. *Der Stechlin*, it was argued, explores similar issues. In this novel, a critically distant stance towards the haste of modern, changing life is presented as desirable, and indeed necessary. Aesthetic perception can only occur slowly and through contemplation, and this gradual process is hindered by the modernity of Berlin as represented in this *Zeitroman*. The novel's topography creates in Stechlin an alternative to Berlin: a location where aesthetic experience is possible, a symbol of poetic language and ultimately Fontane's own poetry. Fontane expresses confidence in the continued validity and potential of literature, but acknowledges its dependence on the stance of the individual towards his world.

Considering the texts studied in the ways suggested above, it becomes apparent that spatial representation in Fontane's texts has two main aspects: a functional aspect, and a reflective aspect, and that, in general terms, the reflective aspect is absent in the second group of texts, but plays a significant role in groups one and three, namely *Die Grafschaft Ruppin* and the mature novels. The analysis of the functional aspect illuminates the formal role of space in the text: the way that description, topography, journeys, and so forth contribute to the text's integrity as a structure of meaning. Space is here a mode of literary expression. The term 'reflective aspect' indicates Fontane's tendency in some texts to create a discourse on spatial experience, on the significance of the world and the relationship between individual and environment. Space is here an object of literary exploration. The reflective aspect also marks a trend towards reflexivity in Fontane's work, which is frequently based on notions of observation and aesthetic perception.

Variety and Development in Fontane's Spatial Representation

The functional aspect of space is what is normally understood as being the object of a study of space in literature, that is, the represented space in the text is considered alongside the other major features such as themes and plot, with a view to uncovering the meaning of space in relation to these other textual elements. In analysing the function of space, this study has drawn on two basic critical perspectives broadly considered: on the one hand, structural approaches, which focus on topography and the relationship between spaces; and on the other, methodologies for analysing individual descriptions, particularly the concept of focalization, in which the main concern is the relationship between the represented world and the viewer.

In Fontane's work, a variety of techniques for rendering spatial representation meaningful and relevant to wider thematic and narrative concerns may be observed. At the most basic level, descriptions of private spaces are used to provide characterization, as is evident in *Vor dem Sturm* for example. Here, the state of a room and the objects in it relay information about a character's past and psychology.[2] Significantly, the value of this method of characterization is the relative objectivity which such descriptions display. In most cases, the rooms in question are focalized through a reliable narrator, and can contradict impressions created in conversation or through a character's actions. Examples here would be the positive edge given to Adelheid von Stechlin through the presentation of her room, or the relativization of the generally favourable image of Berndt von Vitzewitz through his untidy, darkened rooms. This form of spatial characterization can also function within wider thematic frameworks which are themselves spatially expressed. This is the case in *Vor dem Sturm* and *Der Stechlin*, but may also be observed in the Vienna descriptions in *Graf Petöfy*, for example.

At a more complex level, Fontane's descriptions often include allegorical details, whose associative meanings are manipulated for the purposes of prefiguration. Although criticized by some, this technique can often be subtle and unobtrusive: the toads croaking in Tempelhof in *Schach von Wuthenow* is a good example.[3] Whereas a passage of description for the purposes of characterization will, for the most part, communicate information to the reader which has validity for the text as a whole, spatial representation of the latter type is frequently embedded in the narrative and has specific relevance to ongoing events, as is the case with Schach's view of Wuthenow am See in the moonlight. Scholars who have sought to see this trait of Fontane's spatial representation as defining, however, such as Brüggemann, risk oversimplifying both the referential complexity of the signs themselves, and the variety of Fontane's work: as Ohl persuasively argued, it is within the thematic tapestry of the literary text that Fontane's symbols gain their pregnancy.[4] The analysis of *Die Grafschaft Ruppin* offered here may be seen as providing a more differentiated view of Fontane's use of signs and textual reference, while accepting Ohl's basic premise with regard to the symbol within Fontane's literary works. Perhaps most significantly, however, the range of spatial strategies Fontane employs needs to be stressed.

Fontane's texts also have frequent recourse to topographical or structural spatial symbolism, a technique which varies considerably in scope. In *Unwiederbringlich* and *Der Stechlin* for example, whole narratives may be related to single topographical structures, complex and contradictory though these may be. In *Graf Petöfy*, a meaningful landscape is constructed in Arpa, but this is separate from other locations such as Öslau, while 'east' and 'west' as markers have validity throughout the text. In *Schach von Wuthenow*, topographical symbolism is important, as in *Graf Petöfy*, for the representation of a changing state of mind, but in contrast to *Unwiederbringlich* or *Der Stechlin*, *Schach von Wuthenow*'s topography is composed of a set of successive and related descriptive passages, each one charting a progression in line with the narrative. In other works, such as *Vor dem Sturm* and *Irrungen Wirrungen*, topographical considerations appear subordinated to other spatial agendas: in *Vor dem Sturm* the varied use of spatial representation is a means of promoting critical commentary, while in *Irrungen Wirrungen* the focus is on individual spatial experience. Topographical or structural spatial symbolism is more limited in these novels, to the representation of Hohen Vietz village, for example. Individual description and all-encompassing topographical structures are, however, not mutually exclusive, they work interdependently: thus the distinct forms of personal space in *Der Stechlin* can be seen as a variant of the Berlin/Stechlin opposition. Furthermore, individual descriptions may be said to create structural symbolism or topographies on a small scale: the repeated representation of places which oppose internal and external spheres in *Schach von Wuthenow* for example; conversely, one symbol created in a single description may become part of a wider overall topographical structure, as is the case in *Der Stechlin*. A flexible analytical approach, which takes account of the text's various, complementary strategies of spatial representation, is thus required.

Examining literary sections in *Die Grafschaft Ruppin* reveals that both of these types of spatial representation, the individual pregnant description ('Am Wall') and the topographical network ('Rheinsberg'), are in evidence from an early stage in Fontane's oeuvre, and both continue to be used in the later novels. There can thus be no suggestion of an evolution from one to the other. Progression occurs rather in the complexity of spatial representation and in the extent to which the reflective aspect of Fontane's spatial representation is present. In group one (*Die Grafschaft Ruppin*), leaving aside rhetorical space, the poetic function of space is relatively rare, while reflection on the significance of spatial experience is common.

In group two, spatial representation is of course functional — these are literary texts, but the spatial representation has little or no reflective aspect. There are occasional hints at themes which will become important in the later novels, but these are limited in scope. The theme of awareness in *Schach von Wuthenow* and *Graf Petöfy* may be related to the reflection in the later texts, but it is not a discussion of aesthetic issues. These Fontane explores with non-spatial means, as in the discussion of beauty in *Schach von Wuthenow*, or poetry in *Vor dem Sturm*. These discussions form a constant of Fontane's oeuvre, but are not developed via spatial representation in these early novels. The significance of this second group of texts is that the various possibilities and uses of spatial representation as a literary means of expression are explored. In *Vor dem Sturm* Fontane develops spatial means of contextualization, comparison, and relativization to a high level of sophistication and variety. In *Schach von Wuthenow*, an integrated topographical structure is introduced, which had not featured in the earlier works analysed, and this shorter novel shows the potential of the novel's spatial world to represent the inner workings of one individual. In *Graf Petöfy*, Fontane engages in a greater exploration of spatial techniques, employing subtle syntagmatic structures, operating, for example, around the antipodes left/right, which have been observed in a more fully developed form in later works.[5]

The third group of texts is characterized by a refinement of the techniques seen in the previous group. This can be observed in terms of extent: the partial topographical structures in *Schach von Wuthenow* and *Graf Petöfy* are succeeded by larger, more inclusive ones in *Der Stechlin* and, though problematically, in *Unwiederbringlich*. More significantly, however, the spatial representation in these later novels is distinguished by a greater complexity, subtlety, and *chiaroscuro*. The ambiguities in these later spatial structures are in part due to the fact that 'zones' in the imaginary world created by the texts are not differentiated in an absolute sense. For example, the opposition between Berlin and Stechlin in *Der Stechlin* is not clear cut: the reader is shown the potential for stillness and *Verklärung* in Berlin as well as in Stechlin. This seems paradoxical:

at about the same stage where Fontane is expanding the degree of topographical integration, the capacity of a single overarching structure to reflect complex problems, frequently involving more than one character, is undermined, as is the case with the antithetical topography in *Unwiederbringlich*. This change appears to be due to an increased emphasis on characters' subjective experiences and thus on focalization. Individual perception and constructed meaning are the primary foci of *Irrungen Wirrungen*; in *Unwiederbringlich*, it is not the topographical structure, but rather Holk and Christine's flawed reading of their world which is the key to understanding space in the novel, while in *Der Stechlin* contemplation and observation become the themes which are expressed topographically. It is significant that both *Irrungen Wirrungen* and *Unwiederbringlich* begin with descriptions seen through the eyes of an unnamed observing figure. Fontane announces through these figures the distinctive focus of these works.

This is a tendency rather than a rule, and it is true that the perceiving individual is important in many of Fontane's descriptions in the earlier texts. In *Vor dem Sturm* for example, Bohlsdorf church is presented clearly through Lewin's eyes. Yet the relationship between character and description in the earlier novels is usually simply one of relevance, and more often than not description is presented by a narrator in order to give information about characters or events. The world is related to the reader by a narrator; the characters are placed in, and do not create or transmit, their world. Tau's comparison of Fontane's landscapes with stage scenery as is appropriate here, if it is taken without its implied negative connotations.[6] In the later novels where Fontane focuses more on individual subjectivity, the way the world is perceived by a character acquires heightened value: the topography of *Unwiederbringlich* is in fact a product of Holk's imagination, whereas that of *Graf Petöfy* is more akin to an encrypted set of signs against which the characters' actions are to be followed. This amounts, in the end, to a change in the relationship between the narrative components — narrator, character, represented world — on the one hand, and the reader on the other, in that the boundaries between the world presented by the narrator and the world experienced by the characters, between externally and internally focalized space, become increasingly blurred. We must be cautious not to overstate the generalization: identifying the focalizer, whether narrator or character, is often difficult in Fontane's writing, and in all the later novels the narrator (and author) continues to communicate via spatial representation independently of figural focalization. Space continues to have a functional aspect. This explanation would, however, accord with the generally accepted view that in Fontane's work it is increasingly the case that individuals are presented and characterized through the medium of conversation, and the reader is often left with a series of subjective images of a character, rather than an authoritative one. It seems then that in spatial representation a similar process occurs: the world is presented frequently through the eyes of individuals, who all have their own ideas and emotional influences, and who are thus not disinterested parties, but whose presentation of the world is filtered and transformed. However, while it is typically argued that characterization through dialogue is a means of creating objectivity and distance, it seems that in these later novels spatial representation becomes a means of exploring and expressing issues which are close to Fontane's concerns as an artist.

Space and Fontane's Poetics

Fontane's spatial representation is thus reflective, in that spatial experience becomes an object of literature, a thematic concern of the literary text. More significantly, however, in his focalizing, observing characters, Fontane examines the relationship between man and the world, and the meaning that the environment has for individuals. Characters are seen interpreting reality in the text, reading signs in the world, in *Irrungen Wirrungen* and *Unwiederbringlich*. In *Der Stechlin*, the capacity to perceive beauty becomes a central concern of the novel. Focalization can also entail a representation — and thus a literary exploration of — aesthetic perception.

The special importance that this theme gains in Fontane's work, and its particular interest to the reader is, however, the relationship between this kind of perception and presentation, and Fontane's own poetics. In his critical writings Fontane returns time and again to the idea that an art work must portray reality (in a broad sense, meaning either the real world, or something which is believable), but at the same the art work must portray beauty and goodness. Reality must thus be refined and transfigured, seen from a particular perspective and imbued with specific ideals. The represented observer and represented process of observing thus also provide a vehicle for the exploration and representation of the evaluative process of *Verklärung*. Fontane creates an image of the artistic process within his works, and in so doing, he explores the relevance of art and artistic ways of understanding in human life, the potential of art as he sees it in the modern age. This is extremely significant, and an aspect of Fontane's work which previous spatial studies have overlooked. Insight into this aspect of Fontane's spatial representation adds a new dimension to our appreciation of Fontane as a self-aware artist and critic, and may suggest that the relationship between Fontane the critic and Fontane the writer is closer than previously thought. An awareness of these tendencies in Fontane's writings, both fictional and journalistic, should furthermore stimulate increased interest in his aesthetic thought.

This process of representation and exploration of creative processes is not, however, something which is restricted in its relevance to the creative artist. In fact, what Fontane depicts here more than anything is a way of life, a way of looking relevant to all. Indeed, the observers in Fontane's texts are not poets or writers, but people whose lives are, or could be, improved by learning to see the world in the way Fontane suggests.

In the texts studied, Fontane appears to portray an observer of the world who is capable of seeing symbolism in his or her surroundings. This then raises the question, symbolism of what? Wolfgang Jung argues that Fontane continues the German Classical tradition by linking beauty to the perception of wider truths, but in rejecting art's claims to metaphysical revelations about the relationship between man and the universe, Fontane leaves an aesthetic or philosophical void.[7] Indeed what Hans Blumenberg theorizes in the twentieth century, man's 'desire for meaning' as a result of living in a secularized world,[8] appears to be explored by Fontane from the *Wanderungen* onwards. This correspondence should, however, not be overstated. If Fontane's texts eschew absolute and transcendental truths, they do nevertheless deal in private and potential ones. Fontane frequently ascribes truth value to myth, saga, and other 'irrational elements', as has been previously demonstrated.[9] Having a sensitivity for the symbolic meaning of the world might be said to equate to having an appreciation of the unknowable, or empirically unprovable truths which nevertheless have human value and relevance to the lives and concerns of individuals. It is precisely the ability to construct and transmit these meanings which gives literature value and relevance in the modern age. As I. A. Richards argues, literature is no longer a pseudo-statement of a magical truth. We moderns have

> 'cut our pseudo-statements free from belief, and yet retain them, in this released state, as the main constituents by which we order our attitudes to one another and the world'.[10]

Just as frequently, however, it seems that the capacity to perceive is valued in itself: being contemplative, having critical distance, having the capacity to evaluate, these are the qualities which are given positive value throughout the texts in the last group, particularly in *Der Stechlin*. Here again, Fontane's artistic explorations foreshadow twentieth-century theoretical discourses: the Russian formalist Victor Shlovsky's poetics of dehabitualization; Richards, for whom 'the good life is the life of the man fully aware of the world';[11] or Georg Lukács, whose 1920 *Theory of the Novel* argues that: 'A mere glimpse of meaning is the highest that life has to offer, and [. . .] this glimpse is the only thing worth the commitment of an entire life'.[12]

Thus not only the capacity to feel a wider *Zusammenhang der Dinge*, but also a more modest significance relevant to oneself is valued — aesthetic perception and reflection make life richer in emotion. This can be a *Hilfskonstruktion*: the ability to see beauty in the world is presented in these texts as an aid in modern life. For Botho it permits him to access values beyond his narrow sphere, for

Holk and Christine it would have taught them to live according to the aesthetic laws of harmony and moderation. Thus perception as a way of becoming more conscious of ourselves as human beings is linked to the wider human meaning which Fontane sees as the purpose of art: that it should present and promote a specific view of man in the modern age.[13] That view of man is as a critical observer. What we see in the representation of space is thus that this view of man is not detached, abstracted from his surroundings, but perceived and presented within them.

Research Context

This research project has inevitably been limited in its scope. Had time and space permitted, the number and variety of texts could have been extended. In consequence of these constraints, some of the established masterpieces, such as *Effi Briest*, have been avoided, and other less well-known works in which space plays an important role, such as *Ellernklipp*, have also remained unexamined. It might equally have proven fruitful to include more non-fiction, such as *Jenseit des Tweed*, or to have examined evidence of the author's real-life relationship with his environment as documented in letters, autobiographical writings and diaries. That is not to mention the other material that the texts studied offered, but which could not be addressed, the further potential readings which have had to remain unexplored, and the range of secondary material of which only a fraction could be brought into the small compass of this study.

Nevertheless, within these unavoidable limitations, this research has produced findings which are relevant to current scholarship. The relationship of the particular readings in this study to existing Fontane research has already been noted in the appropriate chapters, and need not be reiterated here. Of greater interest at this stage of the discussion are more general considerations with regard to the research presented here and current scholarship. In terms of methodology, this research demonstrates that analysis of literary space is a productive mode of textual study, particularly with regard to Fontane's texts, but that the approach must be flexible and the analysis conducted with sensitivity to the text in question. Furthermore, in the case of *Die Grafschaft Ruppin* it has been demonstrated that a spatial focus provides a means of discussing difficult grey areas in a transparent and clear manner.

The functional aspect of spatial representation in Fontane's work had been previously recognized. In fact, much earlier research has proved to be of continued relevance, such as the early work by Max Tau in the 1920s on associative symbolism, or Hermann Fricke's essay on lakes in Fontane's works.[14] The main contribution of this research with regard to the functional aspect of space has thus been to expand the number of readings, by providing alternative interpretations of texts where spatial readings already exist, and more particularly by incorporating both analyses of spatial structures and individual descriptions.

The most significant outcome of this study, however, is the identification and exploration of what has been termed here the 'reflective aspect' in these texts. Here the project develops earlier research by Hubert Ohl, which stressed the subjectivity of focalizing figures in the creation of symbolic meaning in Fontane's texts,[15] essentially by expanding the extent of interest in the observing figures, while at the same time not negating the possibility that the textual world may itself communicate meaning to the reader, independently of focalizers, as is particularly the case in the earlier work and in *Der Stechlin*.[16]

This research has also clearly drawn on and complements earlier work on the imagination and poetry and prose in Fontane's texts.[17] This is still a current area of interest, as Nora Hoffmann's related work on photography in Fontane's novels illustrates.[18] However, by linking this theme more explicitly to Fontane's aesthetic concerns, this study takes this aspect of Fontane research in a new direction. Similarly, this research may also be considered alongside scholarship which addresses the portrayal and narrative influence of individual characters' subjective experiences of the text's reality, though the focus on space means that the relationship between the observer and object is highlighted here, and the emphasis is on objects and environments, rather than on reading people or events, as in Bowman's essay on *Cécile*, for example.[19]

It is also clear from this project that there is still much work to be done in the area of Fontane's aesthetics. While there are studies of Fontane as a critic of the drama, as an art critic, and of his literary criticism, this needs to be brought together and considered alongside the scattered reflections in the travel writings, autobiographical works, and novels. Returning to space more properly, this study has continually been compelled to stress the ambiguity and multivalency of overarching spatial structures in Fontane's later works and the increased emphasis on the creation of these structures through the figures in the texts. Whether this view is compatible with scholarship which emphasizes structural symbolism, such as Haberkamm's interpretations of *Effi Briest* and *Irrungen Wirrungen*, remains an area open for debate.[20] In his interpretations of these works, Haberkamm argues that relative markers connote fixed values, whereas the analysis here has shown that what appears to be fixed is more usually exposed as relative, as a construct created by a viewing individual, although the two positions are not necessarily mutually exclusive, as the discussion of *Der Stechlin* shows. Above all, this research suggests that a greater appreciation of the nuances of Fontane's spatial poetics is needed.

The Final Word

Theodor Fontane's represented worlds have long been recognized as meaningful, as displaying an underlying sense of coherence. This study has drawn on earlier methodological and critical sources to provide new readings of a range of works, from the *Wanderungen* to the late novels. More significantly, however, it has demonstrated that space in Fontane's works is an object of literature, a thematic concern. The meaning of the world, the relationship between viewer and viewed, is a recurrent theme. Through spatial representation Fontane explores how we create symbolism, and how we perceive beauty. Spatial representation performs a poetic function, but also has a reflective aspect. Through spatial representation Fontane communicates a 'poetische Betrachtung des Lebens'. He gives us an image of literature as a way of life.

Notes to the Conclusion

1. Arnold Bennet, *Literary Taste*, ed. by Frank Swinnerton (Harmondsworth: Penguin, 1938), p. 20.
2. Contrast here Sabina Becker (p. 167), who sees characterization of this sort in Poetic Realism primarily as a means of establishing a character's social milieu, rather than providing evidence of individual traits. Becker is considering spatial representation as product and expression of the bourgeois ideology she proposes, but she arguably goes too far here. As has been shown in this study, the description of interior spaces can equally be related to the novel's particular thematic concerns, as in *Der Stechlin*.
3. Tau (p. 22) both identifies this aspect of Fontane's writing and sees it as limiting.
4. See Ohl, *Bild und Wirklichkeit*, pp. 205–06
5. Haberkamm, '"Links und rechts umlauert"'.
6. Tau, p. 18.
7. Wolfgang Jung, *Das 'Menschliche' im 'Alltäglichen': Fontanes Literaturtheorie in ihrer Beziehung zur klassischen Ästhetik und seine Rezeption der Dichtung Goethes und Schillers* (Frankfurt a. M.: Lang, 1985), p. 98.
8. Franz-Josef Wetz, *Hans Blumenberg zur Einführung* (Hamburg: Junius, 1993), p. 116.
9. Chambers, *Supernatural and Irrational Elements*.
10. I. A. Richards, *Science and Poetry* (London: Kegan Paul, Trench, and Trubner, 1926), p. 61.
11. *Russian Formalist Criticism: Four Essays*, trans. and ed. by Lee T. Lemon and Marion J. Reis (Lincoln, NB and London: University of Nebraska Press, 1965), p. 5.
12. Georg Lukács, *The Theory of the Novel: A Historico-philosophical Essay on the Forms of Great Epic Literature*, trans. by Anna Bostock (London: Merlin, 1978).
13. Jung, p. 94 and p. 97.
14. Fricke, 'Das Auge der Landschaft'.
15. Ohl, *Bild und Wirklichkeit*.
16. Ohl (ibid., p. 213) argues that space in Fontane's texts can only be understood in terms of the observing character.
17. Such as Bance, *The Major Novels*, or Howe, 'Reality and Imagination'.
18. Nora Hoffmann, 'Photographien in Fontanes Romanen', *FBl*, 87 (2009), 38–54.

19. Peter James Bowman, 'Theodor Fontane's *Cécile*: An allegory of Reading', *German Life and Letters*, 53 (2000), 17–36.
20. Haberkamm, '"Links und rechts umlauert"'; "Nein, nein, die Linke "'.

BIBLIOGRAPHY

Bibliographical Sources

BARNER, WILFRIED and OTHERS, eds, *Germanistik: Internationales Referatenorgan mit bibliographischen Hinweisen* (Tübingen: Niemeyer, 1960-)
CHAMBERS, HELEN E., *Theodor Fontanes Erzählwerk im Spiegel der Kritik: 120 Jahre Fontane Rezeption* (Würzburg: Königshausen & Neumann, 2003)
JOLLES, CHARLOTTE, *Theodor Fontane*, 4th rev. edn (Stuttgart: Metzler, 1993)
JOLLES, CHARLOTTE and WALTER MÜLLER-SEIDEL, *Die Briefe Theodor Fontanes: Verzeichnis und Register* (Munich: Hanser, 1987)
RASCH, WOLFGANG, and OTHERS, eds, *Theodor Fontane Bibliographie: Werk und Forschung*, 3 vols (Berlin and New York: de Gruyter, 2006)
SCHMIDT, WILHELM R., ed., *Bibliographie der deutschen Sprach- und Literaturwissenschaft* (Frankfurt a. M.: Klostermann, 1970-)
Fontane-Blätter, cited as *FBl*

Primary Sources

Fontane

FONTANE, THEODOR, *Briefe an Georg Friedlaender*, ed. by Kurt Schreinert (Heidelberg: Quelle & Meyer, 1954)
—— *Sämtliche Werke*, ed. by Edgar Gross and others, 24 vols (Munich: Nymphenburger Verlagshandlung, 1959-75), 'Nymphenburger Ausgabe', cited as NyA
—— *Werke, Schriften und Briefe* [originally *Sämtliche Werke*], ed. by Walter Keitel and Helmuth Nürnberger, 21 vols in 4 sections (Munich: Hanser, 1962-97), 'Hanser Ausgabe', cited as HA
—— *Briefe an Julius Rodenberg: Eine Dokumentation*, ed. by Hans-Heinrich Reuter (Berlin and Weimar: Aufbau, 1969)
—— *Romane und Erzählungen*, ed. by Peter Goldammer and others, 8 vols (Berlin and Weimar: Aufbau, 1969), 'Aufbau Ausgabe', cited as AA
—— *Briefe*, ed. by Gotthard Erler, 2nd edn, 2 vols (Munich: Nymphenburger Verlagshandlung, 1981)
—— *Gedichte*, 3 vols, ed. by Joachim Krueger and Anita Golz (Berlin and Weimar: Aufbau, 1989)
—— *Wanderungen durch die Mark Brandenburg*, ed. by Helmuth Nürnberger, 3 vols (Munich: Deutscher Taschenbuch Verlag, 2006)

Other Authors

[GOETHE, JOHANN WOLFGANG VON], *Goethes Werke*, ed. by Erich Trunz and others, 15 vols (Hamburg: Wegner, 1948-60)

HÖLDERLIN, FRIEDRICH, *Sämtliche Werke*, ed. by Norbert von Hellingrath, Friedrich Seebass, and Ludwig von Pigenot, 6 vols (Berlin: Propyläen, 1922–23)
LESSING, GOTTHOLD EPHRAIM, *Gesammelte Werke*, 2 vols, ed. by Wolfgang Stammler (Munich: Hanser, 1959)
MANN, THOMAS, *Der Zauberberg* (Frankfurt a. M.: Fischer, 1960)
MICHA, ALEXANDRE, ed., *Verlaine et les poètes symbolistes* (Paris: Larousse, 1943)
ROUSSEAU, JEAN-JACQUES, *Émile ou de l'éducation*, ed. by François and Pierre Richard (Paris: Garnier, 1964)
[SCHILLER, FRIEDRICH VON], *Schillers Sämtliche Werke*, ed. by Eduard von der Hellen and others, 16 vols (Stuttgart and Berlin: Cotta, 1904–05)
TIECK, LUDWIG, *Werke in vier Bänden*, ed. by Marianne Thalmann (Darmstadt: Wissenschaftliche Buchgesellschaft, 1973)
WORDSWORTH, WILLIAM, *The Prelude, or Growth of a Poet's Mind*, ed. by Ernest de Selincourt, rev. by Helen Darbyshire (Oxford: Clarendon Press, 1959)

Secondary Literature

Spatial theory and theorists

BACHELARD, GASTON, *La poétique de l'espace* (Paris: Presses Universitaires de France, 1967)
—— *The Poetics of Space*, trans. by Maria Jolas (Boston, M.A.: Beacon Press, 1994)
BAL, MIEKE, *On Story-Telling* (Sonoma, CA: Polebridge Press, 1991)
BLANCHOT, MAURICE, *L'espace littéraire* (Paris: Gallimard, 1955)
BOURNEUF, ROLAND, *L'univers du roman* (Paris: Presses Universitaires de France, 1981)
BUTOR, MICHEL, 'L'espace du roman', in Michel Butor, *Essais sur le roman* (Paris: Gallimard, 1969), pp. 48–58
FRANK, JOSEPH, 'Spatial Form in Modern Literature', in Joseph Frank, *The Widening Gyre: Crisis and Masters in Modern Literature* (Brunswick, NJ: Rutgers University Press, 1963), pp. 3–62
GENETTE, GÉRARD, 'Espace et langage', in Gérard Genette, *Figures, essais* (Paris: Seuil, 1969), pp. 101–08
—— 'La littérature et l'espace', in Gérard Genette, *Figures II* (Paris: Seuil, 1969), pp. 43–49
HAMON, PHILIPPE, 'Introduction à l'analyse du descriptif (1981)', in Philippe Hamon, *La Description littéraire. De L'Antiquité à Roland Barthes: une anthologie* (Paris: Macula, 1991), pp. 264–73
LOTMAN, JURIJ, 'The Problem of Artistic Space', in Jurij Lotman, *The Structure of the Artistic Text*, trans. by Ronald Vroon (Ann Arbor: University of Michigan, 1977), pp. 217–31
MILLER, J. HILLIS, *Topographies* (Stanford, CA: Stanford University Press, 1995)
O'TOOLE, LAURENCE M., 'Dimensions of Semiotic Space in Narrative', *Poetics Today*, 1 (1980), 135–49
PRIEST, STEPHEN, *Merleau-Ponty* (London: Routledge, 1998)
RIMMON-KENAN, SCHLOMITH, *Narrative Fiction, Contemporary Poetics*, 4th edn (London: Routledge, 1993)

Ronen, Ruth, 'Space in Fiction', *Poetics Today*, 7 (1986), 421–38
Smith, Roch C., *Gaston Bachelard* (Boston, MA: Twayne, 1982)
Weigel, Sigrid, '"On the Topographical Turn": Concepts of Space in Cultural Studies and *Kulturwissenschaften*. A Cartographic Feud', *European Review*, 17 (2009), 187–201
Zoran, Gabriel, 'Towards a Theory of Space in Narrative', *Poetics Today*, 5 (1984), 309–35

Literature on Fontane, his works, and Realism

Amberg, Andreas, 'Poetik des Wassers. Theodor Fontanes *Stechlin*. Zur protagonistischen Funktion des See-Symbols', *Zeitschrift für deutsche Philologie*, 115 (1996), 541–59
Andermatt, Michael, *Haus und Zimmer im Roman: Die Genese des erzählten Raumes bei Eugenie Marlitt, Theodor Fontane und Franz Kafka* (Berne: Lang, 1988)
Arnold, Heinz Ludwig, ed., *Text + Kritik: Sonderband Theodor Fontane* (Munich: edition text + kritik, 1989)
Attwood, Kenneth, *Fontane und das Preußentum* (Berlin: Haude und Spenersche Verlagsbuchhandlung, 1970)
Auerbach, Erich, *Mimesis: Dargestellte Wirklichkeit in der abendländischer Literatur* (Berne: Francke, 1946)
Aust, Hugo, *Theodor Fontane: 'Verklärung': Eine Untersuchung zum Ideengehalt seiner Werke* (Bonn: Bouvier, 1974)
—— ed., *Fontane aus heutiger Sicht* (Munich: Nymphenburger Verlagshandlung, 1980)
—— *Der historische Roman* (Stuttgart and Weimar: Metzler, 1994)
—— 'Zur Modernität des vaterländischen Romans bei Theodor Fontane', *FBl*, 60 (1995), 83–102
—— *Literatur des Realismus* (Stuttgart: Metzler, 2000)
Bance, Alan, *Theodor Fontane: The Major Novels* (Cambridge: Cambridge University Press, 1982)
Bance, Alan, Helen Chambers, and Charlotte Jolles, eds, *Theodor Fontane: The London Symposium*, Publications of the Institute of Germanic Studies LXII (Stuttgart: Heinz; London: University of London, 1995)
Bange, Pierre, *Ironie et dialogisme dans les romans de Theodor Fontane* (Grenoble: Presses Universitaires de Grenoble, 1974)
—— 'Zwischen Mythos und Kritik: Eine Skizze über Fontanes Entwicklung bis zu den Romanen', in Aust, *Fontane aus heutiger Sicht*, pp. 17–55
Barlow, Derek, 'Symbolism in Fontane's *Der Stechlin*', *German Life and Letters*, 12 (1958–59), 282–86
Barthes, Roland, 'L'effet de réel', in Roland Barthes, *Œuvres complètes*, ed. by Eric Marty, 4 vols (Paris: Seuil, 2002), III, 25–32
Beaton, Kenneth Bruce, 'Fontanes *Irrungen, Wirrungen* und Fanny Lewalds *Wandlungen*: Ein Beitrag zur Motivgeschichte der vom Adel verführten Unschuld aus dem Volke', *Jahrbuch der Raabe-Gesellschaft* (1984), 208–24
Becker, Sabina, *Bürgerlicher Realismus: Literatur und Kultur im bürgerlichen Zeitalter 1840–1900* (Tübingen: Francke, 2003)

BECKMANN, MARTIN, 'Theodor Fontanes *Der Stechlin* als ästhetisches Formgefüge', *Wirkendes Wort*, 39 (1989), 218–39
BERBIG, ROLAND, 'Mediale Textprozesse: Theodor Fontanes Romanerstling *Vor dem Sturm*', in *Theodor Fontane: Neue Wege der Forschung*, ed. by Bettina Plett (Darmstadt: Wissenschaftliche Buchgesellschaft, 2007), pp. 154–73
BERMAN, RUSSEL A., *Between Fontane and Tucholsky: Literary Criticism and the Public Sphere in Imperial Germany* (New York: Lang, 1983)
BETZ, FREDERICK, ed., *Erläuterungen und Dokumente: Theodor Fontane 'Irrungen, Wirrungen'* (Stuttgart: Reclam, 1979)
—— 'Fontanes *Irrungen, Wirrungen*: Eine Analyse der zeitgenössischen Rezeption des Romans', in Aust, *Fontane aus heutiger Sicht*, pp. 258–81
BLESSIN, STEFAN, '*Unwiederbringlich* — ein historisch-politischer Roman? Bemerkungen zu Fontanes Symbolkunst', *Deutsche Vierteljahresschrift für Literaturwissenschaft und Geistesgeschichte*, 48 (1974), 672–703
BLOMQUIST, CLARISSA, 'Der Fontane-Ton: Typische Merkmale der Sprache Theodor Fontanes', in *Sprachkunst*, 35 (2004), 23–34
BÖSCHENSTEIN, RENATE, 'Idyllischer Todesraum und agrarische Utopie: Zwei Gestaltungsformen des Idyllischen in der erzählenden Literatur des 19. Jahrhunderts', in Seeber and Klussmann, *Idylle und Modernisierung*, pp. 25–40
—— 'Fontane's Writing and the Problem of "Reality" in Philosophy and Literature', in Howe and Chambers, *Theodor Fontane and the European Context*, pp. 15–32
—— 'Prägnante Mikrostrukturen in Fontanes *Wanderungen durch die Mark Brandenburg*', in Delf von Wolzogen, *Geschichte und Geschichten*, pp. 453–70
BOSSHART, ADELHEID, *Theodor Fontanes historische Romane* (Winterthur: Keller, 1957)
BOWMAN, DEREK, '"Unser Herz hat Platz für allerlei Widersprüche": Aspekte von Liebe und sexueller Gier in Fontanes Roman *Irrungen, Wirrungen*', *FBl*, 37 (1984), 443–56
BOWMAN, PETER JAMES, 'Theodor Fontane's *Cécile* as an Allegory of Reading', *German Life and Letters*, 53 (2000), 17–36
—— 'Fontane's *Der Stechlin*: A fragile Utopia', *MLR*, 97 (2002), 877–91.
—— 'Fontane's *Unwiederbringlich*: A Bakhtinian Reading', *German Quarterly*, 77 (2004), 170–87
—— 'The Lover's Discourse in Theodor Fontane's *Irrungen, Wirrungen*', *Orbis Litterarum*, 62 (2007), 139–58
BRINKMANN, RICHARD, *Theodor Fontane: Über die Verbindlichkeit des Unverbindlichen* (Munich: Piper, 1967)
—— 'Der angehaltene Moment. Requisiten — Genre — Tableau bei Fontane', *Deutsche Vierteljahresschrift für Literaturwissenschaft und Geistesgeschichte*, 58 (1979), 429–62
BRÜGGEMANN, DIETRICH, 'Fontanes Allegorien', *Neue Rundschau*, 82 (1971), 290–310 and 486–505
BRUMM, ANNE-MARIE, 'The Lovesong of J. Botho von Rienäcker — Theodor Fontane's Portrayal of the Wasteland in *Irrungen, Wirrungen*', in *Acta Germanica*, 18 (1985), 98–140
BUFFAGNI, CLAUDIA, 'Aspekte der Reise in *Vor dem Sturm* und dem *Stechlin*', *FBl*, 76 (2003), 62–79
—— 'Das Motiv der Reise als Strukturbildendes Element im Prosawerk Theodor

Fontanes: Die *Wanderungen durch die Mark Brandenburg*', in Delf von Wolzogen, *Geschichte und Geschichten*, pp. 433-52
CHAMBERS, HELEN E., *Supernatural and Irrational Elements in the Works of Theodor Fontane* (Stuttgart: Heinz, 1980)
—— 'Mond und Sterne in Fontanes Werken', *FBl*, 37 (1987), 457-76
—— 'Großstädte in der Provinz: Topographie bei Theodor Fontane und Joseph Roth', in Delf von Wolzogen and Nürnberger, *Theodor Fontane am Ende des Jahrhunderts*, III, 215-25
—— 'Afterword', in Theodor Fontane, *No Way Back*, trans. by Hugh Rorrison and Helen Chambers (London: Angel, 2010), pp. 233-45
CZUCKA, ECKHARD, 'Faktizität und Sprachskepsis: Fontanes *Stechlin* und die Sprachskepsis der Jahrhundertwende', in Delf von Wolzogen and Nürnberger, *Theodor Fontane am Ende des Jahrhunderts*, II, 27-39
DELF VON WOLZOGEN, HANNA, ed., *'Geschichte und Geschichten aus Mark Brandenburg': Fontanes 'Wanderungen durch die Mark Brandenburg' im Kontext der europäischen Reiseliteratur. Internationales Symposium des Theodor-Fontane-Archivs in Zusammenarbeit mit der Theodor Fontane Gesellschaft 18.-22. September 2002 in Potsdam* (Würzburg: Königshausen & Neumann, 2003)
DELF VON WOLZOGEN, HANNA, and HELMUTH NÜRNBERGER, eds, *Theodor Fontane am Ende des Jahrhunderts: Internationales Symposium des Theodor-Fontane-Archivs zum 100. Todestag Theodor Fontanes 13.-17. September 1998 in Potsdam*, 3 vols (Würzburg: Königshausen & Neumann, 2000)
DELF VON WOLZOGEN, HANNA, and OTHERS, eds, *Renate Böschenstein. Verborgene Facetten. Studien zu Fontane* (Würzburg: Königshausen & Neumann, 2006)
DELIUS, F. C., *Der Held und sein Wetter: Ein Kunstmittel und sein ideologischer Gebrauch im Roman des bürgerlichen Realismus* (Munich: Hanser, 1971)
DEMETZ, PETER, *Formen des Realismus: Theodor Fontane. Kritische Untersuchungen* (Munich: Hanser, 1964)
DOWNING, ERIC, 'Tragödie/Spiel: An essay on Fontane's "Glücksbegriff" in *Irrungen, Wirrungen*', *Deutsche Vierteljahresschrift für Literaturwissenschaft und Geistesgeschichte*, 59 (1985), 290-312
DUTSCHKE, MANFRED, 'Geselliger Spießrutenlauf: Die Tragödie des lächerlichen Junkers Schach von Wuthenow', in Arnold, *Text + Kritik*, pp. 103-16
EHLICH, KONRAD, ed., *Fontane und die Fremde: Fontane und Europa* (Würzburg: Königshausen & Neumann, 2002)
ERLER, GOTTHARD, 'Fontanes *Wanderungen* heute', *FBl*, 21 (1975), 353-68
EWERT, MICHAEL, 'Heimat und Welt: Fontanes Wanderungen durch die Mark', in Ehlich, *Fontane und die Fremde*, pp. 167-77
—— 'Theodor Fontanes Wanderungen durch die märkische Historiographie', in Delf von Wolzogen, *Geschichte und Geschichten*, pp. 471-86
FIELD, GEORGE WALLIS, ed., THEODOR FONTANE, *Irrungen, Wirrungen* (London: Macmillan; New York: St Martin's Press, 1967)
FINLAY, ROSEMARY, and HELGA DUNN, 'The Pictures in Fontane's *Irrungen, Wirrungen*', *Seminar*, 24 (1988), 221-36
FISCHER, HUBERTUS, 'Märkische Bilder: Ein Versuch über Fontanes *Wanderungen durch die Mark Brandenburg*, ihre Bilder und ihre Bildlichkeit', *FBl*, 60 (1995), 117-42

FRANK, PHILIPP, *Theodor Fontane und die Technik* (Würzburg: Königshausen & Neumann, 2005)
FRICKE, HERMANN, 'Das Auge der Landschaft: Mit Fontane am märkischen Seen', *Brandenburgische Jahrbücher*, 3 (1936), 41–47
—— 'Theodor Fontanes *Wanderungen durch die Mark Brandenburg* als Vorstufe seiner epischen Dichtung', *Jahrbücher für brandenbürgische Landesgeschichte*, 13 (1962), 119–35
FRIEDRICH, GERHARD, 'Die Frage nach dem Glück in Fontanes *Irrungen, Wirrungen*', *Der Deutschunterricht*, 11 (1959), 76–87
FÜRSTENAU, JUTTA, *Fontane und die märkische Heimat*, Germanistische Studien, CCXXXII (Berlin: Ebering, 1941)
GARLAND, HENRY, *The Berlin Novels of Theodor Fontane* (Oxford: Clarendon Press, 1980)
GAUGER, HANS-MARTIN, 'Sprachbewußtsein im *Stechlin*', in *Bild und Gedanke: Festschrift für Gerhart Baumann zum 60. Geburtstag*, ed. by Günter Schnitzler and Gerhard Neumann (Munich: Fink, 1980), pp. 311–23
GRATZKE, MICHAEL, '"Das Opfer war Gebot, war Leidenschaft": Männlichkeit und Heldentum in Fontanes *Wanderungen durch die Mark Brandenburg*', in *Masculinities in German Culture*, ed. by Sarah Colvin and Peter Davies, Edinburgh German Yearbook, II (Rochester, NY: Camden House, 2008), pp. 65–80
GRAWE, CHRISTIAN, 'Fontanes neues Sprachbewußtsein in *Der Stechlin*', in Christian Grawe, *Sprache im Prosawerk* (Bonn: Bouvier, 1974), pp. 38–62
—— 'Käthe von Sellenthins *Irrungen, Wirrungen*: Anmerkungen zu einer Gestalt in Fontanes gleichnamigem Roman', *FBl*, 33 (1982), 84–100
—— ed., *Interpretationen: Fontanes Novellen und Romane*, (Stuttgart: Reclam, 1991)
GRAWE, CHRISTIAN, and HELMUTH NÜRNBERGER, eds, *Fontane-Handbuch* (Stuttgart: Kröner, 2000)
GRETER, HEINZ EUGEN, *Fontanes Poetik* (Frankfurt. a. M.: Lang, 1973)
GUARDA, SYLVAIN, '*Schach von Wuthenow*', '*Die Poggenpuhls*' und '*Der Stechlin*': *Fontanes innere Reisen in die Unterwelt* (Würzburg: Königshausen & Neumann, 1997)
GÜNTHER, VINCENT J., *Das Symbol im erzählerischen Werk Fontanes* (Bonn: Bouvier, 1967)
HABERKAMM, KLAUS, '"Links und rechts umlauert": Zu einem symbolischen Schema in Fontanes *Effi Briest*', *MLN*, 101 (1986), 553–91
—— '"Nein, nein, die Linke, die kommt von Herzen." Zur Rechts-Links-Dichotomie in Fontanes *Irrungen, Wirrungen*', *FBl*, 82 (2006), 88–109
HAHN, ANSELM, *Theodor Fontanes 'Wanderungen durch die Mark Brandenburg' und ihre Bedeutung für das Romanwerk des Dichters* (Breslau: Friedrich-Wilhelms-Universität, 1935)
HAJEK, SIEGFRIED, 'Anekdoten in Theodor Fontanes Roman *Vor dem Sturm*', *Jahrbuch der Raabe-Gesellschaft* (1979), 72–93
HAYENS, KENNETH, *Theodor Fontane: A Critical Study* (London: Collins, 1920)
HEHLE, CHRISTINE, 'Unterweltsfahrten: Reisen als Erfahrung des Versagens im Erzählwerk Fontanes', in Delf von Wolzogen and Nürnberger, *Theodor Fontane am Ende des Jahrhunderts*, III, 65–76

—— 'Venus und Elisabeth: Beobachtungen zu einigen Bildfeldern in Theodor Fontanes Roman *Unwiederbringlich*', in *'Spielende Vertiefung ins Menschliche.' Festschrift für Ingrid Mittenzwei*, ed. by Monika Hahn (Heidelberg: Winter, 2002), pp. 219–33

HENSCHEL, UWE, '"Märkische Bilder" oder "Wanderungen"? Anmerkungen zur Textproblematik', in Delf von Wolzogen, *Geschichte und Geschichten*, pp. 81–94

HERTLING, GUNTHER H., *Theodor Fontanes 'Irrungen, Wirrungen': Die erste Seite als Schlüssel zum Werk* (New York: Lang, 1985)

HETTCHE, WALTER, '*Irrungen, Wirrungen*: Sprachbewußtsein und Menschlichkeit', in Grawe, *Interpretationen*, pp. 136–56

—— 'Die Handschriften zu Theodor Fontanes *Vor dem Sturm*: Erste Ergebnisse ihrer Auswertung', *FBl*, 58 (1994), 193–211

HILLEBRAND, BRUNO, *Mensch und Raum im Roman: Studien zu Keller, Stifter und Fontane* (Munich: Winkler, 1971)

HOFFMANN, NORA, 'Photographien in Fontanes Romanen', *FBl*, 87 (2009), 38–54

HOWALD, ERNST, 'Fontanes *Wanderungen durch die Mark Brandenburg*', in Ernst Howald, *Deutsch-Französisches Mosaik* (Zurich: Artemis, 1962), pp. 269–89

HOWE, PATRICIA, 'Reality and Imagination in Fontane's *Irrungen, Wirrungen*', *German Life and Letters*, 38 (1985), 346–56

—— 'Realism and Moral Design', in *Perspectives on German Realist Writing: Eight Essays*, ed. by Mark G. Ward (Lewiston: Edwin Mellen, 1995), pp. 45–63

HOWE, PATRICIA, and HELEN CHAMBERS, eds, *Theodor Fontane and the European Context: Literature, Culture and Society in Prussia and Europe* (Amsterdam: Rodopi; London: University of London, 2001)

IRETON, SEAN, 'The Problem of Language in Nietzsche's *Ueber Wahrheit und Lüge im aussermoralischen Sinne* and Fontane's *Der Stechlin*', *Colloquia Germania*, 35 (2002), 239–61

JOLLES, CHARLOTTE, '"Und am Themse wächst man sich anders aus als am Stechlin": Zum Englandmotiv in Fontanes Erzählwerk', *FBl*, 5 (1967), 173–91

—— 'Theodor Fontane als Essayist und Journalist', *Jahrbuch für Internationale Germanistik*, 7 (1975), 98–119

—— '*Der Stechlin*: Fontanes Zaubersee', in Aust, *Fontane aus heutiger Sicht*, pp. 239–57

—— *Fontane und die Politik: Ein Beitrag zur Wesensbestimmung Theodor Fontanes* (Berlin and Weimar: Aufbau, 1983)

—— 'Weltstadt-verlorene Nachbarschaft: Berlin-Bilder Raabes und Fontanes', *Jahrbuch der Raabe-Gesellschaft* (1988), 52–75

—— '"Berlin wird Weltstadt": Theodor Fontane und der Berliner Roman seiner Zeit', in *Berlin: eine Großstadt im Spiegel der Literatur*, ed. by Derek Glass and others, Publications of the Institute of Germanic Studies, XLII (London: University of London; Berlin: Schmidt, 1989), pp. 50–69

—— '*Unwiederbringlich* — Der Irrweg des Grafen Holk', *FBl*, 61 (1996), 66–83

JOST, ERDMUT, 'Das poetische Auge: Visuelle Programmatik in Theodor Fontanes Landschaftsbildern aus Schottland und der Mark Brandenburg', in Delf von Wolzogen, *Geschichte und Geschichten*, pp. 63–80

JUNG, WOLFGANG, *Das 'Menschliche' im 'Alltäglichen': Fontanes Literaturtheorie in ihrer Beziehung zur klassischen Ästhetik und seine Rezeption der Dichtung Goethes und Schillers* (Frankfurt a. M.: Lang, 1985)

KAHRMANN, CORDULA, *Idyll im Roman: Theodor Fontane* (Munich: Fink, 1973)
KEILER, OTFRIED, 'Vor dem Sturm: Das große Gefühl der Befreiung und die kleinen Zwecke der Opposition', in Grawe, *Interpretationen*, pp. 13–43
KILLY, WALTER, 'Abschied vom Jahrhundert. Fontane: *Irrungen, Wirrungen*', in Walter Killy, *Wirklichkeit und Kunstcharakter: Neun Romane des 19. Jahrhunderts* (Munich: Beck, 1963), pp. 193–211
KITTELMANN, JANA, '". . .die ganze Welt ein Idyll"? Gartenbeschreibungen bei Theodor Fontane und Hermann von Pückler-Muskau', *FBl*, 85 (2008), 132–49
KLOEPPER, ALBRECHT, 'Fontanes Berlin: Funktion und Darstellung der Stadt in seinen Zeitromanen', *Germanisch-Romanische Monatsschrift*, 42 (1992), 67–86
KRAUSCH, HEINZ-DIETER, 'Die natürliche Umwelt in Fontanes *Stechlin*: Dichtung und Wirklichkeit', *FBl*, 7 (1968), 342–53
KRIBBEN, KARL-GERT, 'Großstadt- und Vorstadtschauplätze in Theodor Fontanes Roman *Irrungen, Wirrungen*', in *Studien zur deutschen Literatur: Festschrift für Adolf Beck zum siebzigsten Geburtstag*, ed. by Ulrich Fülleborn and Johannes Krogoll (Heidelberg: Winter, 1979), pp. 225–45
KUCZYNSKI, INGRID, 'Reisen in fiktive Räume — der Umgang mit Landschaftskonstrukten in der britischen Reiseliteratur des 19. Jahrhunderts', in Delf von Wolzogen, *Geschichte und Geschichten*, pp. 175–89
LAU, HEIKE, 'Betrachtungen zu Raum und Zeit in Theodor Fontanes *Irrungen Wirrungen*', *FBl*, 45 (1988), 71–77
LIMLEI, MICHAEL, *Geschichte als Ort der Bewährung: Menschenbild und Gesellschaftsverständnis in den deutschen historischen Romanen (1820–1890)* (Frankfurt a. M.: Lang, 1988)
LÖCK, ALEXANDER, '"Auge und Liebe gehören zusammen". Fontanes Begriff der Verklärung', *FBl*, 85 (2008), 84–102
LORENZ, DAGMAR C. G., 'Fragmentierung und Unterbrechung als Struktur- und Gehaltprinzipien in Fontanes Roman *Unwiederbringlich*', *German Quarterly*, 51 (1978), 493–510
MANN, THOMAS, 'Der alte Fontane', in Preisendanz, *Theodor Fontane*, pp. 1–24
MANTHEY, JÜRGEN, 'Die zwei Geschichten in einer: Über eine Lesart der Erzählung *Schach von Wuthenow*', in Arnold, *Text + Kritik*, pp. 117–30
MARTINI, FRITZ, 'Zur Theorie des Romans im deutschen "Realismus"', in *Deutsche Romantheorie*, ed. by Reinhold Grimm (Frankfurt a. M.: Athenäum,1968), pp. 186–208
——*Deutsche Literatur im bürgerlichen Realismus 1848–1898*, 4th edn (Stuttgart: Metzler, 1981)
MCDONALD, EDWARD R., 'Charakterdarstellung in Theodor Fontanes *Unwiederbringlich*', *Weimarer Beiträge*, 17 (1971), 197–205
MCHAFFIE, MARGARET A., 'Fontane's *Irrungen, Wirrungen* and the Novel of Realism', in *Periods of German Literature*, ed. by J. M. Ritchie (London: Wollf, 1969), pp. 157–61
MECKLENBURG, NORBERT, *Theodor Fontane: Romankunst der Vielstimmigkeit* (Frankfurt a. M.: Suhrkamp, 1998)
MINDEN, MICHAEL, 'Realism versus Poetry: Theodor Fontane, *Effi Briest*', in *The German Novel in the Twentieth Century*, ed. by David Midgley (Edinburgh: Edinburgh University Press; New York: St Martin's Press, 1993), pp. 18–29

MITTENZWEI, INGRID, *Die Sprache als Thema: Untersuchungen zu Fontanes Gesellschaftsromanen* (Bad Homburg: Gehlen, 1970)
MÜLLER, KARLA, *Schloßgeschichten: Eine Studie zum Romanwerk Theodor Fontanes* (Munich: Fink, 1986)
MÜLLER-SEIDEL, WALTER, 'Fontane: *Der Stechlin*', in *Der deutsche Roman*, ed. by Benno von Wiese (Düsseldorf: Bagel, 1963), IIb, 146–89
—— 'Der Fall des Schach von Wuthenow', in, Theodor-Fontane-Archiv, *Theodor Fontanes Werk in unserer Zeit*, pp. 53–66
—— *Theodor Fontane: Soziale Romankunst in Deutschland* (Stuttgart: Metzler, 1975)
NEUHAUS, STEFAN, 'Und nichts als die Wahrheit? Wie der Journalist Fontane Erlebtes wiedergab', *FBl*, 65–66 (1998), 188–213
—— 'Archäologie der Poesie: Überlegungen zum Kompositionsprinzip von Fontanes *Wanderungen*', in Delf von Wolzogen, *Geschichte und Geschichten*, pp. 398–415
NÜRNBERGER, HELMUTH, *Theodor Fontane in Selbstzeugnissen und Bilddokumenten* (Reinbeck bei Hamburg: Rowohlt, 1973)
—— '"Sie kennen ja unsren berühmten Sänger": Künstler und ihre Welt als Thema Fontanescher Gedichte', *FBl*, 51 (1991), 115–40
—— 'Die England-Erfahrung Theodor Fontanes', *FBl*, 58 (1994), 12–28
—— *Fontanes Welt: Eine Biographie des Schriftsellers* (Munich: Pantheon, 2007)
NÜRNBERGER, HELMUTH, and DIETMAR STORCH, *Fontane Lexikon: Namen — Stoffe — Zeitgeschichte* (Munich: Hanser, 2007)
OHL, HUBERT, *Bild und Wirklichkeit: Studien zur Romankunst Raabes und Fontanes* (Heidelberg: Stiehm, 1968)
—— 'Bilder, die die Kunst stellt: Die Landschaftsschilderung in den Romanen Theodor Fontanes (1967)', in Preisendanz, *Theodor Fontane*, pp. 447–64
—— 'Zwischen Tradition und Moderne: Der Künstler Theodor Fontane am Beispiel von *Unwiederbringlich*', in Bance, *The London Symposium*, pp. 235–52
OSBORNE, JOHN, '*Schach von Wuthenow*: "Das rein Äußerliche bedeutet immer viel. . ."', in Grawe, *Interpretationen*, pp. 92–112
—— '*Graf Petöfy*: Eine Separatvorstellung', *FBl*, 80 (2005), 70–90
PAULSEN, WOLFGANG, 'Warum ausgerechnet "Nimptsch"?', *FBl*, 43 (1987), 561–66
PETERSEN, JULIUS, 'Theodor Fontanes Altersroman', *Euphorion*, 29 (1928), 1–74
PLETT, BETTINA, *Die Kunst der Allusion: Formen literarischer Anspiegelungen in den Romanen Theodor Fontanes* (Cologne and Vienna: Böhlau, 1986)
—— 'Der Platz an dem man gestellt ist: Ein Topos Fontanes und seine bewußtseinsgeschichtliche Topographie', in Delf von Wolzogen and Nürnberger, *Theodor Fontane am Ende des Jahrhunderts*, II, 97–105
PLUMPE, GERHARD, 'Das Reale und die Kunst: Ästhetische Theorie im 19. Jahrhundert', in *Hansers Sozialgeschichte der deutschen Literatur vom 16. Jahrhundert bis zur Gegenwart*, ed. by Rolf Grimminger and others (Munich: Hanser, 1980–2009), VI: *Bürgerlicher Realismus und Gründerzeit 1848–1890*, ed. by Edward McInnes and Gerhard Plumpe (1996), pp. 242–307
—— *Theorie des bürgerlichen Realismus: Eine Textsammlung* (Stuttgart: Reclam, 2005)
POST, KLAUS DIETER, '"Das eigentliche Parfüm des Wortes": Zum Doppelbild des Heliotrop in Theodor Fontanes Roman *Effi Briest*', *FBl*, 49 (1990), 32–39

PREISENDANZ, WOLFGANG, ed., *Theodor Fontane*, Wege der Forschung, CCCLXXXI (Darmstadt: Wissenschaftliche Buchgesellschaft, 1973)
—— *Humor als dichterische Einbildungskraft* (Munich: Fink, 1976)
—— 'Reduktionsformen des Idyllischen im Roman des 19. Jahrhunderts (Flaubert, Fontane)', in Seeber and Klussmann, *Idylle und Modernisierung*, pp. 81–92
RADECKE, GABRIELE, 'Vom Reisen zum Schreiben: Eine textgenetische Betrachtung der *Wanderungen* am Beispiel des "Pfaueninsel"-Kapitels', in Delf von Wolzogen, *Geschichte und Geschichten*, pp. 231–52
REUTER, HANS-HEINRICH, *Fontane*, 2 vols (Munich: Nymphenburger Verlagshandlung, 1968)
—— 'Entwicklung und Grundzüge der Literatur Kritik Fontanes', in Preisendanz, *Theodor Fontane*, pp. 111–68
—— 'Die englische Lehre: Zur Bedeutung und Funktion Englands für Fontanes Schaffen', in Thunecke and Sagarra, pp. 282–99
RICHTER, KARL, *Resignation: Eine Studie zum Werk Theodor Fontanes* (Stuttgart: Kohlhammer, 1966)
—— 'Die späte Lyrik Theodor Fontanes', in Aust, *Fontane aus heutiger Sicht*, pp. 118–42
ROBINSON, A., '"Bei Frau Hulen": An Examination of Chapter 40 in Fontane's Novel *Vor dem Sturm*', in Thunecke and Sagarra, pp. 471–77
RODENBERG, JULIUS, 'Vor dem Sturm. Roman aus dem Winter 1812 auf 13', in Reuter, *Briefe an Julius Rodenberg*, pp. 120–24
ROSENFELD, HANS-FRIEDRICH, *Zur Entstehung Fontanescher Romane* (Groningen and The Hague: Wolters, 1926)
ROST, WOLFGANG. E., *Örtlichkeit und Schauplatz in Fontanes Werken* (Berlin: de Gruyter, 1930)
RYCHNER, MAX, 'Fontanes *Unwiederbringlich* (1952)', in Max Rychner, *Aufsätze zur Literatur* (Zurich: Manesse, 1966), pp. 237–50
SAGARRA, EDA, *Tradition and Revolution: German Literature and Society 1830–1890* (London: Weidenfeld and Nicholson, 1971)
—— *Theodor Fontane: 'Der Stechlin'* (Munich: Fink, 1986)
SAGAVE, PIERRE-PAUL, 'Un roman berlinois de Fontane', in Pierre-Paul Sagave, *Recherches sur le roman social en Allemagne* (Paris: Gap, 1961), pp. 55–83
—— '*Schach von Wuthenow* als politischer Roman', in *Fontanes Realismus: Wissenschaftliche Konferenz zum 150. Geburtstag Theodor Fontanes in Potsdam*, ed. by Hans-Erich Teitge and Joachim Schobeß (Berlin: Akademie Verlag, 1972), pp. 87–94
—— ed., *Theodor Fontane. 'Schach von Wuthenow'. Vollständiger Text der Erzählung, Dokumentation* (Frankfurt a. M: Ullstein, 1966)
SASSE, H. C., *Theodor Fontane: An Introduction to the Man and his Works* (Oxford: Blackwell, 1968)
SCHERPE, KLAUS R., 'Rettung der Totalität durch Konstruktion: Fontanes vierfacher Roman *Der Stechlin*', in Klaus R. Scherpe, *Poesie der Demokratie* (Cologne: Pahl-Rügenstein, 1980), pp. 227–67
—— 'Ort oder Raum? Fontanes literarische Topographie', in Delf von Wolzogen and Nürnberger, *Theodor Fontane am Ende des Jahrhunderts*, III, 161–69
SCHILLEMEIT, JOST, *Theodor Fontane: Geist und Kunst seines Alterswerks* (Zurich: Atlantis, 1961)

SCHMIDT-BRÜMMER, HORST, *Formen des perspektivischen Erzählens: Fontanes 'Irrungen, Wirrungen'* (Munich: Fink, 1971)
SCHÜRMANN, UTA, 'Tickende Gehäuseuhr, gefährliches Sofa: Interieurbeschreibungen in Fontanes Romanen', *FBl*, 85 (2008), 115-31
SEEBER, HANS ULRICH and PAUL GERHARD KLUSSMANN, eds, *Idylle und Modernisierung in der europäischen Literatur des 19. Jahrhunderts* (Bonn: Bouvier, 1986)
SOMMER, DIETRICH, 'Prädestination und soziale Determination im Werk Theodor Fontanes', in Theodor-Fontane-Archiv, *Theodor Fontanes Werk in unserer Zeit*, pp. 37-52
SPEIRS, RONALD, '"Un schlimm is eigentlich man bloß das Einbilden": Zur Rolle der Phantasie in *Irrungen, Wirrungen*', *FBl*, 39 (1985), 67-78
STCOSZECK, HAUKE, 'Schwalben: Ein Nachtrag zu Fontanes poetischer Avi fauna', *FBl*, 70 (2000), 76-92
STETLAND, DIETER, 'Momento Mori: Ein kryptisches Zitat und seine epische Integration in Theodor Fontanes *Vor dem Sturm*', *FBl*, 81 (2006), 46-79
STROOP, CONSTANTIN, 'Raum und Erzählen in *Vor dem Sturm*: Eine Mikroanalyse', *FBl*, 85 (2008), 103-14
STORCH, DIETRICH, '"Immer berlinischer Geschichten — will auch andres mal berichten...": Theodor Fontane, Österreich und Ungarn', *FBl*, 80 (2005), 49-69
STRECH, HEIKO, *Theodor Fontane: Die Synthese von Alt und Neu* (Berlin: Schmidt, 1970)
SUBIOTTO, FRANCES M., 'The Use of Memory in Fontane's *Irrungen, Wirrungen*', in Thunecke and Sagarra, pp. 478-89
—— 'The Function of Letters in Fontanes *Unwiederbringlich*', *MLR*, 65 (1970), 306-18
TAU, MAX, *Der assoziative Faktor in der Landschafts- und Ortsdarstellung Theodor Fontanes* (Kiel: Schwartz, 1928)
THEODOR-FONTANE-ARCHIV DER BRANDENBURGISCHEN LANDES UND HOCHSCHULBIBLIOTHEK, ed., *Theodor Fontanes Werk in unserer Zeit: Symposion zur 30-Jahr-Feier des Fontane-Archivs der Brandenburgischen Landes- und Hochschulbibliothek Potsdam* (Potsdam: Brandenburgische Landes- und Hochschulbibliothek, 1966)
THUNECKE, JÖRG, and EDA SAGARRA, eds, *Formen realistischer Erzählkunst: Festschrift für Charlotte Jolles* (Nottingham: Sherwood Press, 1979)
TREBEIN, BERTHA E., *Theodor Fontane as a Critic of the Drama* (New York: AMS, 1966)
VELLUSIG, ROBERT, 'Ein "Wiederspiel *des* Lebens, das wir führen": Fontane und die Authentizität des poetischen Realismus', *Zeitschrift für deutsche Philologie*, 125 (2006), 209-34
VOLKOV, EVGENIJ, 'Der Begriff des Raumes in Fontanes später Prosa', *FBl*, 63 (1997), 144-51
VOSS, LIESELOTTE, *Literarische Präfiguration dargestellter Wirklichkeit bei Fontane: Zur Zitatstruktur seines Romanwerks* (Munich: Fink, 1985)
WAGNER, WALTER, *Die Technik der Vorausdeutung in Fontanes 'Vor dem Sturm' und ihre Bedeutung im Zusammenhang des Werkes* (Marburg: Elwert, 1966)
WALKER, COLIN, 'Inheritance, Allegiance, and Conversation in *Graf Petöfy*', in Bance, *The London Symposium*, pp. 253-72

WALTER-SCHNEIDER, MARGARET, 'Randfiguren im Roman Fontanes: Bemerkungen zu *Irrungen, Wirrungen* und *Effi Briest*', *Jahrbuch der Deutschen Schiller-Gesellschaft*, 27 (1983), 303–25

WANDREY, CONRAD, *Theodor Fontane* (Munich: Beck, 1919)

WEBBER, ANDREW, *Berlin in the Twentieth Century: A Cultural Topography* (Cambridge: Cambridge University Press, 2008)

WEBER, KURT, '"Au fond sind Bäume besser als Häuser": Über Theodor Fontanes Naturdarstellung', *FBl*, 64 (1997), 134–59

WENDE, WALTRAUD, '"Es gibt [. . .] viele Leben, die keine sind": Effi Briest und Baron von Innstetten im Spannungsfeld zwischen gesellschaftlichen Verhaltensmaximen und privatem Glückanspruch', in Delf von Wolzogen and Nürnberger, *Theodor Fontane am Ende des Jahrhunderts*, II, 147–60

WIESE, BENNO VON, 'Theodor Fontane: *Schach von Wuthenow*', in Benno von Wiese, *Die deutsche Novelle von Goethe bis Kafka* (Düsseldorf: Bagel, 1962)

WILHELM, GISELA, *Die Dramaturgie des epischen Raumes bei Fontane* (Frankfurt a. M.: Fischer, 1981)

WITTE, BERNDT, 'Ein preußisches Wintermärchen: Theodor Fontanes erster Roman *Vor dem Sturm*', in Delf von Wolzogen and Nürnberger, *Theodor Fontane am Ende des Jahrhunderts*, I, 143–55

WRUCK, PETER, 'Zum Zeitgeschichtsverständnis in Theodor Fontanes Roman *Vor dem Sturm*', *FBl*, 1 (1965), 1–9

—— 'Viel Freud, viel Leid. Irrungen Wirrungen. Das alte Lied', *FBl*, 39 (1985), 79–97

—— 'Fontanes Berlin: Durchlebte, erfahrene und dargestellte Wirklichkeit', in *Literarisches Leben in Berlin 1871–1933*, ed. by Peter Wruck, 2 vols (Berlin: Akademie Verlag, 1987), I, 22–87

—— '"Moderne Welt" und "alte Götter" bei Fontane: Die märkische Projekte des Romanciers', in *Roman und Ästhetik im 19. Jahrhundert: Festschrift für Christian Grawe zum 65. Geburtstag*, ed. by Tim Mehigan and Gerhard Sauder (St-Ingbert: Röhrig Universitäts Verlag, 2001), pp. 255–71

—— 'Fontane als Erfolgsautor: Zur Schlüsselstellung der Makrostruktur in der ungewöhnlichen Produktions- und Rezeptionsgeschichte der *Wanderungen durch die Mark Brandenburg*', in Delf von Wolzogen, *Geschichte und Geschichten*, pp. 373–96

WÜLFING, WULF, '"Aber nur dem Auge des Geweihten sichtbar": Mythisierende Strukturen in Fontanes Narrationen', *FBl*, 65/66 (1998), 72–86

WUNBERG, GOTTHARD, 'Rondell und Poetensteig: Topographie und implizierte Poetik in Fontanes "Stechlin"', in *Literaturwissenschaft und Geistesgeschichte: Festschrift für Richard Brinkmann*, ed. by Jürgen Brummach and others (Tübingen: Niemeyer, 1981), pp. 458–73

WÜSTEN, SONJA, 'Die historischen Denkmale im Schaffen Theodor Fontanes', *FBl*, 11 (1970), 187–94

ZERNER, MARIANNE, 'Zu Fontanes *Vor dem Sturm*', *German Quarterly*, 13 (1940), 201–06

—— 'Zur Technik von Fontanes *Irrungen, Wirrungen*', in *Monatshefte*, 45 (1953), 25–34

ZUBERBÜHLER, ROLF, *Fontane und Hölderlin: Romantik-Auffassung und Hölderlin-Bild in 'Vor dem Sturm'* (Tübingen: Niemeyer, 1997)

Secondary sources related to literary theory and aesthetics

[BAUMGARTEN, ALEXANDER GOTTLIEB], *Alexander Gottlieb Baumgarten's 'Reflections on Poetry'*, trans. by Karl Aschenbrenner and William B. Holther (Berkeley: University of California Press, 1954)

BENNET, ARNOLD, *Literary Taste*, ed. by Frank Swinnerton (Harmondsworth: Penguin, 1938)

BROOKS, CLEANTH and ROBERT PENN WARREN, *Understanding Poetry* (New York: Holt, Rinehart, and Winston, 1960)

BROOKS, CLEANTH, *The Well Wrought Urn: Studies in the Structure of Poetry* (London: Methuen, 1968)

DE MAN, PAUL, 'The Resistance to Theory', *Yale French Studies*, 63 (1982), 2–20

FRENZEL, ELISABETH, *Stoff-, Motif-, und Symbolforschung* (Stuttgart: Metzler, 1978)

HAMM, HEINZ, 'Symbol', in *Ästhetische Grundbegriffe: Historisches Wörterbuch in sieben Bänden*, ed. by Karlheinz Barck and others (Weimar and Stuttgart: Metzler, 2003), V, 805–39

LEMON, LEE T., and MARION J. REIS, TRANS. and eds, *Russian Formalist Criticism: Four Essays* (Lincoln, NB and London: University of Nebraska Press, 1965)

LOTMAN, YURY M., 'The Content and Structure of Literature', in *Twentieth-Century Literary Theory: A Reader*, ed. by K. M. Newton (Basingstoke: Macmillan, 1980), pp. 176–80

LUKÁCS, GEORG, *The Theory of the Novel: A Historico-philosophical Essay on the Forms of Great Epic Literature*, trans. by Anna Bostock (London: Merlin, 1978)

MÜLLER, JAN-DIRK, and OTHERS, eds, *Reallexikon der deutschen Literaturwissenschaft: Neubearbeitung des Reallexikons der deutschen Literaturgeschichte* (Berlin: de Gruyter, 2007)

MÜLLER-SEIDEL, WALTER, *Probleme der literarischen Wertung* (Stuttgart: Metzler, 1969)

PREMINGER, ALEX, and OTHERS, *The New Princeton Encyclopedia of Poetry and Poetics* (Princeton: Princeton University Press, 1993)

RICHARDS, I. A., *Science and Poetry* (London: Kegan Paul, Trench, and Trubner, 1926)

RUTHVEN, KENNETH KNOWLES, *Critical Assumptions* (Cambridge: Cambridge University Press, 1979)

SCHULTE-SASSE, JOCHEN, *Literarische Wertung* (Stuttgart: Metzler, 1971)

SHLOVSKY, VICTOR, 'Art as Technique', in Lemon, *Russian Formalist Criticism*, pp. 3–25

VICE, SUSAN, *Introducing Bakhtin* (Manchester and New York: Manchester University Press, 1997)

WELLEK, RENÉ, *A History of Modern Criticism: 1750–1950*, 8 vols (London: Cape, 1955–92), IV: *The later Nineteenth Century* (1966)

WELLEK, RENÉ and AUSTIN WARREN, *Theory of Literature* (Harmondsworth: Penguin, 1976)

WETZ, FRANZ-JOSEF, *Hans Blumenberg zur Einführung* (Hamburg: Junius, 1993).

WILPERT, GERO VON, *Sachwörterbuch der Literatur* (Stuttgart: Kröner, 1969)

WIMSATT, WILLIAM K. and CLEANTH BROOKS, *Literary Criticism: A Short History* (New York: Vintage, 1957)

Reference

BÄCHTOLD-STÄUBLI, HANNS, and others, eds, *Handwörterbuch des deutschen Aberglaubens*, 10 vols (Berlin and Leipzig: de Gruyter, 1927–42)

ERICH, OSWALD A., and RICHARD BEITH, eds, *Wörterbuch der deutschen Volkskunde* (Stuttgart: Kröner, 1955)

INDEX

Alexis, Willibald 59
Andermatt, Michael 12
allegory 13
allegorical 11, 63, 65, 165
Aust, Hugo 13, 76

Bachelard, Gaston 5–7, 106, 110
Bal, Mieke 9
balcony 74–75, 86, 88, 109, 132–33
Bance, Alan 14, 158
Bange, Pierre 21, 82
Barlow, Derek 13
Becker, Sabina 129, 173 n. 2
Berlin 1, 14, 26, 37, 55–56, 58–60, 62, 65, 71, 74, 77, 79–83, 95–96, 99, 106, 109–10, 128–29, 135, 138–46, 148–50, 153, 156, 164, 166, 167
Bildungsroman 27, 118
Blumenberg, Hans 170
border 27, 31, 42, 82, 153
boundary 7, 80, 87, 122
Bowman, Peter James 101, 172
Brinkmann, Richard 13, 128
Brooks, Cleanth 44 n. 22, 45 n. 40
Brüggemann, Dietrich 13, 166
Butor, Michel 7–8, 58

Chambers, Helen 13–14, 126 n. 56
characterization 49, 50, 53, 61, 73, 76, 84, 87, 123, 129, 131–32, 135–36, 165–66, 169

De Man, Paul 22
Demetz, Peter 13, 54–55, 76
Dunn, Helga 101
Dutschke, Manfred 75

emblem, emblematic 11, 29, 36, 38, 41, 94
England 48–49, 138
Erler, Gotthard 47, 54

Finlay, Rosemary 101
Fischer, Hubertus 14
focalization 6, 8, 9, 15, 96, 101, 143, 165, 168, 169
Fontane, Theodor:
 Aus den Tagen der Okkupation 48

Cécile 101, 172
Der Stechlin 1, 12, 13, 66, 96, 110, 122, 127–61 163–70, 172
Effi Briest 12, 14, 20, 54, 96, 127
Ellernklipp 171
Frau Jenny Treibel 1, 20, 132, 142
'Fritz Katzfuß' 156–57
Graf Petöfy 12, 71, 72
Irrungen Wirrungen 12, 14, 54, 96, 99–112, 119, 122–23, 130, 142, 149, 159, 163–64, 166, 168–69, 172
'Ja, das möcht ich noch erleben' 156
Jenseit des Tweed 1, 10, 171
'Mein Leben' 157
Schach von Wuthenow 10, 71–84, 95–98, 103, 107, 129, 149, 163–67
'Unsere lyrische und epische Poesie seit 1848': 108
Unwiederbringlich 1, 12, 96, 99–100, 112–26, 127, 138, 163–64, 166–69
Vor dem Sturm 10, 46–70, 72, 80–81, 105, 107, 129–30, 135–36, 138, 147, 163, 165–68
Von Zwanzig bis Dreißig 1
Wanderungen durch die Mark Brandenburg 1, 10, 14–15, 20–45, 46–48, 71, 83, 100, 107–08, 134, 147–48, 163, 170, 173
 Die Grafschaft Ruppin 20–45, 71, 127, 163, 166–67, 171; *Das Oderland* 23, 49; *Der Spreewald* 21
'Würd es mir fehlen, würd ich's vermissen?' 156
Frederick the Great 25, 37, 39–41, 53, 64, 73, 81
Fricke, Hermann 33, 171
Friedlaender, Georg 46, 139

Garland, Henry 50
garden 12, 29–30, 34, 82–83, 87, 94, 96, 100–06, 108–09, 111, 122–23, 141–42, 144
Genette, Gérard 3–4
Genrebild 47, 89, 127
Goethe, Johann Wolfgang von 137, 156
Grawe, Christian 97 n. 6, 102, 109
Guarda, Sylvain 76, 79, 97 n. 20
Günther, Vincent 13, 160 n. 42

Hayens, Kenneth 73
Haberkamm, Klaus 12, 37, 96, 172
Hamon, Philippe 6, 8, 132, 147
Hertling, Gunther 14, 124 n. 21
Hettche, Walter 47, 101
Heyse, Paul 47, 56
Hillebrand, Bruno 11–12, 162 n. 42
Howe, Patricia 14, 110
journey 2, 8, 27–28, 34, 36–37, 57–59, 72, 77, 83, 88, 109–10, 117–18, 122, 140–43, 145–46, 164
Jolles, Charlotte 46, 69 n. 64, 142, 153, 158, 161 n. 75
Jung, Wolfgang 170

Kloepper, Albrecht 14

Landpartie 74, 77, 79, 88–89, 143–44
landscape 2, 5, 10, 12–13, 24, 27, 32–33, 37, 85, 89–91, 93–96, 113, 141–47, 164, 166, 168
Lenau, Nikolaus 94–95
Lotman, Jurij 3–4, 7–8, 15, 159 n. 22
Lukács, Georg 108, 170

Mecklenburg, Norbert 49
Merleau-Ponty, Maurice 5–6
Miller, J. Hillis 3
Mittenzwei, Ingrid 124 n. 5, 137, 160 n. 51
Müller, Karla 12–13, 37, 49, 90, 114, 159 n. 10
Müller-Seidel 49, 54, 82, 92, 154, 160 n. 50

Neuhaus, Stefan 14, 21–22
Nürnberger, Helmuth 68 nn. 13 & 25

Ohl, Hubert 13, 166, 172
Osborne, John 89, 92, 98 n. 34

panorama 55–56
perception 2, 9–10, 20, 80, 107, 140, 145, 149, 154, 157–58, 164–65, 168–71
Plett, Bettina 41
poetics 8–9, 12–13, 22, 35–36, 41, 43, 122, 125 n. 43, 139, 145, 149, 158, 169, 170, 172
pond 78, 94
Post, Klaus Dieter 14
prefiguration 54, 78–79, 84, 87, 97 n. 20, 128, 132, 137, 165
Preminger, Alex 16 n. 3, 44 n. 13

Realism 2, 9, 13, 71, 95, 101–02, 108, 125 n. 40, 129, 133, 155, 157, 173 n. 2
Realist 6, 9, 13, 15, 22, 118, 122, 130, 132–33, 136–37, 140–44, 149
Reuter, Hans-Heinrich 54, 68 n. 19, 101, 109, 125 n. 43, 155–57

Richards, I, A. 108, 170
Richter, Karl 155–57
Rimmon-Kenan, Schlomith 8
Ronen, Ruth 8
Rosenfeld, Hans-Friedrich 47, 56
Rost, Wolfgang 11, 13, 47, 54, 147

salon 26, 51, 74–78, 81–82, 130–31
Scheherazade 92
Scherpe, Klaus 12
Shlovsky, Victor 170
Scotland 25, 27, 37
space:
  connoted 4
  definitions of 1–2
  functional aspect of 164–65, 168, 171
  and imagination 2–3, 5–7, 13–14, 100–05, 107, 110–11, 120, 123, 148, 168, 172
  and memory 5, 31, 37, 40, 102, 105–06, 109–10, 120, 122–23
  and metaphor 2–4, 7, 10, 22, 28–30, 34–35, 59, 65, 106, 120, 140–41, 144–45, 150
  reflexive aspect of 164–65, 167, 172–73
Speirs, Ronald 14
Stcoszeck, Hauke 14
structuralist 12, 37
study (*Arbeitszimmer*) 39, 50–53, 55, 61, 135
Subiotto, Frances M. 101
subject, embodied 5
symbolism 2, 11, 13, 22, 34, 36–37, 42, 95–96, 105, 163–64, 166, 170–73

Tau, Max 11, 13, 168, 171
topography 2, 5, 8, 12, 15, 47, 93, 110, 121–22, 138, 140, 150, 156, 158, 164–66, 168
tree 29, 34–37, 55, 63–64, 77–78, 81, 87, 94, 105, 145

Unkenruf 78, 81

veranda 86–88, 113, 135–36, 159 n. 13
Verlaine, Paul 103
Vielstimmigkeit 48, 54
Voß, Lieselotte 14, 41, 94

Wandrey, Conrad 73
Wellek, René 44 n. 23
Wiese, Benno von 97 nn. 2, 7, & 11
Wilhelm, Gisela 12
Wilpert, Gero von 2, 22
Wunberg, Gotthard 12

Zoran, Gabriel 8

www.ingramcontent.com/pod-product-compliance
Lightning Source LLC
Chambersburg PA
CBHW071445150426
43191CB00008B/1246